Cat Massage Therapy

Therapy

1

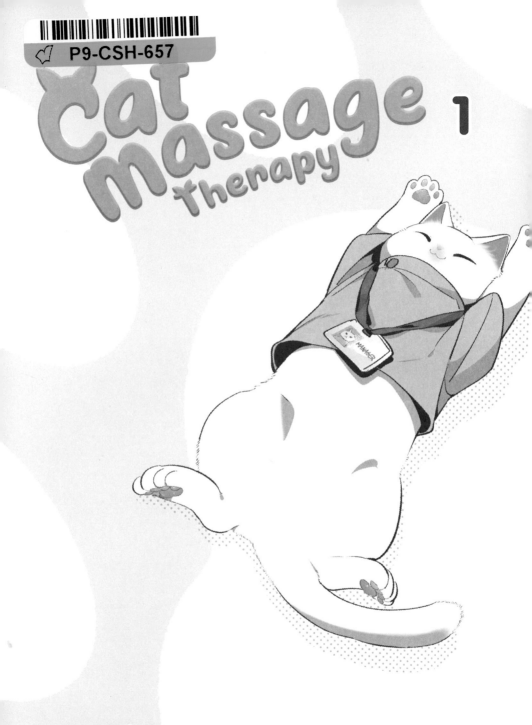

story & art by
Haru Hisakawa

Q1. Where Does It Hurt?

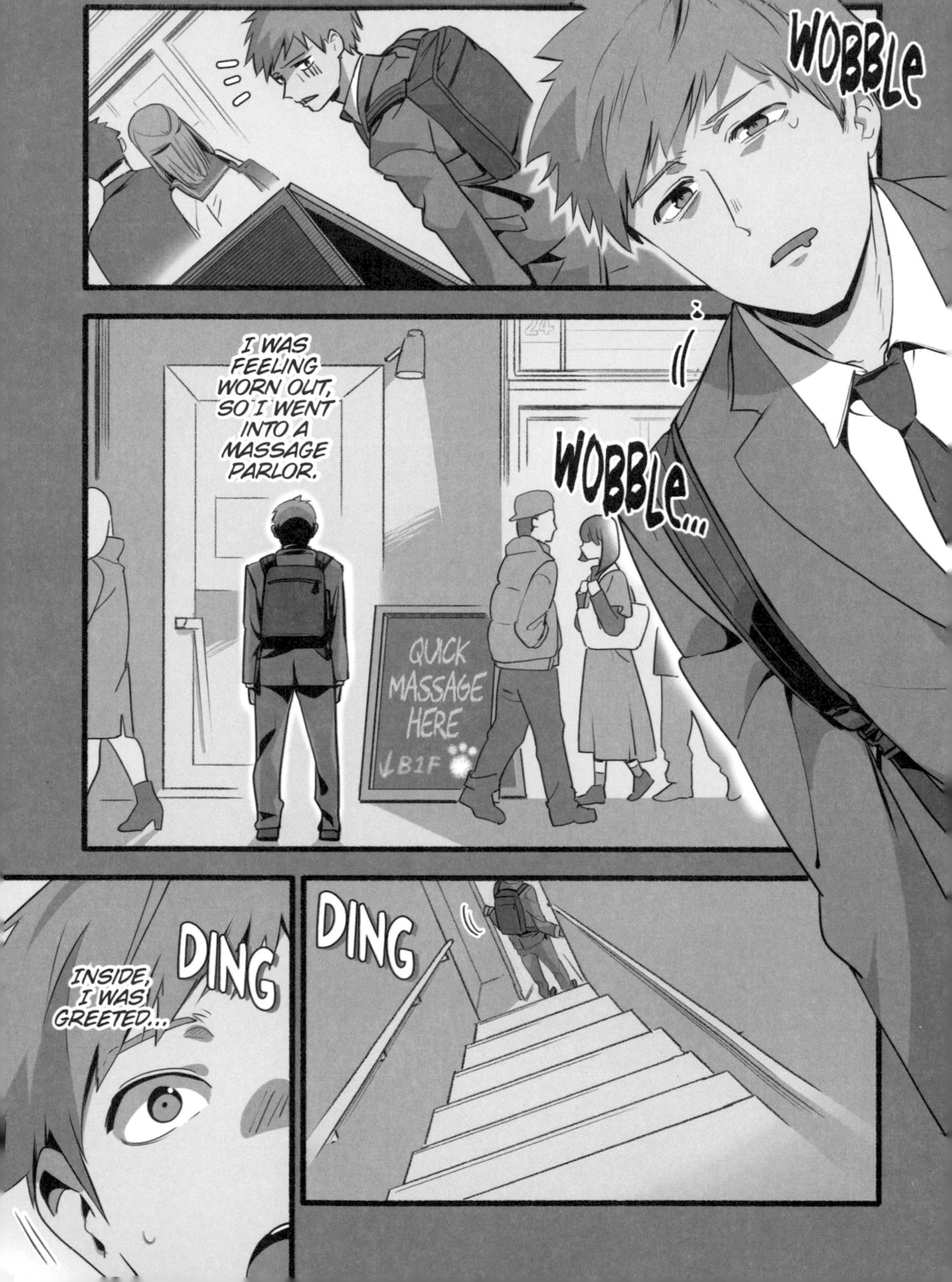
WOBBLE
WOBBLE...
I WAS FEELING WORN OUT, SO I WENT INTO A MASSAGE PARLOR.
QUICK MASSAGE HERE
B1F
DING
DING
INSIDE, I WAS GREETED...

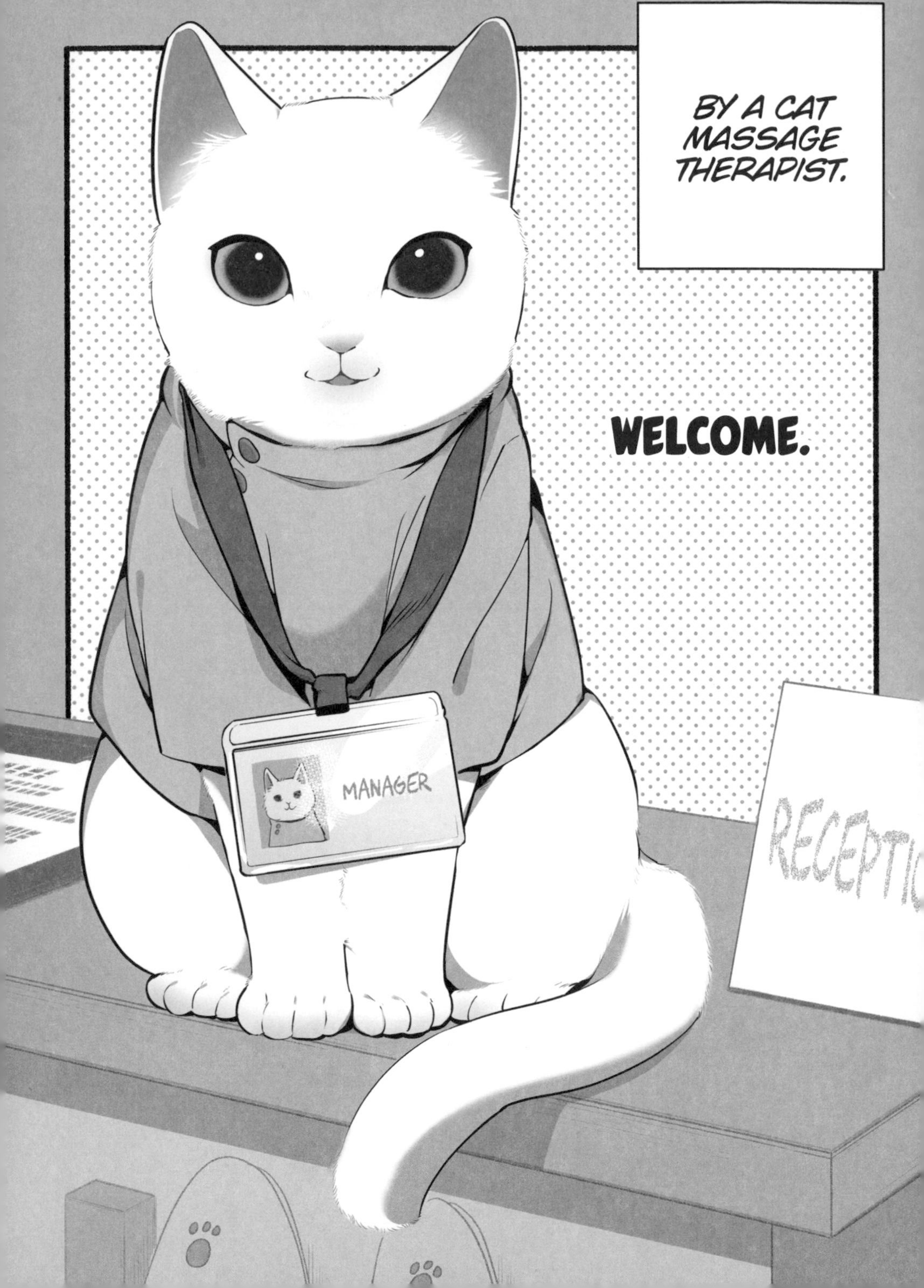
BY A CAT MASSAGE THERAPIST.
WELCOME.
MANAGER

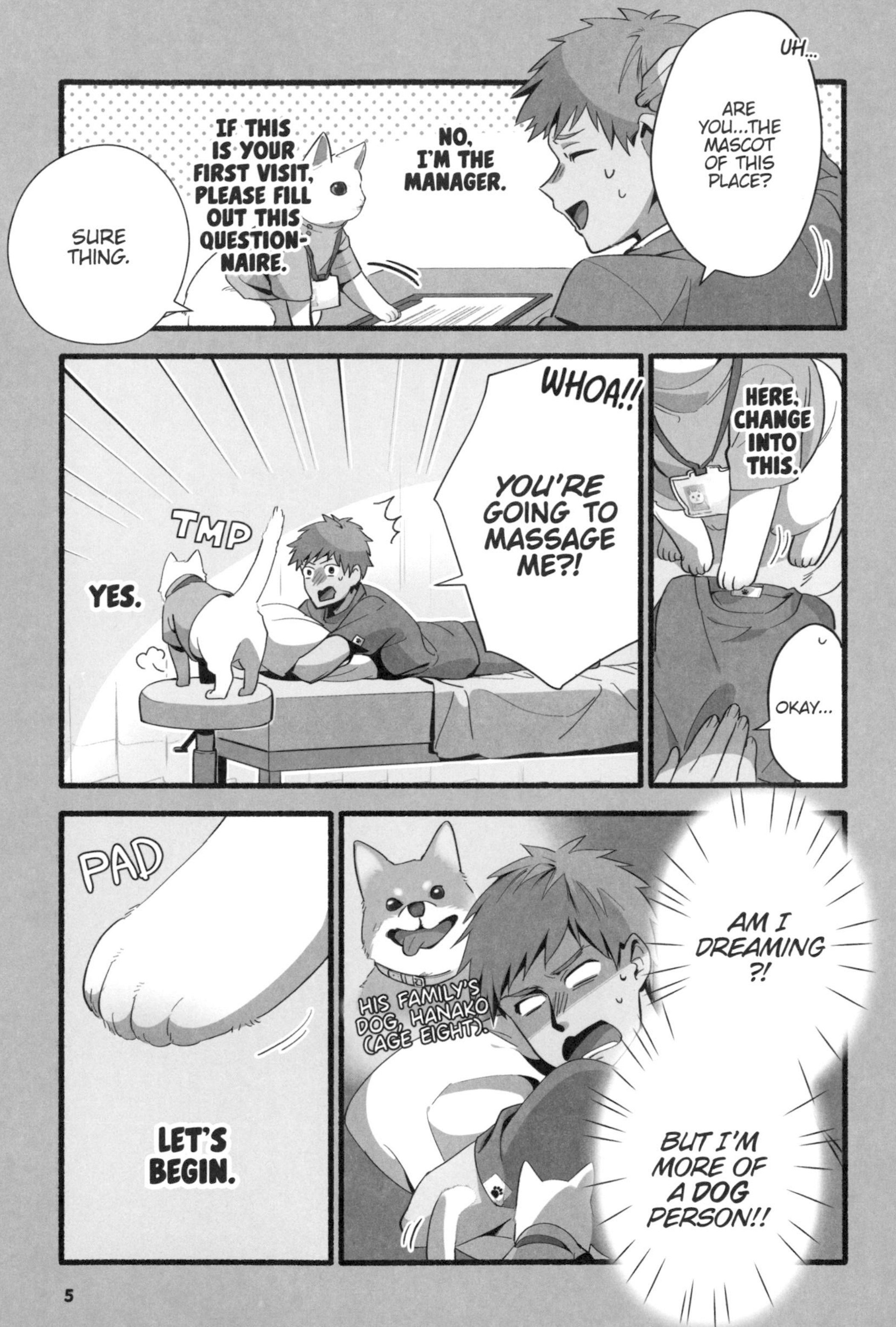
UH...
ARE YOU...THE MASCOT OF THIS PLACE?
NO, I'M THE MANAGER.
IF THIS IS YOUR FIRST VISIT, PLEASE FILL OUT THIS QUESTION-NAIRE.
SURE THING.
HERE. CHANGE INTO THIS.
OKAY...
WHOA!!
YOU'RE GOING TO MASSAGE ME?!
TMP
YES.
AM I DREAMING?!
HIS FAMILY'S DOG, HANAKO (AGE EIGHT).
BUT I'M MORE OF A DOG PERSON!!
PAD
LET'S BEGIN.

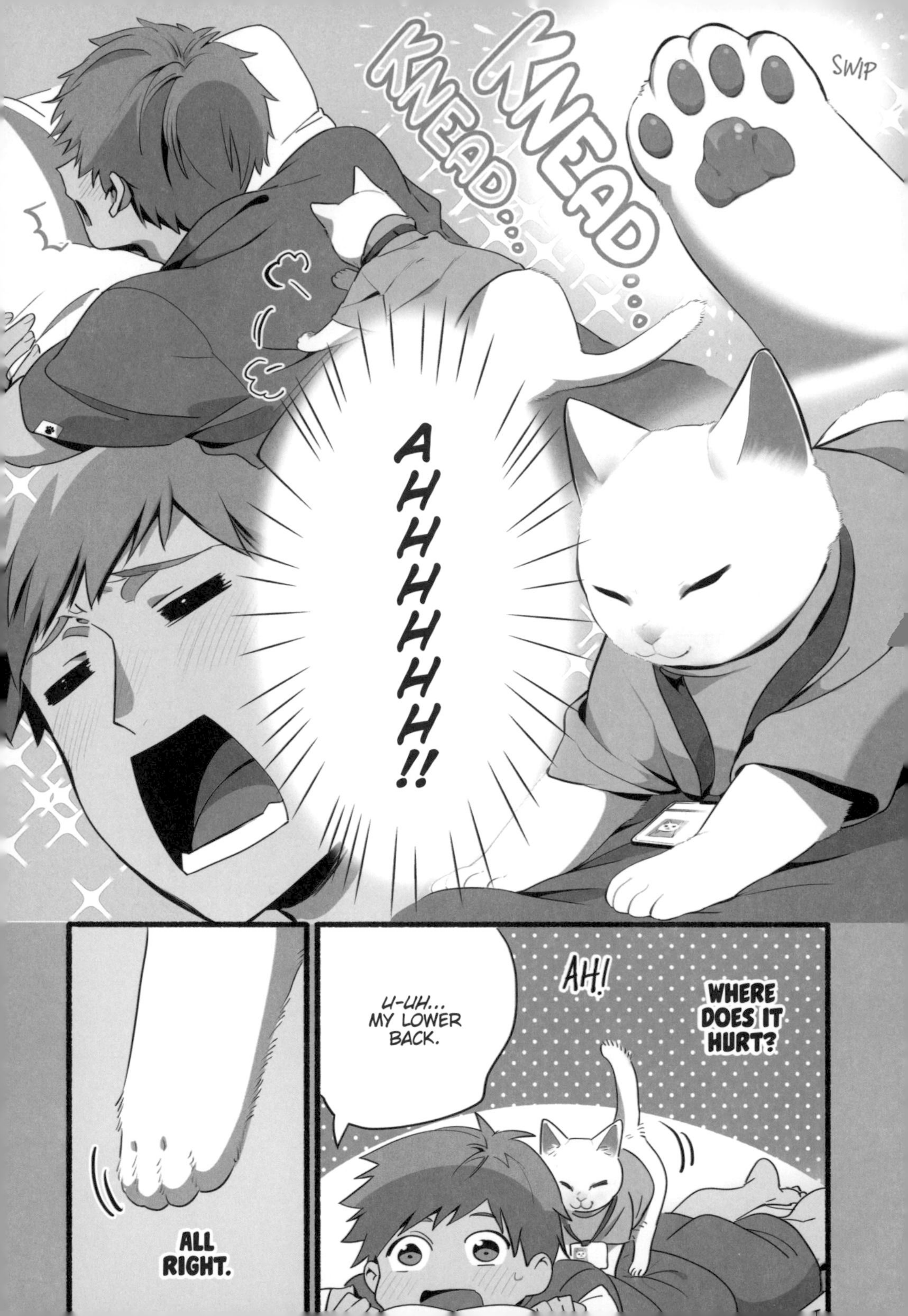
SWIP
KNEAD...
KNEAD...
AHHHHHH!!
AH!
WHERE DOES IT HURT?
U-UH... MY LOWER BACK.
ALL RIGHT.

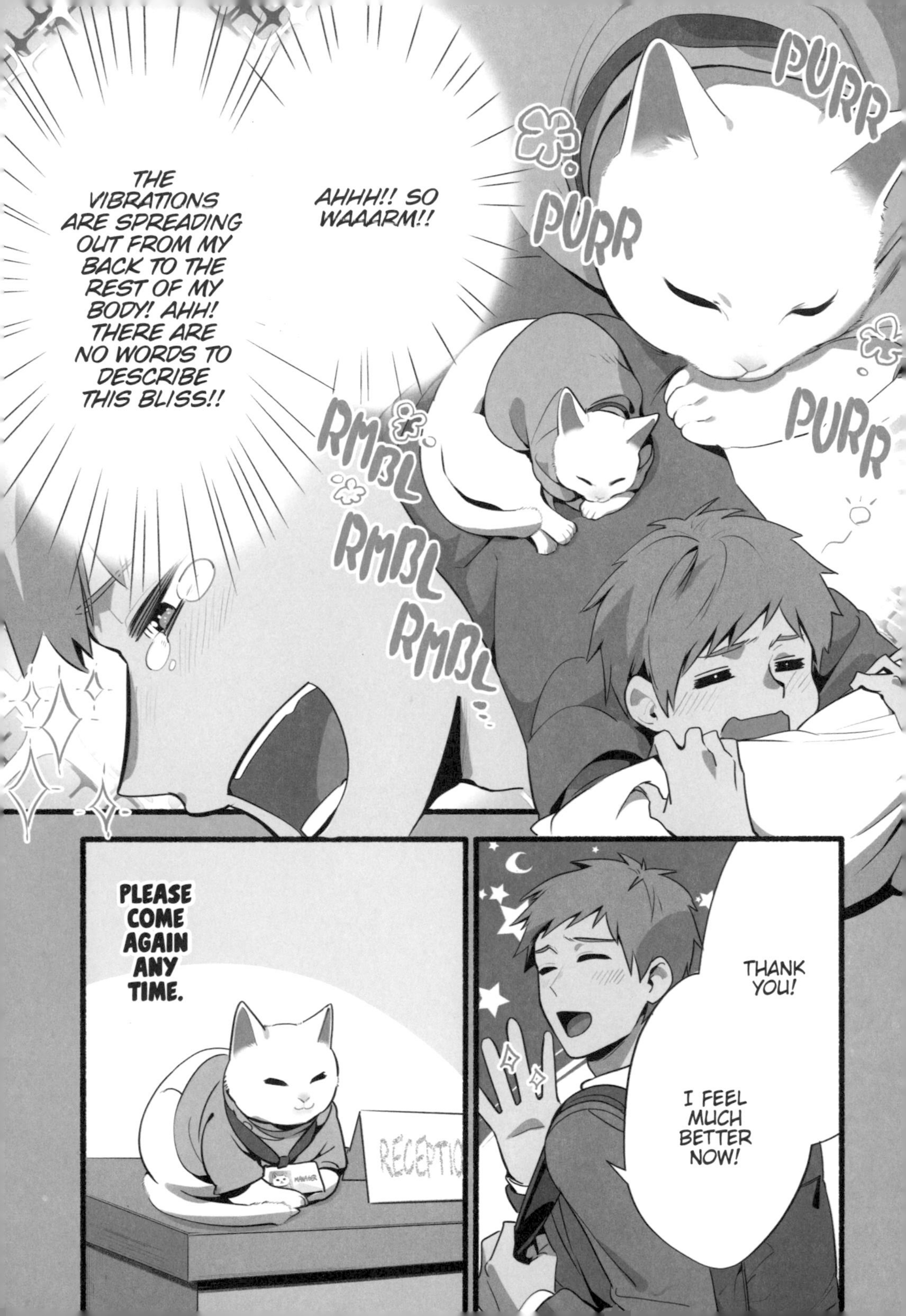
PURR
PURR
PURR
RMBL
RMBL
RMBL
AHHH!! SO WAAARM!!
THE VIBRATIONS ARE SPREADING OUT FROM MY BACK TO THE REST OF MY BODY! AHH! THERE ARE NO WORDS TO DESCRIBE THIS BLISS!!
THANK YOU!
I FEEL MUCH BETTER NOW!
PLEASE COME AGAIN ANY TIME.

CAT MASSAGE THERAPY

Questionnaire

CONTENTS

CAT MASSAGE THERAPY

First-Time Visitor

On-Site Massage

CAT MASSAGE THERAPY
Questionnaire

CONTENTS
CAT MASSAGE THERAPY

Please indicate where you'd like to pet us.

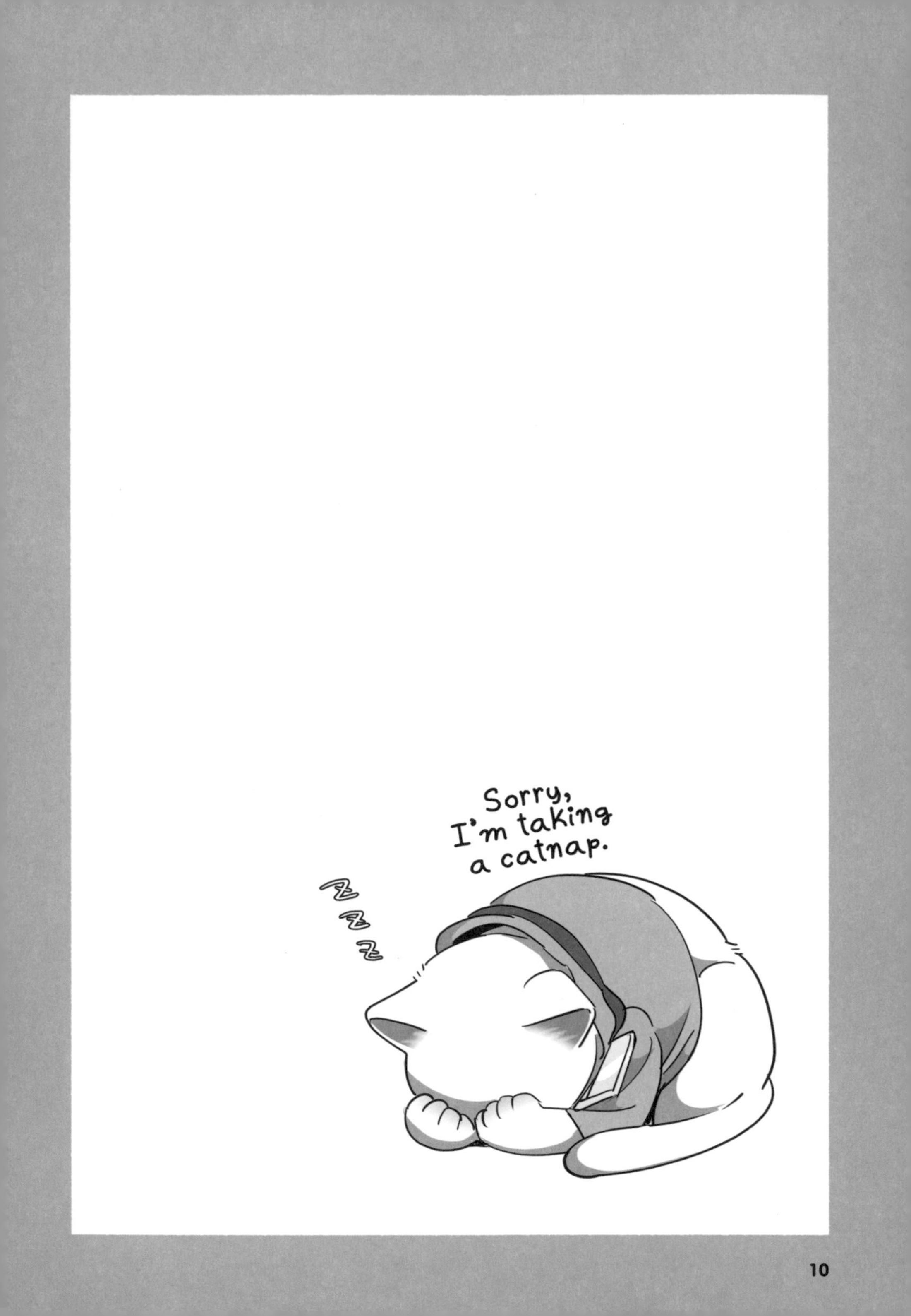
Sorry, I'm taking a catnap.
z z z

Q2. A Task for the Trainees

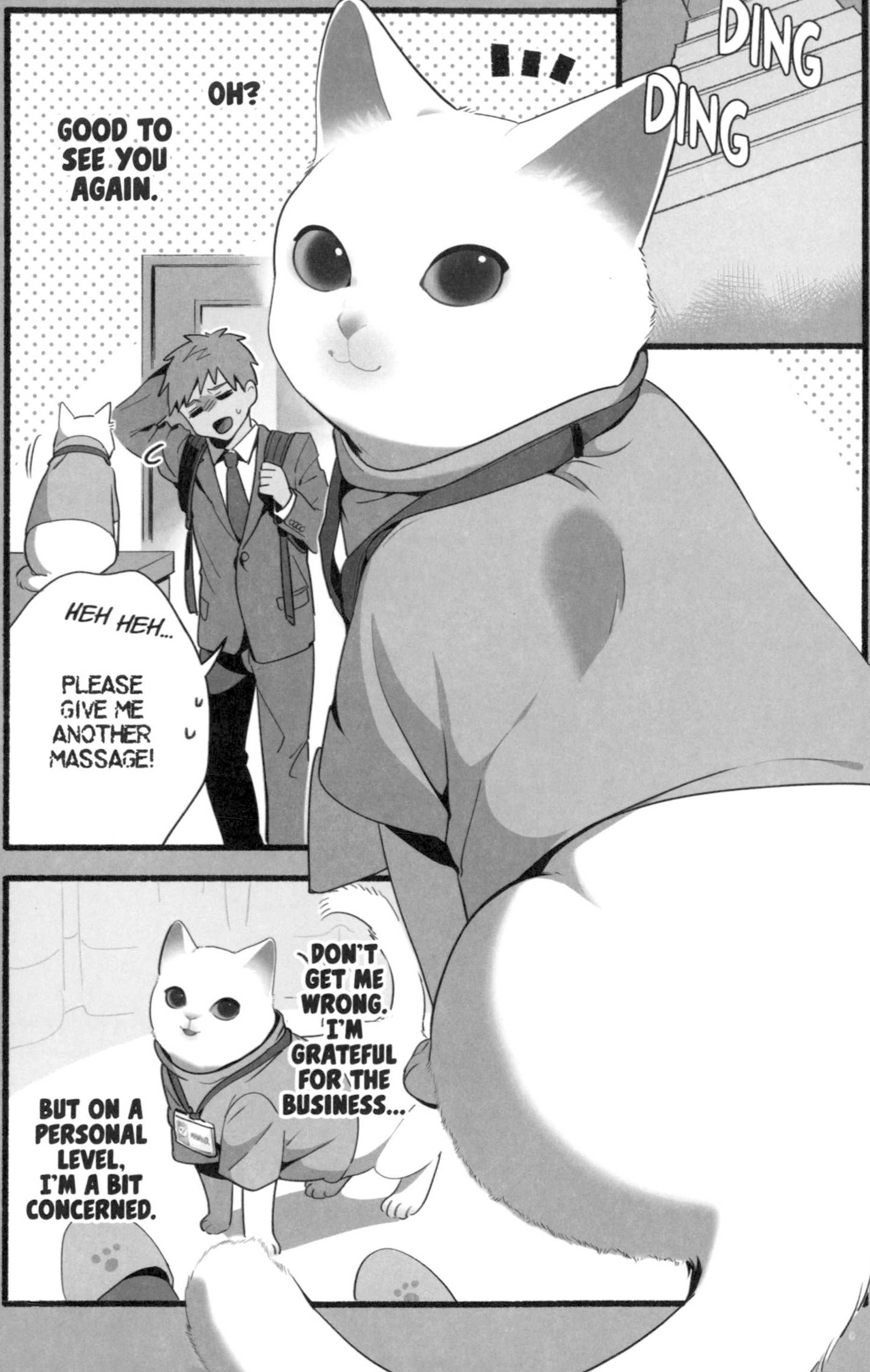
DING
DING
...
OH?
GOOD TO SEE YOU AGAIN.
HEH HEH...
PLEASE GIVE ME ANOTHER MASSAGE!
DON'T GET ME WRONG. I'M GRATEFUL FOR THE BUSINESS...
BUT ON A PERSONAL LEVEL, I'M A BIT CONCERNED.

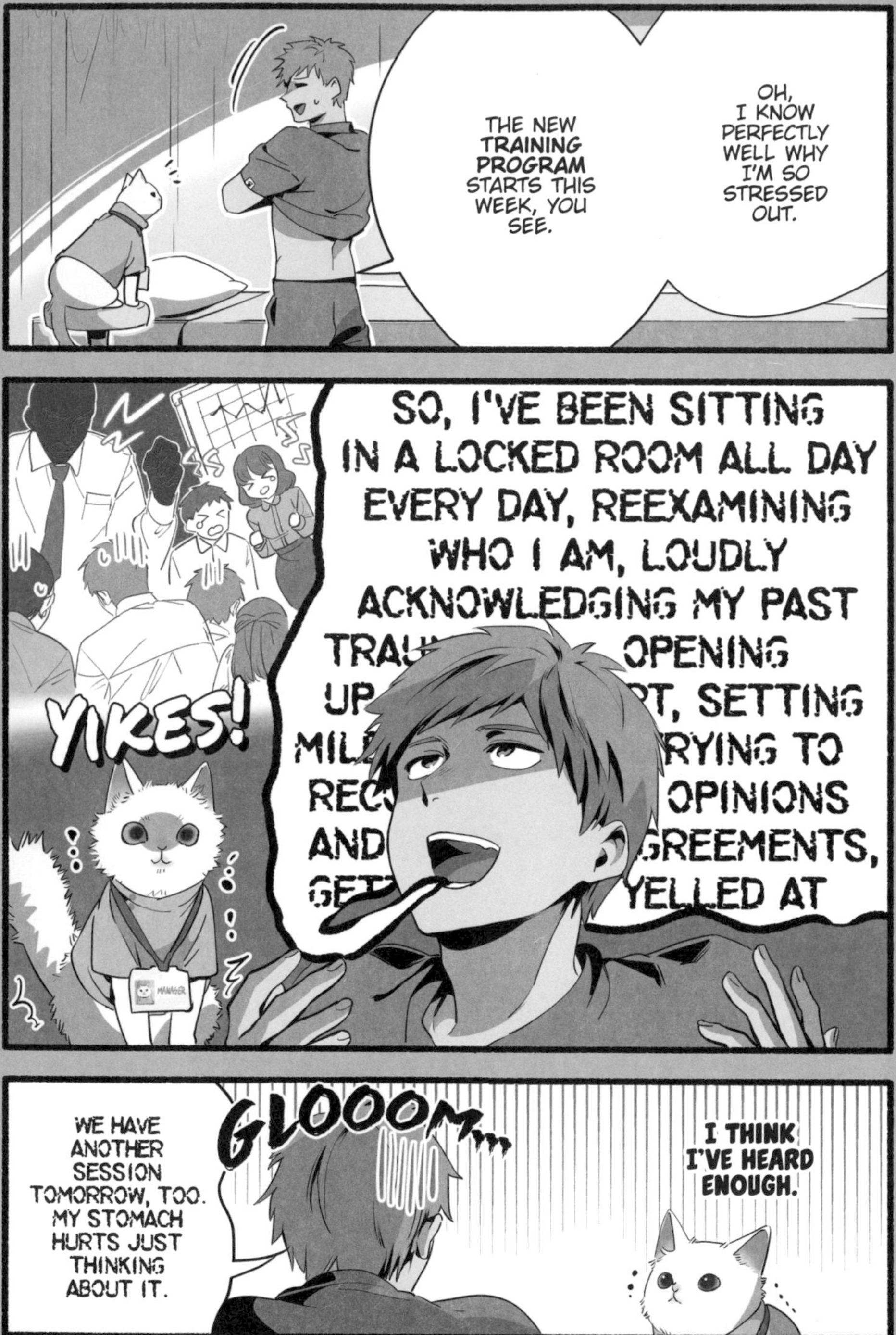
OH, I KNOW PERFECTLY WELL WHY I'M SO STRESSED OUT.
THE NEW **TRAINING PROGRAM** STARTS THIS WEEK, YOU SEE.
SO, I'VE BEEN SITTING IN A LOCKED ROOM ALL DAY EVERY DAY, REEXAMINING WHO I AM, LOUDLY ACKNOWLEDGING MY PAST
OPENING
SETTING
OPINIONS
YELLED AT
YIKES!
I THINK I'VE HEARD ENOUGH.
GLOOOM...
WE HAVE ANOTHER SESSION TOMORROW, TOO. MY STOMACH HURTS JUST THINKING ABOUT IT.

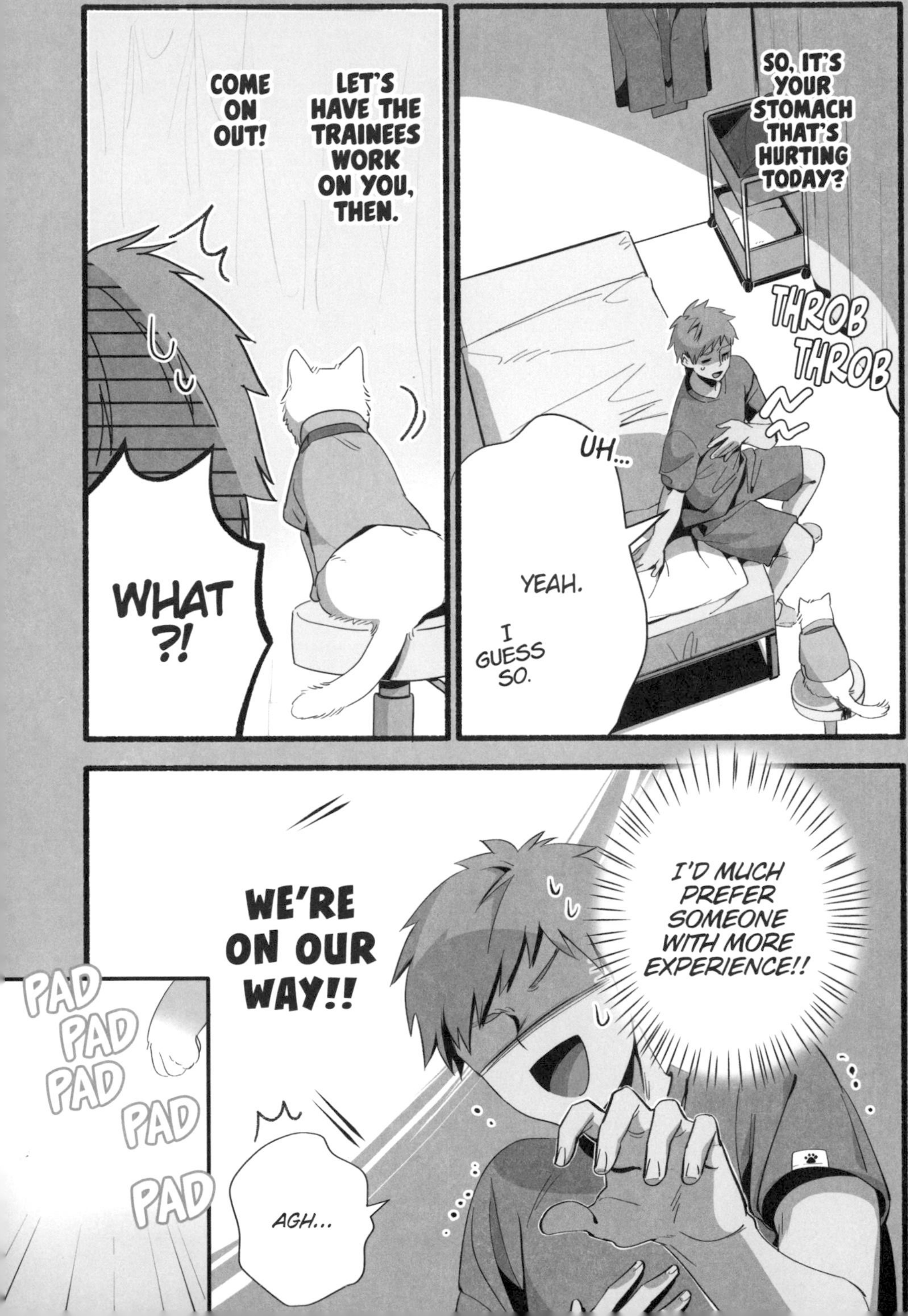
SO, IT'S YOUR STOMACH THAT'S HURTING TODAY?
THROB THROB
UH...
YEAH.
I GUESS SO.
LET'S HAVE THE TRAINEES WORK ON YOU, THEN.
COME ON OUT!
WHAT?!
I'D MUCH PREFER SOMEONE WITH MORE EXPERIENCE!!
WE'RE ON OUR WAY!!
AGH...
PAD PAD PAD PAD PAD

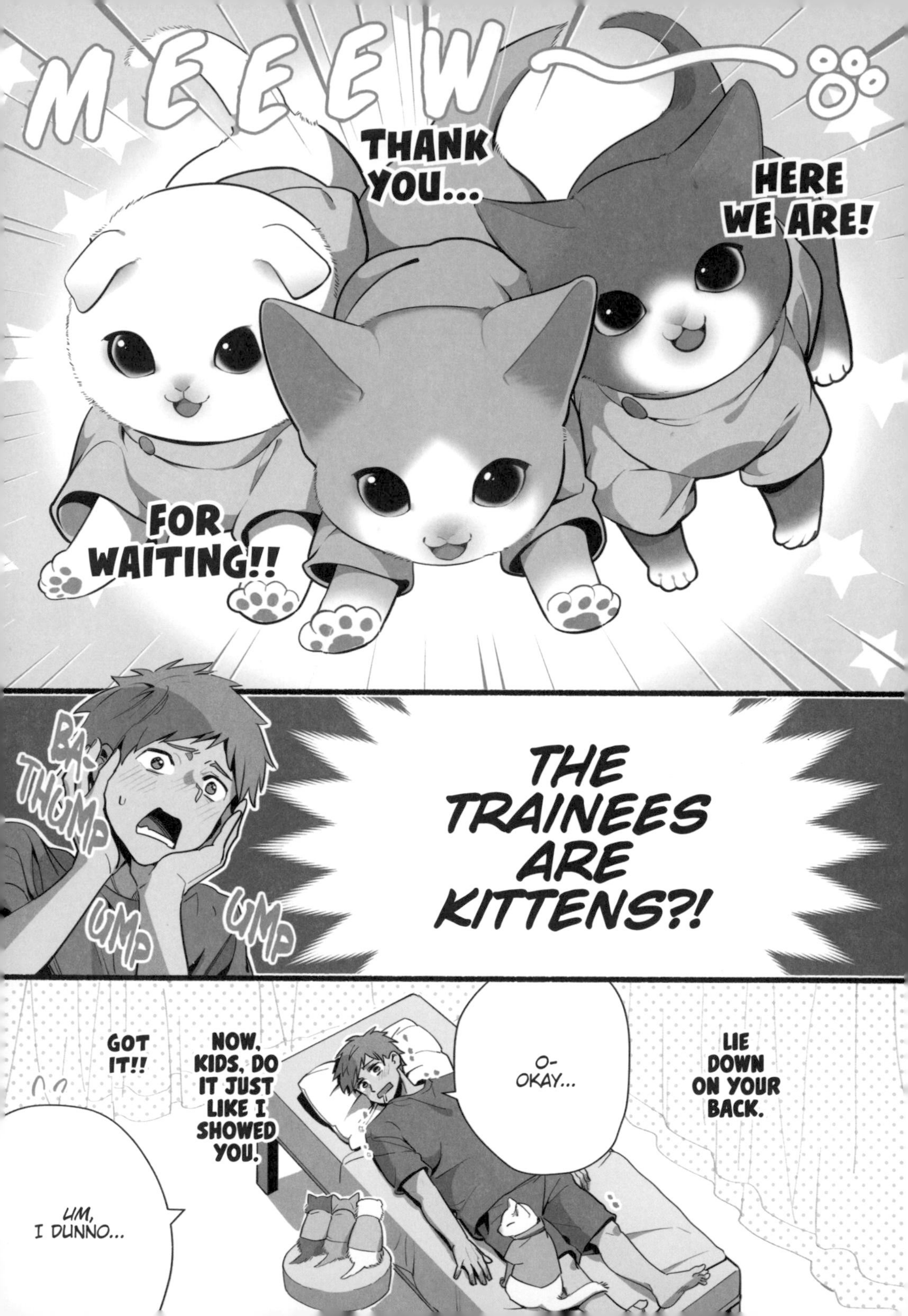
MEEEW
HERE WE ARE!
THANK YOU...
FOR WAITING!!
THE TRAINEES ARE KITTENS?!
BA-THUMP
UMP
UMP
LIE DOWN ON YOUR BACK.
O-OKAY...
NOW, KIDS, DO IT JUST LIKE I SHOWED YOU.
GOT IT!!
UM, I DUNNO...

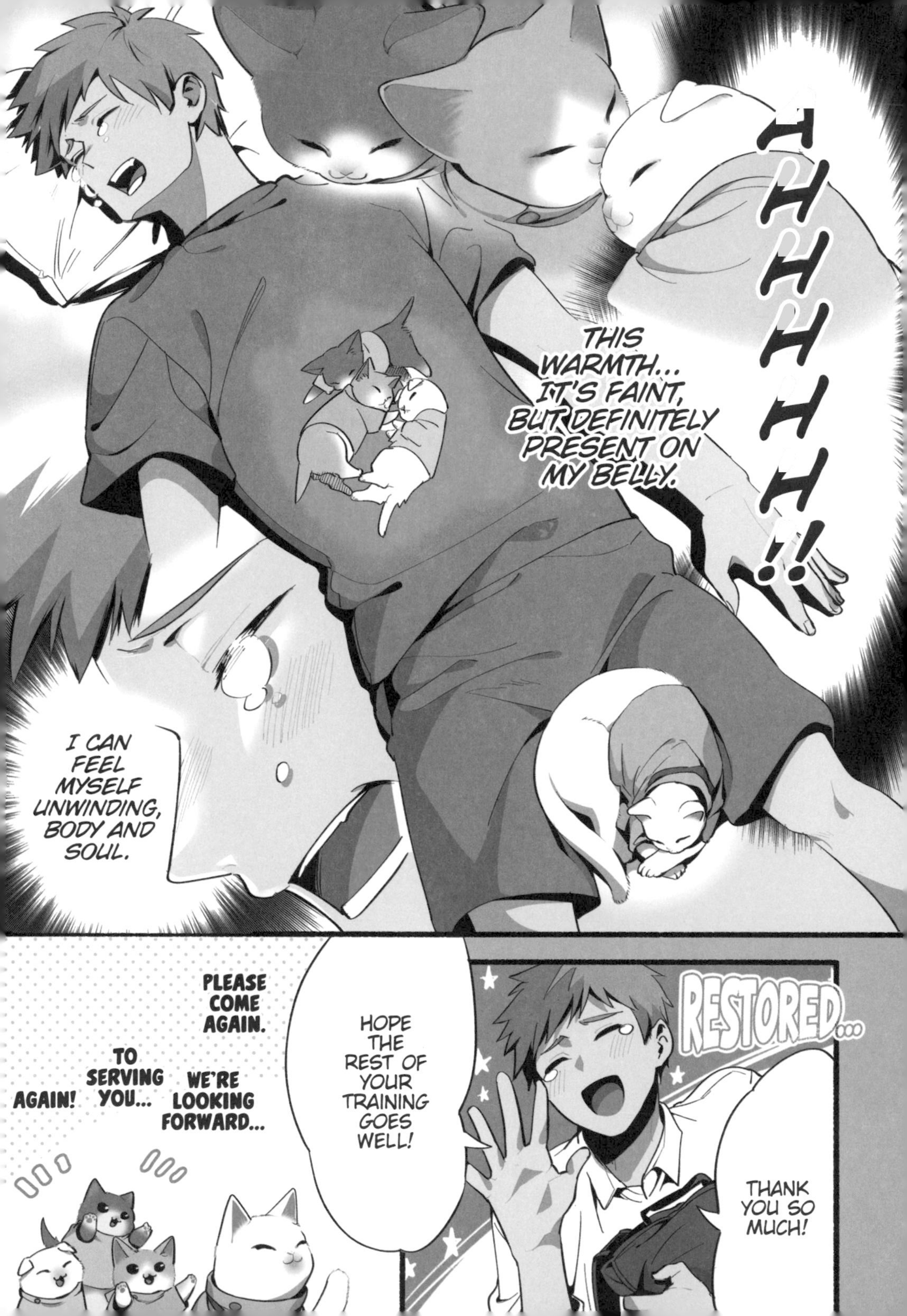
HHHHHH!!
THIS WARMTH... IT'S FAINT, BUT DEFINITELY PRESENT ON MY BELLY.
I CAN FEEL MYSELF UNWINDING, BODY AND SOUL.
RESTORED...
THANK YOU SO MUCH!
HOPE THE REST OF YOUR TRAINING GOES WELL!
PLEASE COME AGAIN.
WE'RE LOOKING FORWARD...
TO SERVING YOU...
AGAIN!

Q3. What Will It Cost?

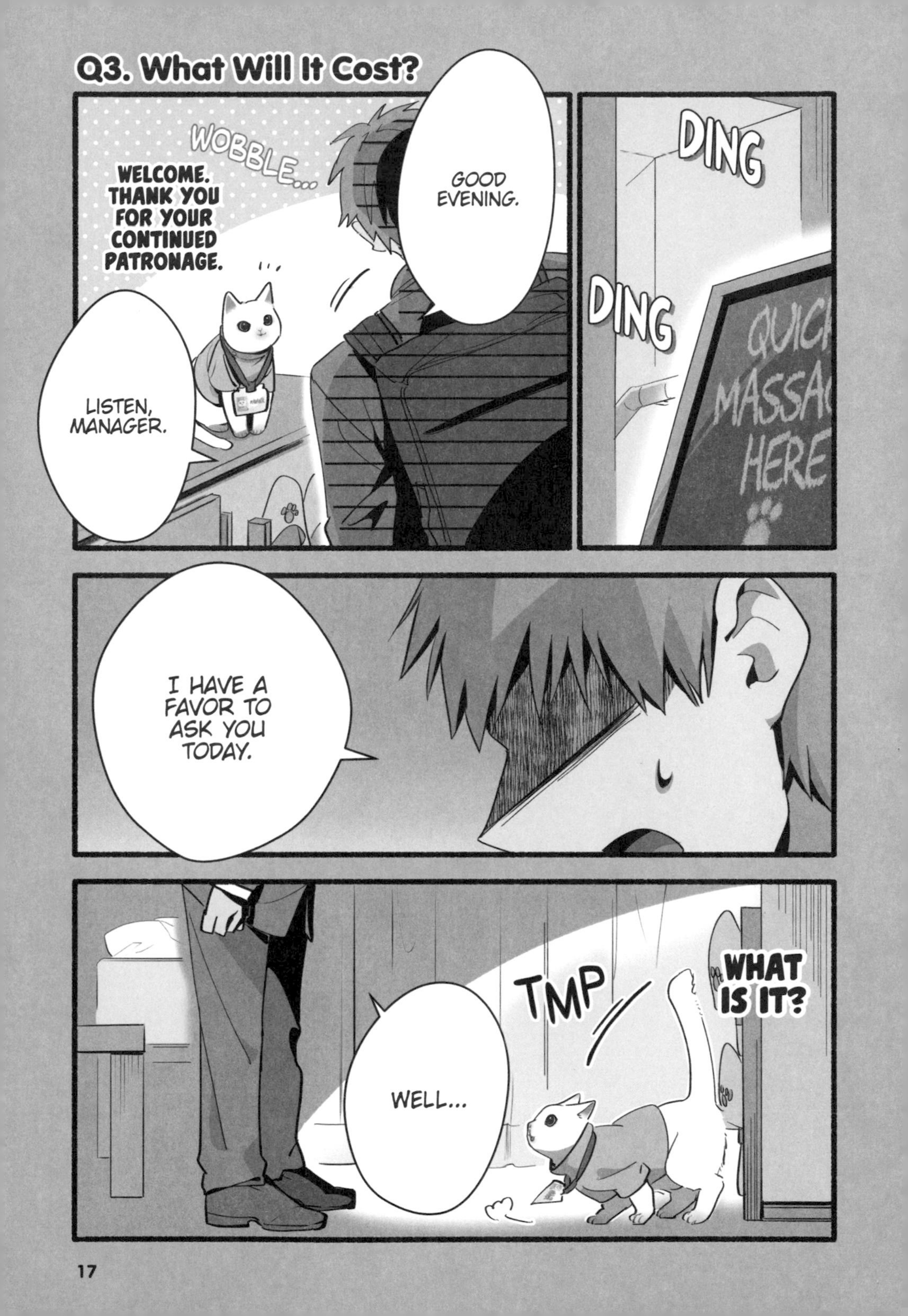
DING
DING
HERE
GOOD EVENING.
WOBBLE...
WELCOME. THANK YOU FOR YOUR CONTINUED PATRONAGE.
LISTEN, MANAGER.
I HAVE A FAVOR TO ASK YOU TODAY.
WHAT IS IT?
TMP
WELL...

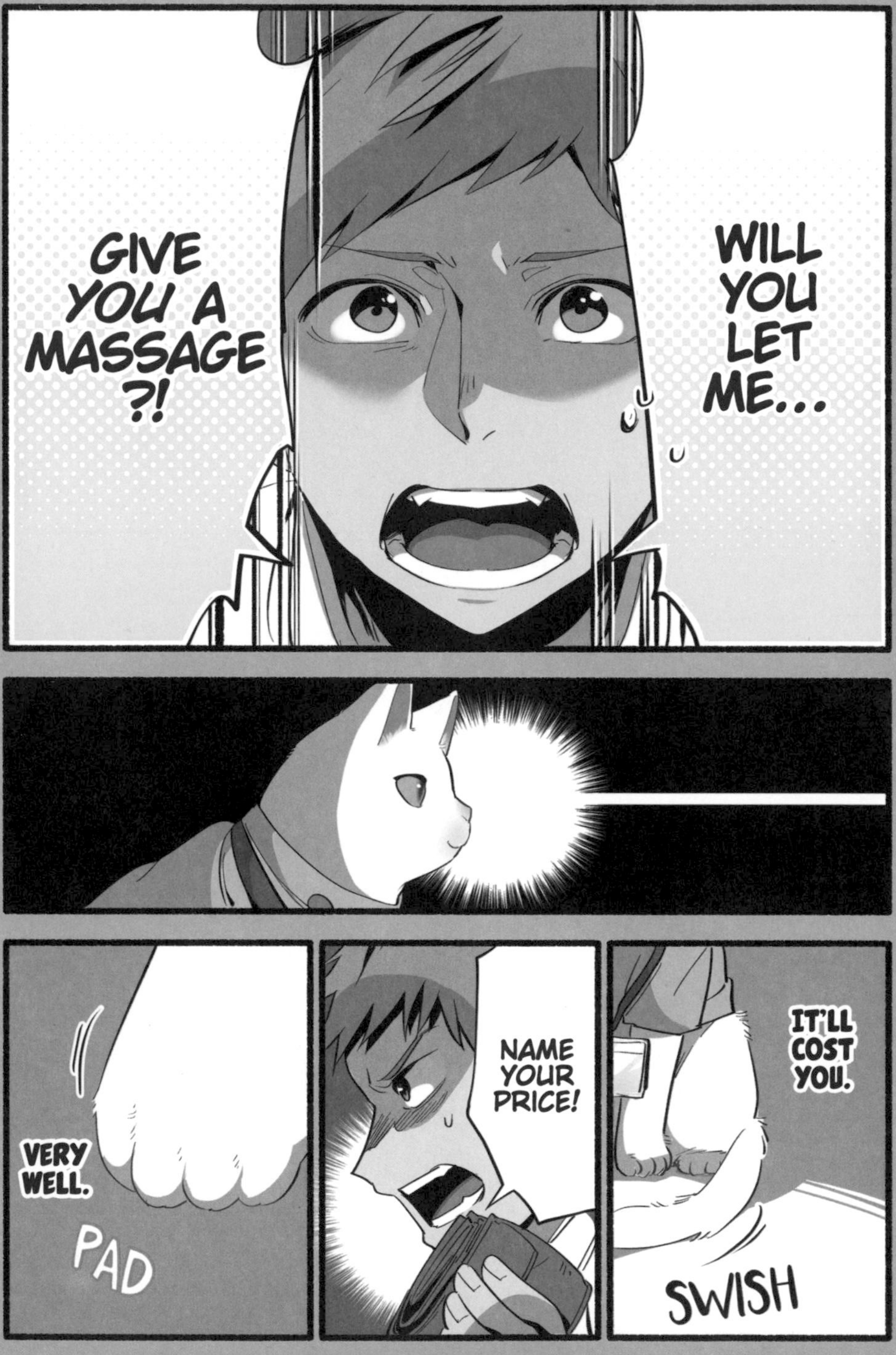
WILL YOU LET ME...
GIVE YOU A MASSAGE?!
IT'LL COST YOU.
SWISH
NAME YOUR PRICE!
VERY WELL.
PAD

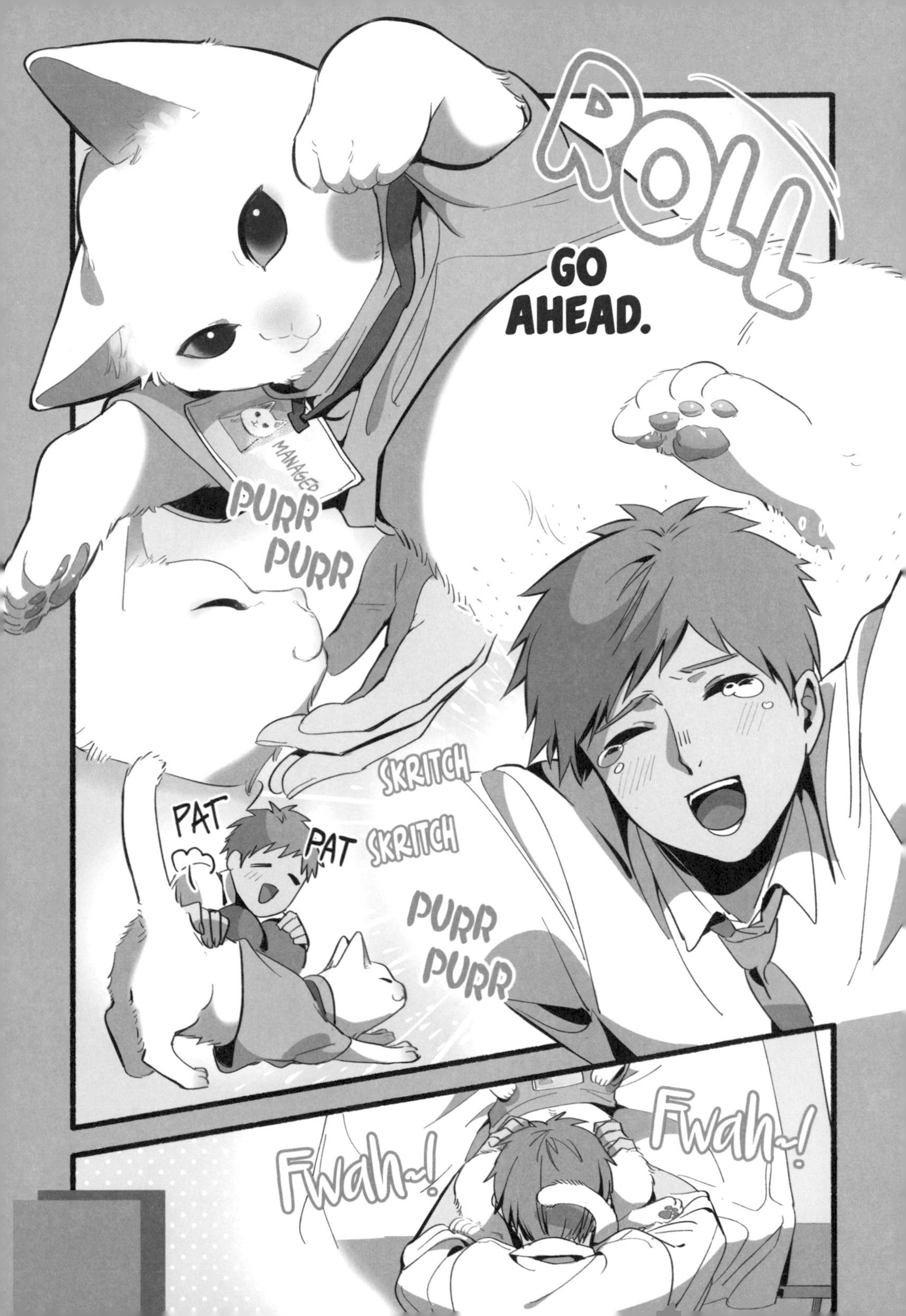
ROLL
GO AHEAD.
MANAGER
PURR PURR
SKRITCH
SKRITCH
PAT PAT
PURR PURR
Fwah~!
Fwah~!

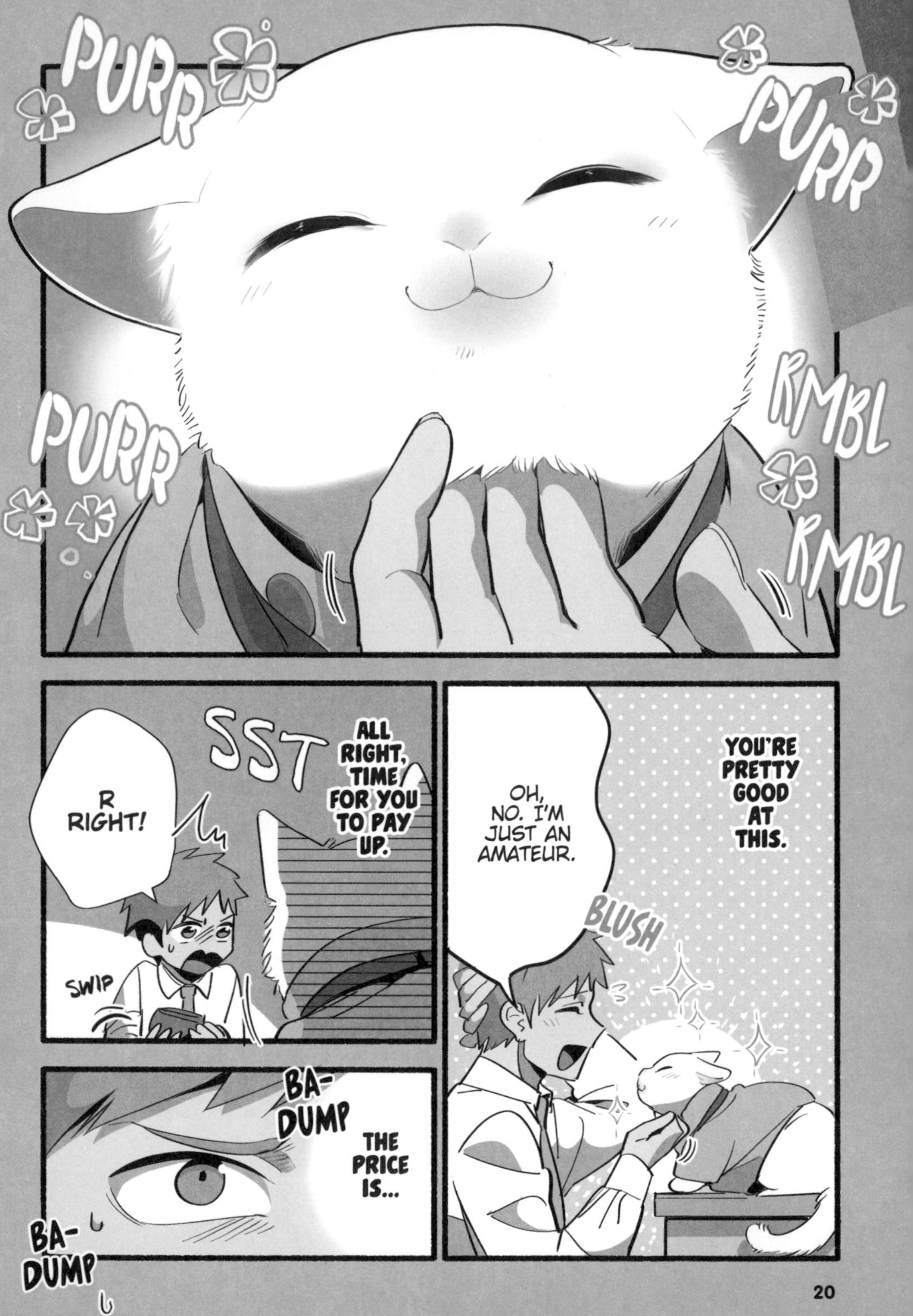
PURR
RMBL
RMBL
PURR
PURR
YOU'RE PRETTY GOOD AT THIS.
OH, NO. I'M JUST AN AMATEUR.
BLUSH
ALL RIGHT, TIME FOR YOU TO PAY UP.
SST
R RIGHT!
SWIP
BA-DUMP
THE PRICE IS...
BA-DUMP

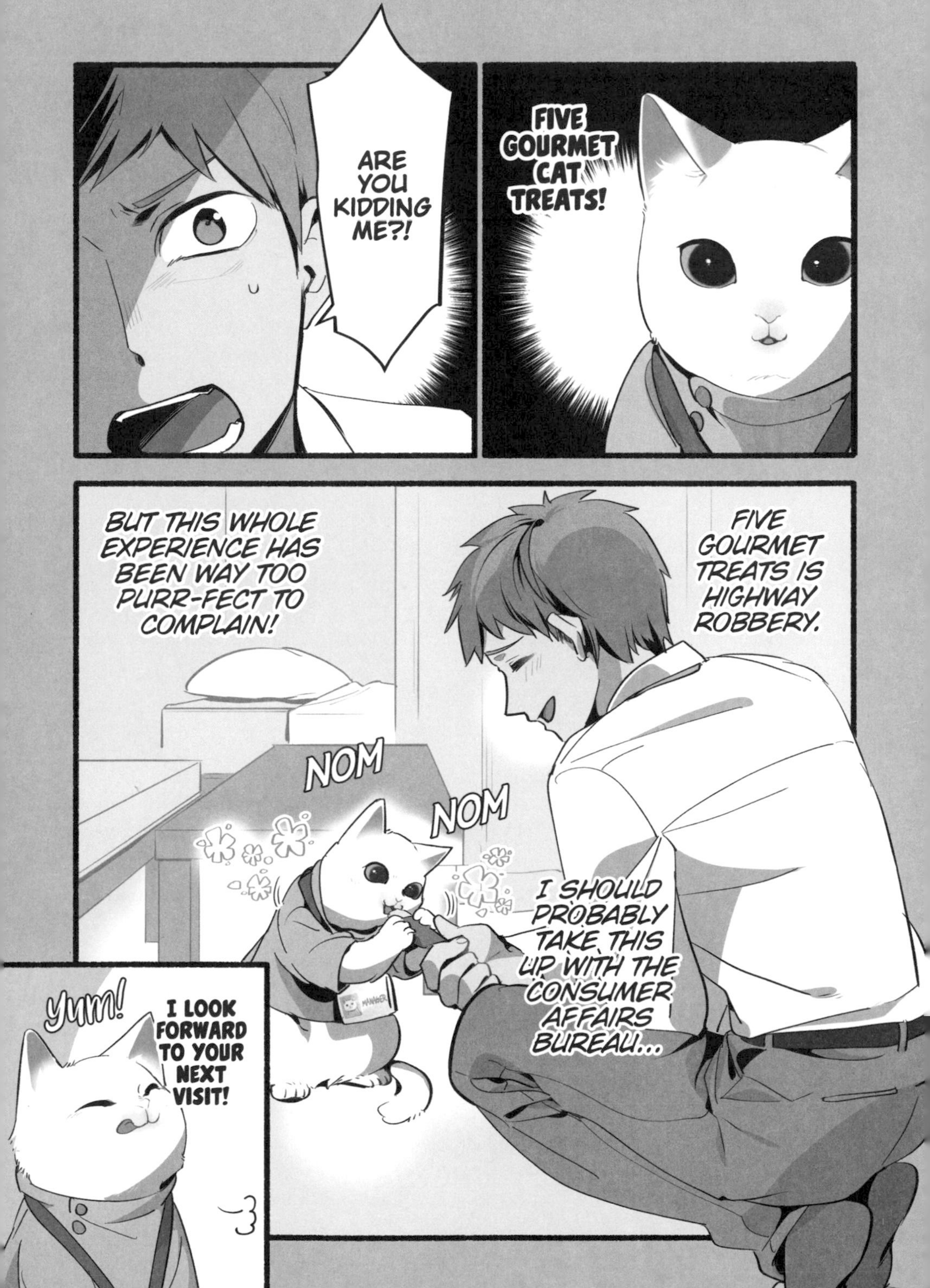
FIVE GOURMET CAT TREATS!
ARE YOU KIDDING ME?!
FIVE GOURMET TREATS IS HIGHWAY ROBBERY.
BUT THIS WHOLE EXPERIENCE HAS BEEN WAY TOO PURR-FECT TO COMPLAIN!
NOM
NOM
I SHOULD PROBABLY TAKE THIS UP WITH THE CONSUMER AFFAIRS BUREAU...
I LOOK FORWARD TO YOUR NEXT VISIT!
Yum!

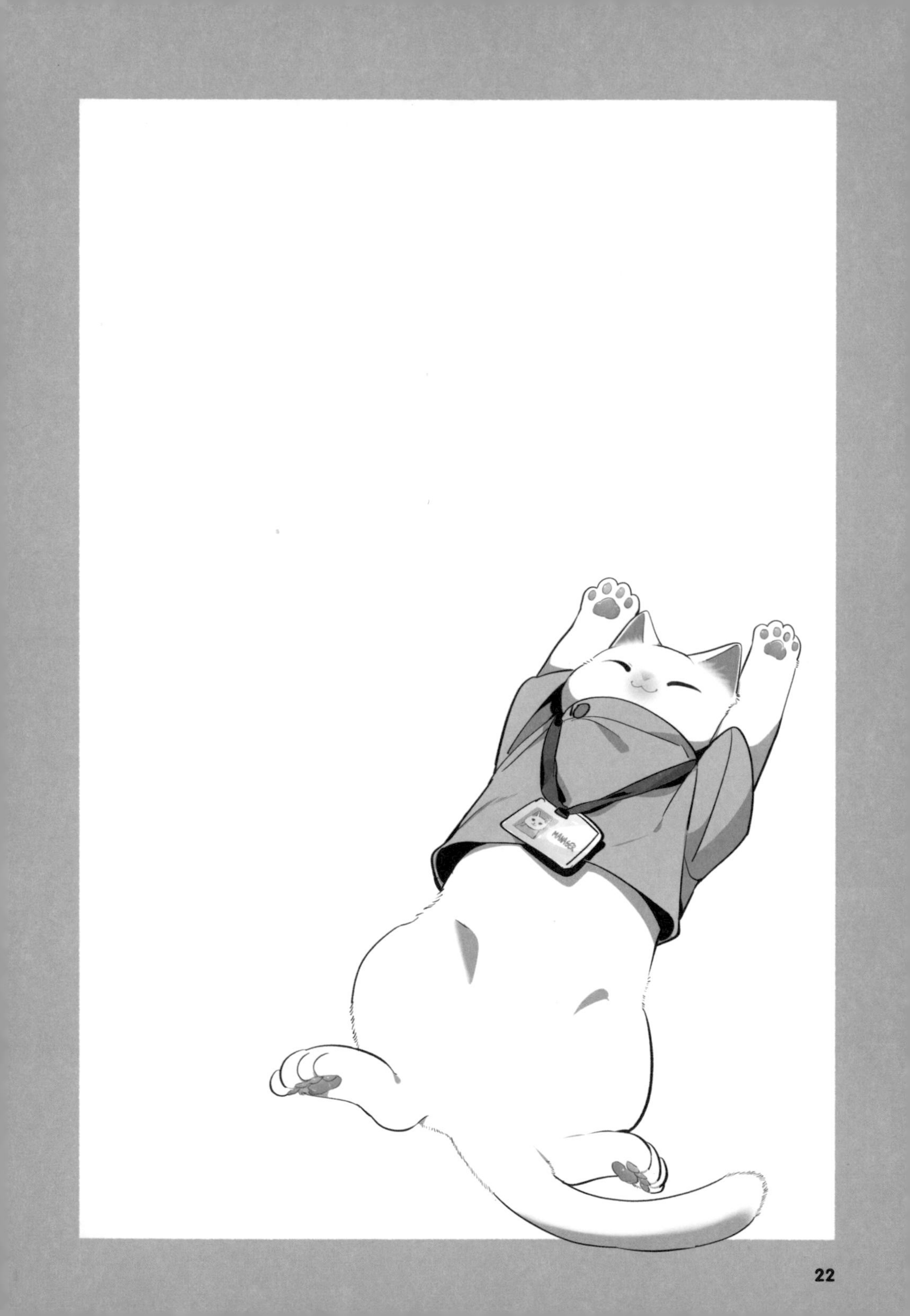
MANAGER

Q4. Time for Your Next Lesson

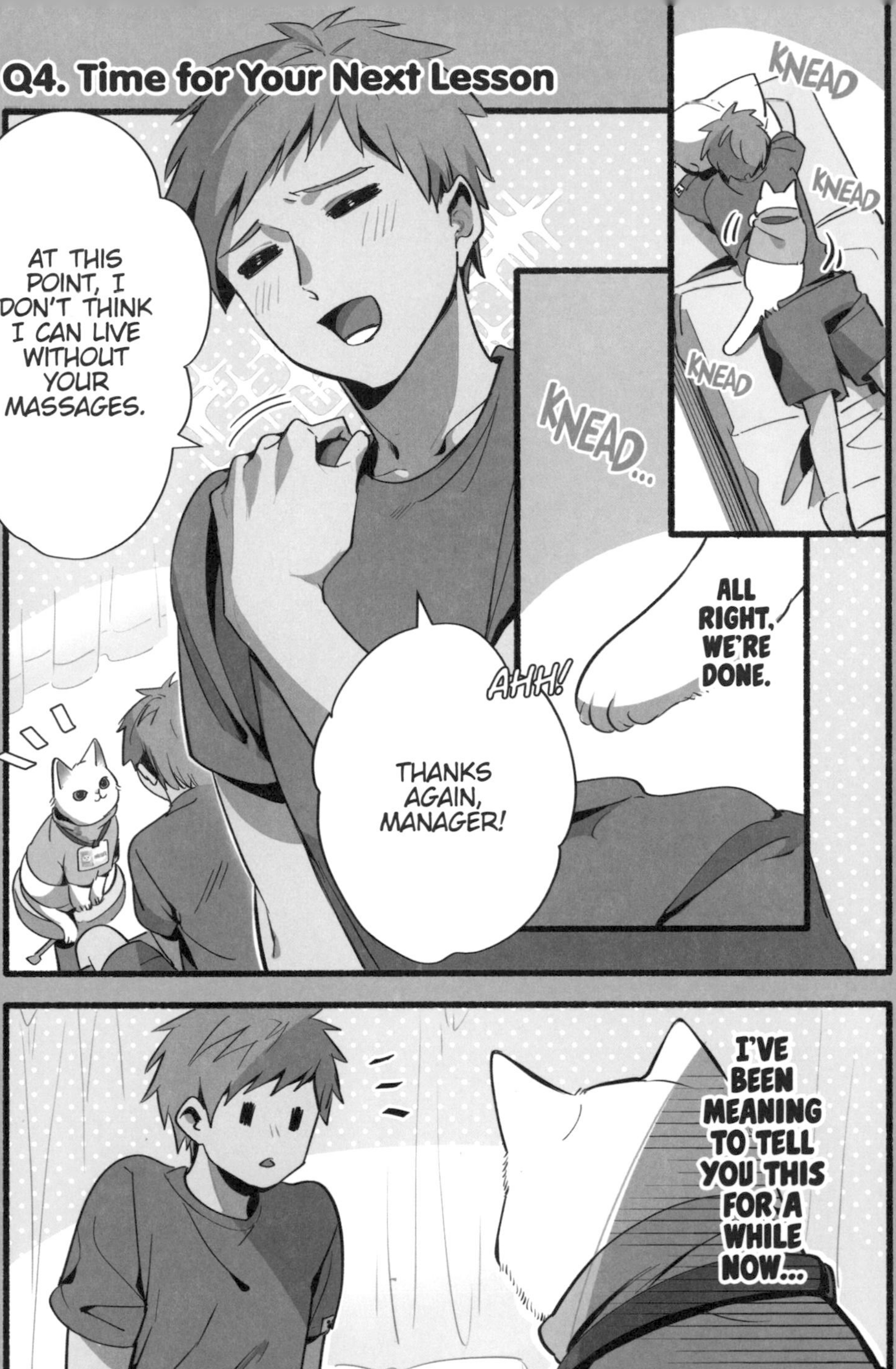
KNEAD
KNEAD
KNEAD
KNEAD...
ALL RIGHT, WE'RE DONE.
AHH!
AT THIS POINT, I DON'T THINK I CAN LIVE WITHOUT YOUR MASSAGES.
THANKS AGAIN, MANAGER!
I'VE BEEN MEANING TO TELL YOU THIS FOR A WHILE NOW...

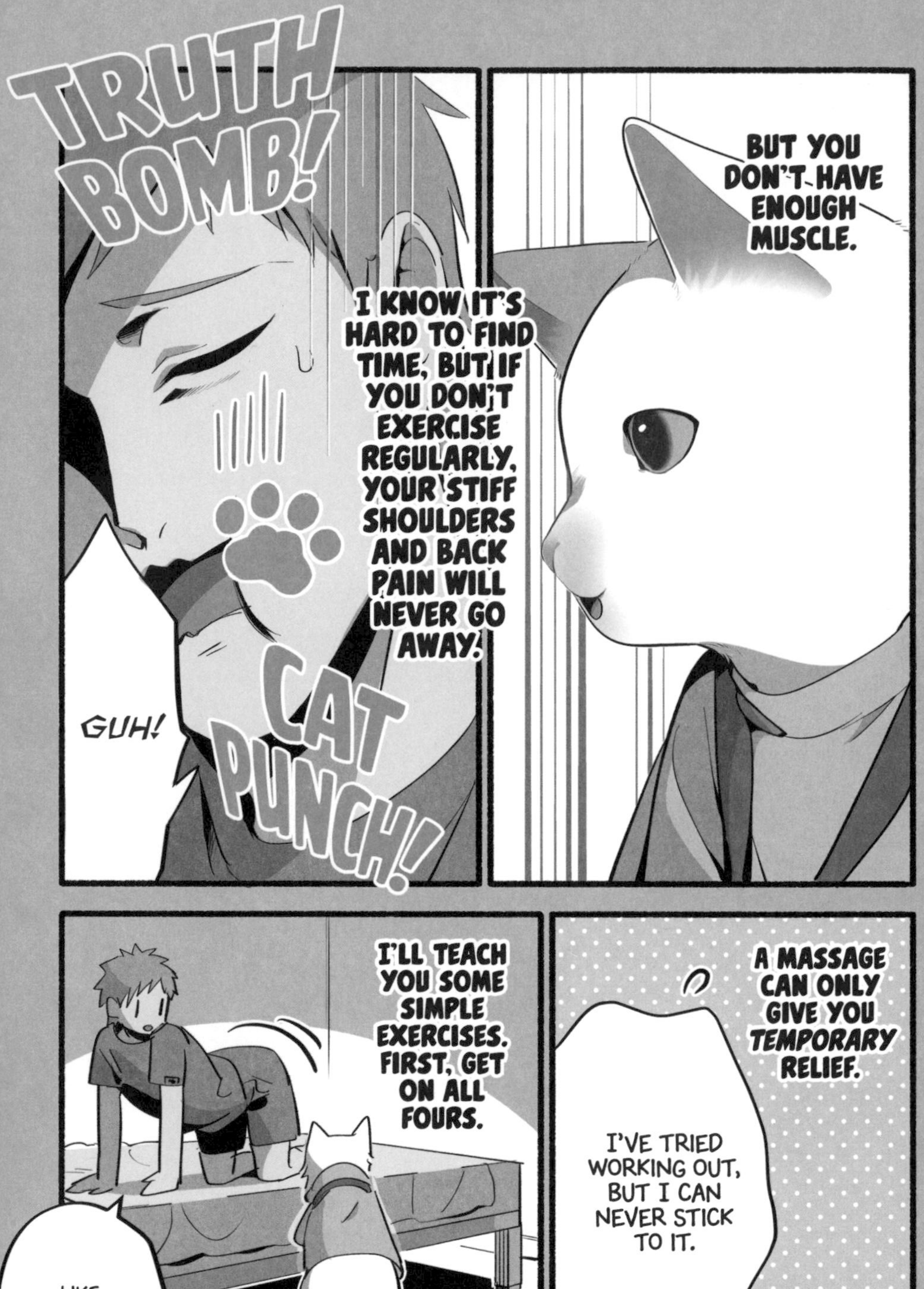
BUT YOU DON'T HAVE ENOUGH MUSCLE.
TRUTH BOMB!
I KNOW IT'S HARD TO FIND TIME, BUT IF YOU DON'T EXERCISE REGULARLY, YOUR STIFF SHOULDERS AND BACK PAIN WILL NEVER GO AWAY.
CAT PUNCH!
GUH!
A MASSAGE CAN ONLY GIVE YOU TEMPORARY RELIEF.
I'VE TRIED WORKING OUT, BUT I CAN NEVER STICK TO IT.
I'LL TEACH YOU SOME SIMPLE EXERCISES. FIRST, GET ON ALL FOURS.
LIKE THIS?

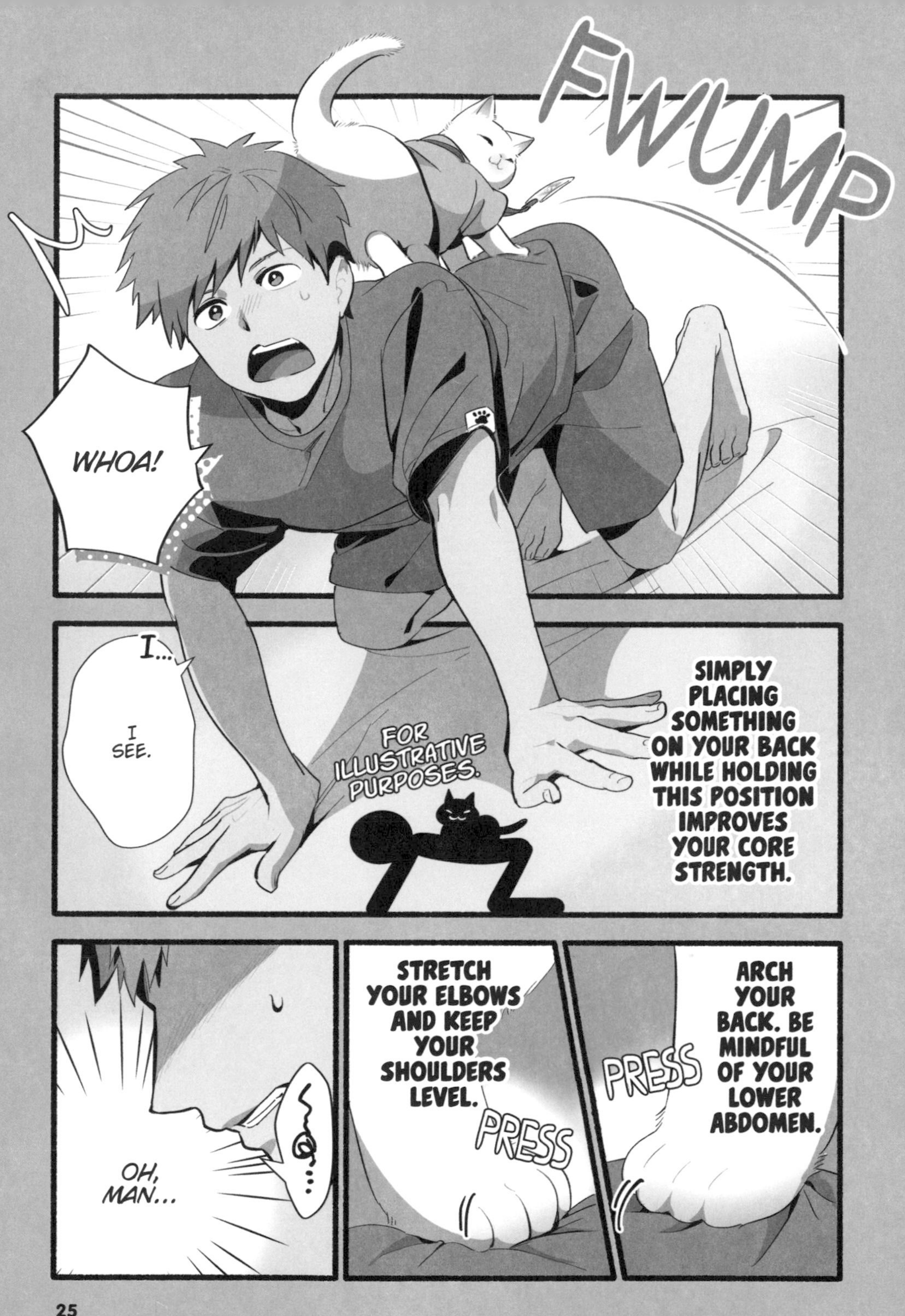
FWUMP
WHOA!
SIMPLY PLACING SOMETHING ON YOUR BACK WHILE HOLDING THIS POSITION IMPROVES YOUR CORE STRENGTH.
FOR ILLUSTRATIVE PURPOSES.
I...
I SEE.
ARCH YOUR BACK. BE MINDFUL OF YOUR LOWER ABDOMEN.
PRESS
STRETCH YOUR ELBOWS AND KEEP YOUR SHOULDERS LEVEL.
PRESS
OH, MAN...

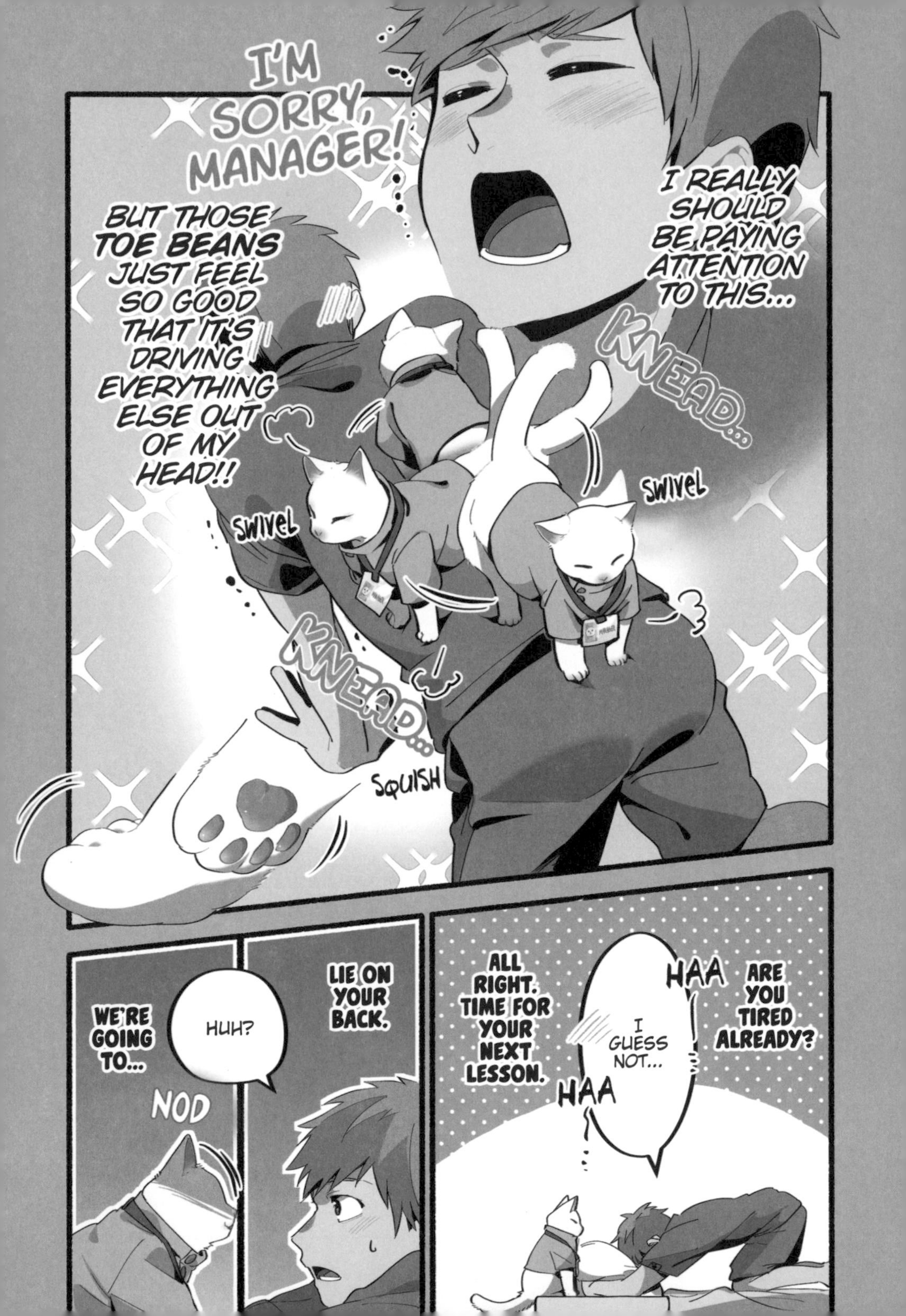
I'M SORRY, MANAGER!
I REALLY SHOULD BE PAYING ATTENTION TO THIS...
BUT THOSE TOE BEANS JUST FEEL SO GOOD THAT IT'S DRIVING EVERYTHING ELSE OUT OF MY HEAD!!
KNEAD...
SWIVEL
SWIVEL
KNEAD...
SQUISH
ARE YOU TIRED ALREADY?
HAA
I GUESS NOT...
HAA
ALL RIGHT. TIME FOR YOUR NEXT LESSON.
LIE ON YOUR BACK.
HUH?
WE'RE GOING TO...
NOD

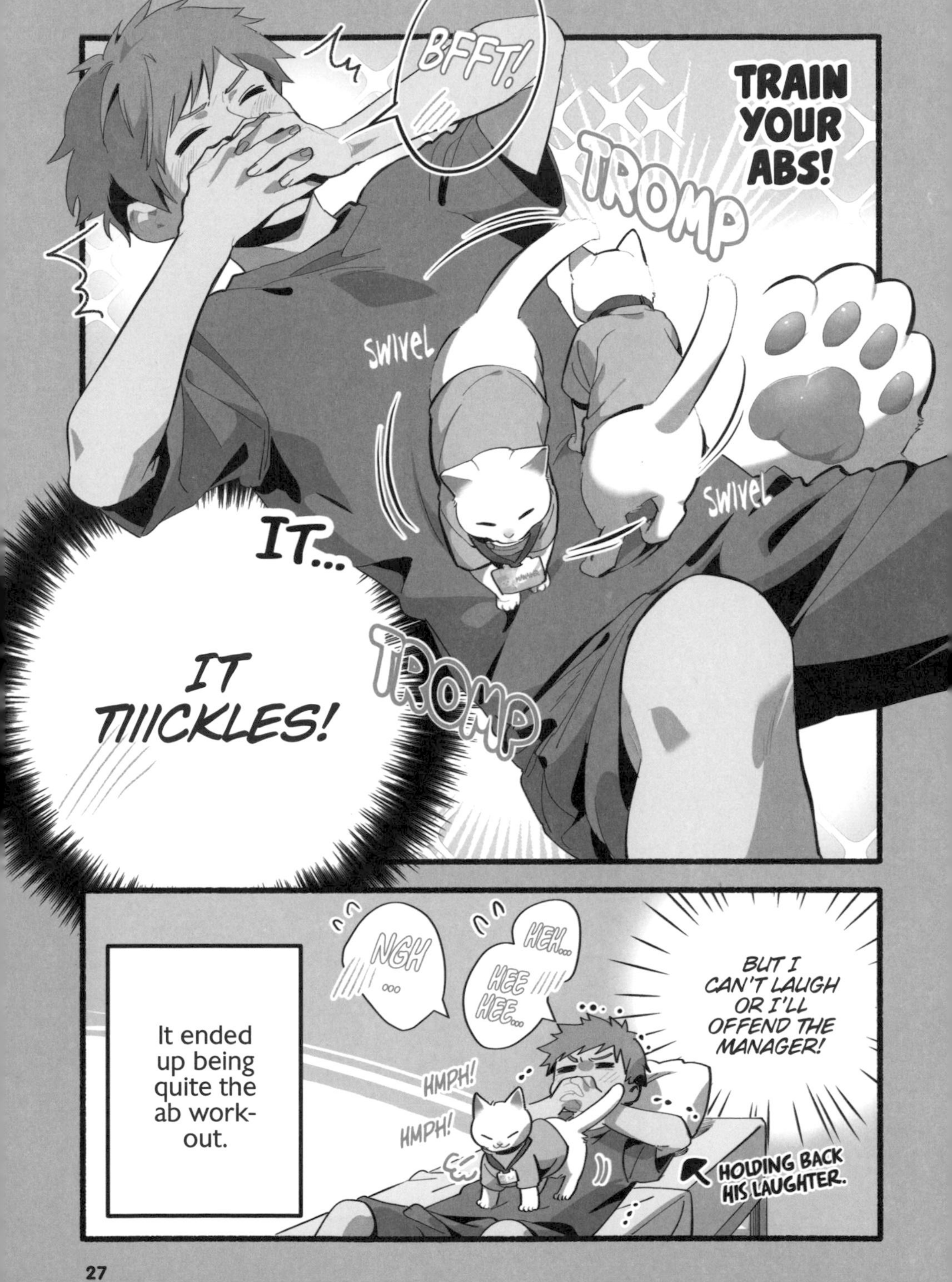
TRAIN YOUR ABS!
BFFT!
TROMP
SWIVEL
SWIVEL
IT...
TROMP
IT TIIICKLES!
BUT I CAN'T LAUGH OR I'LL OFFEND THE MANAGER!
HEH... HEE HEE...
NGH ...
HMPH!
HMPH!
HOLDING BACK HIS LAUGHTER.
It ended up being quite the ab work-out.

Q5. Stretch Your Back!

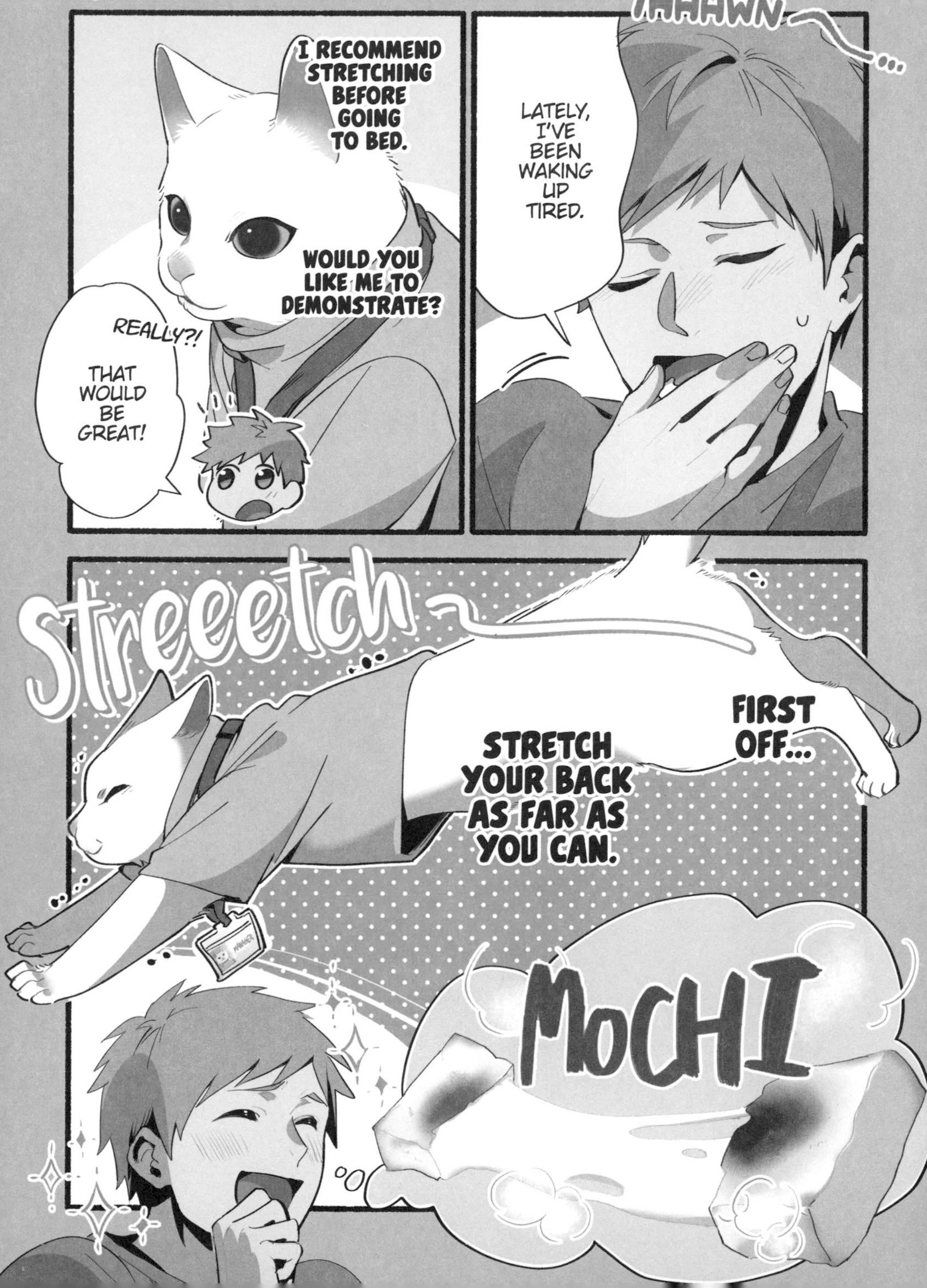
YAAAWN~...
LATELY, I'VE BEEN WAKING UP TIRED.
I RECOMMEND STRETCHING BEFORE GOING TO BED.
WOULD YOU LIKE ME TO DEMONSTRATE?
REALLY?!
THAT WOULD BE GREAT!
FIRST OFF...
STRETCH YOUR BACK AS FAR AS YOU CAN.
streeetch~
MOCHI

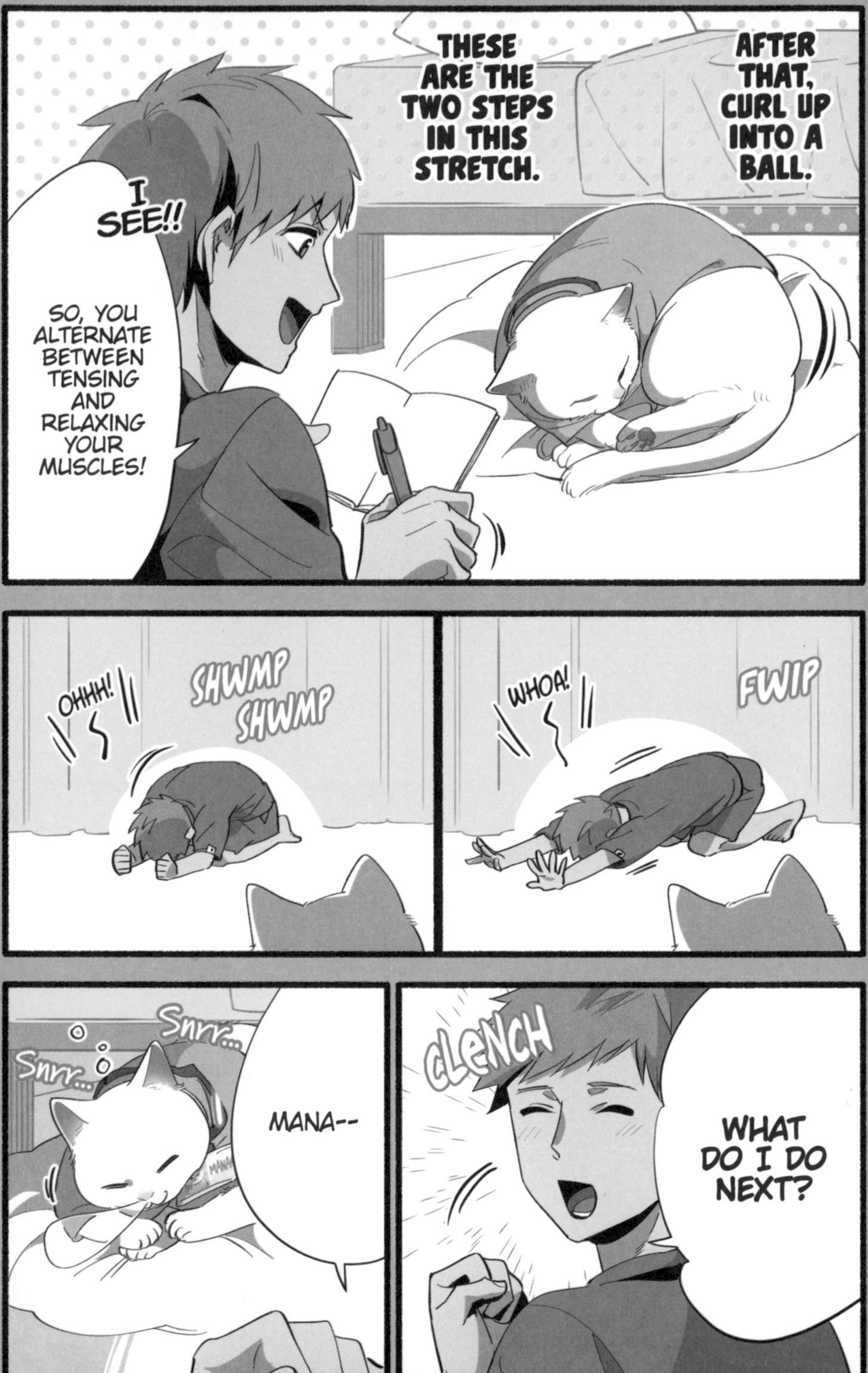
AFTER THAT, CURL UP INTO A BALL.
THESE ARE THE TWO STEPS IN THIS STRETCH.
I SEE!!
SO, YOU ALTERNATE BETWEEN TENSING AND RELAXING YOUR MUSCLES!
FWIP
WHOA!
SHWMP SHWMP
OHHH!
CLENCH
WHAT DO I DO NEXT?
MANA--
Snrr...
Snrr...

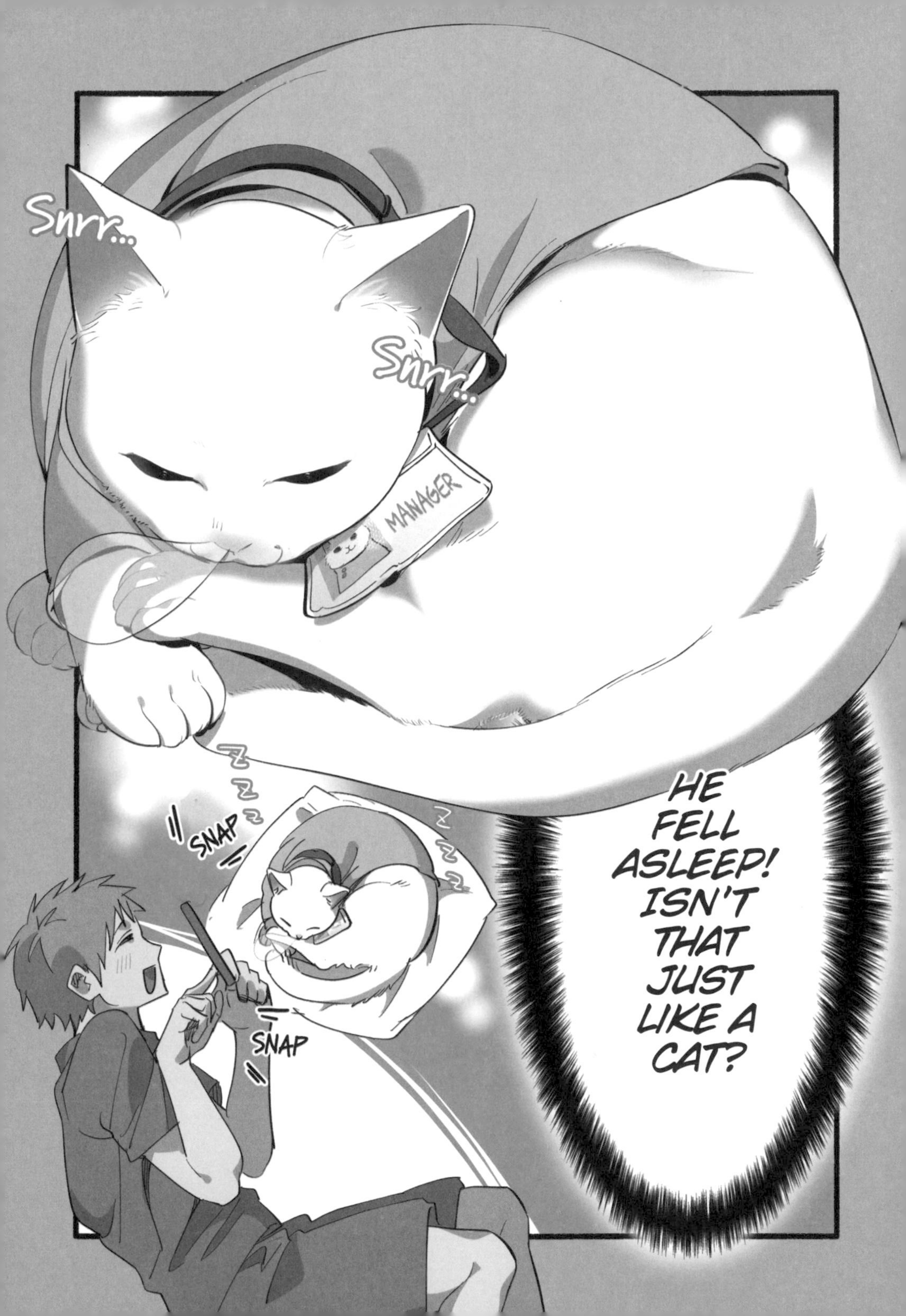
Snrr...
Snrr...
MANAGER
HE FELL ASLEEP! ISN'T THAT JUST LIKE A CAT?
SNAP
SNAP

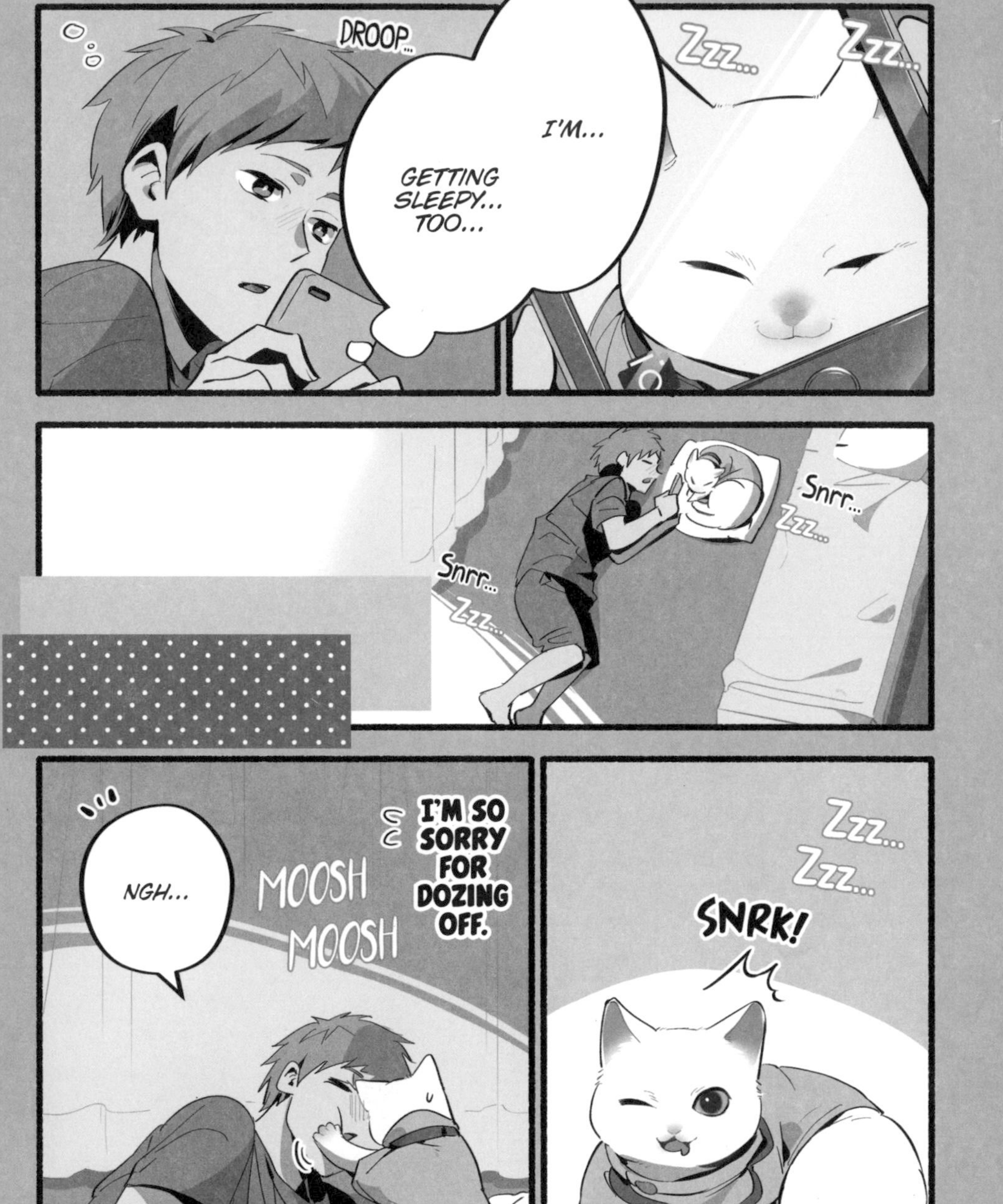
Zzz... Zzz...
DROOP...
I'M... GETTING SLEEPY... TOO...
Snrr... Zzz...
Snrr... Zzz...
Zzz... Zzz...
SNRK!
I'M SO SORRY FOR DOZING OFF.
MOOSH MOOSH
NGH...
MANAGER

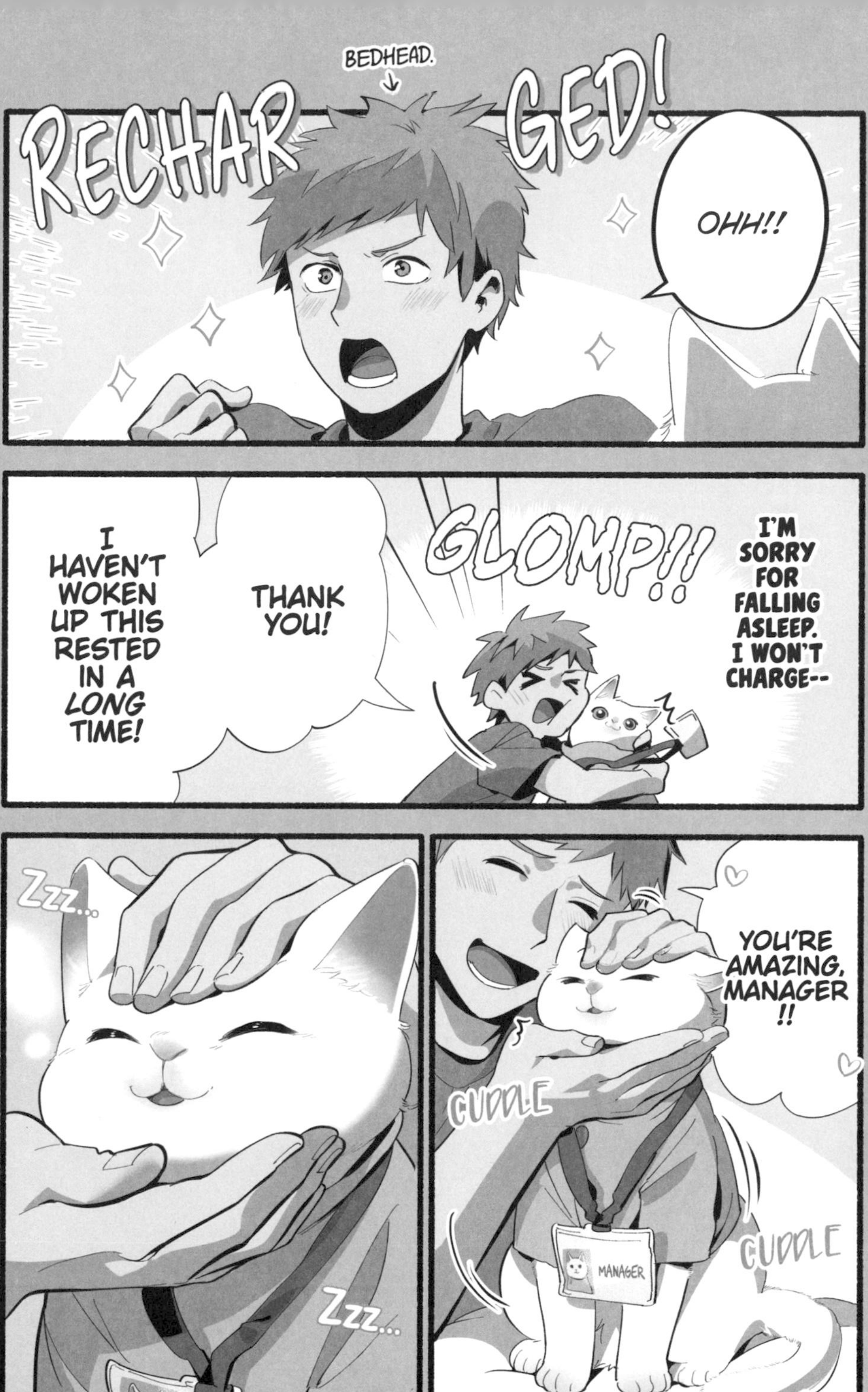
BEDHEAD.
RECHARGED!
OHH!!
I'M SORRY FOR FALLING ASLEEP. I WON'T CHARGE--
GLOMP!!
THANK YOU!
I HAVEN'T WOKEN UP THIS RESTED IN A LONG TIME!
YOU'RE AMAZING, MANAGER!!
CUDDLE
MANAGER
CUDDLE
Zzz...
Zzz...

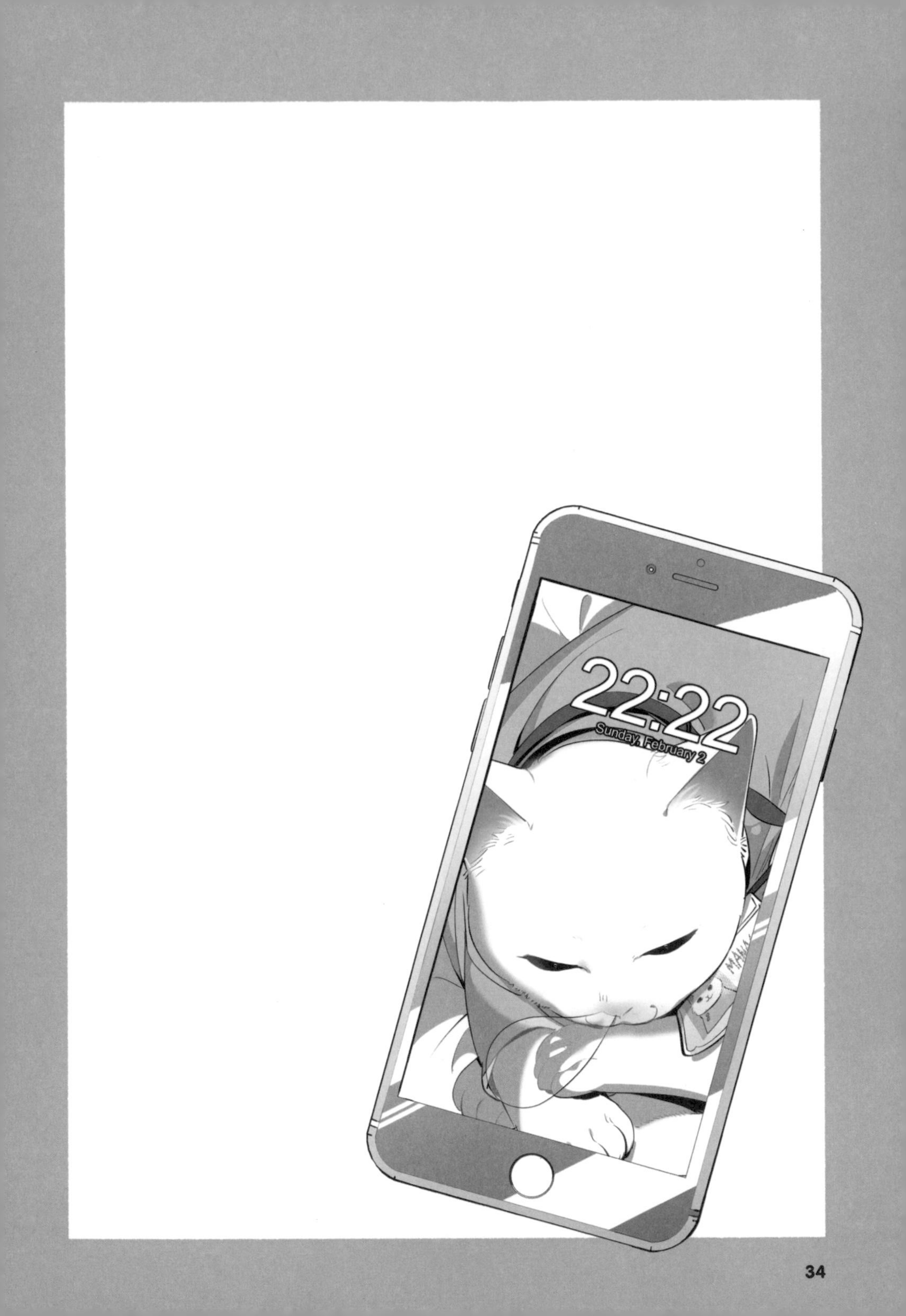
22:22
Sunday, February 2

Q6. Our Policies Are Quite Strict

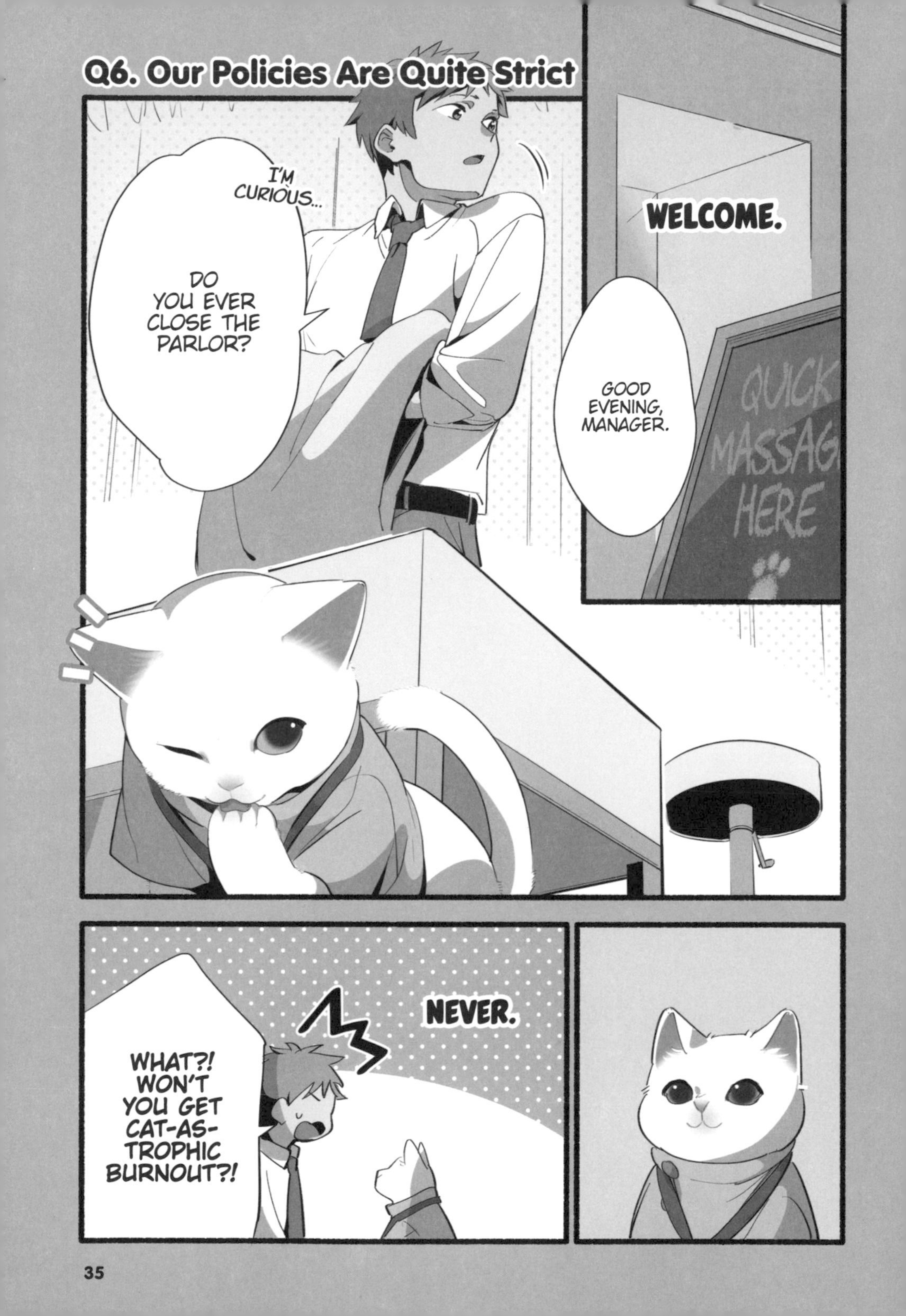

WELCOME.
GOOD EVENING, MANAGER.
QUICK MASSAGE HERE
I'M CURIOUS...
DO YOU EVER CLOSE THE PARLOR?
NEVER.
WHAT?! WON'T YOU GET CAT-AS-TROPHIC BURNOUT?!

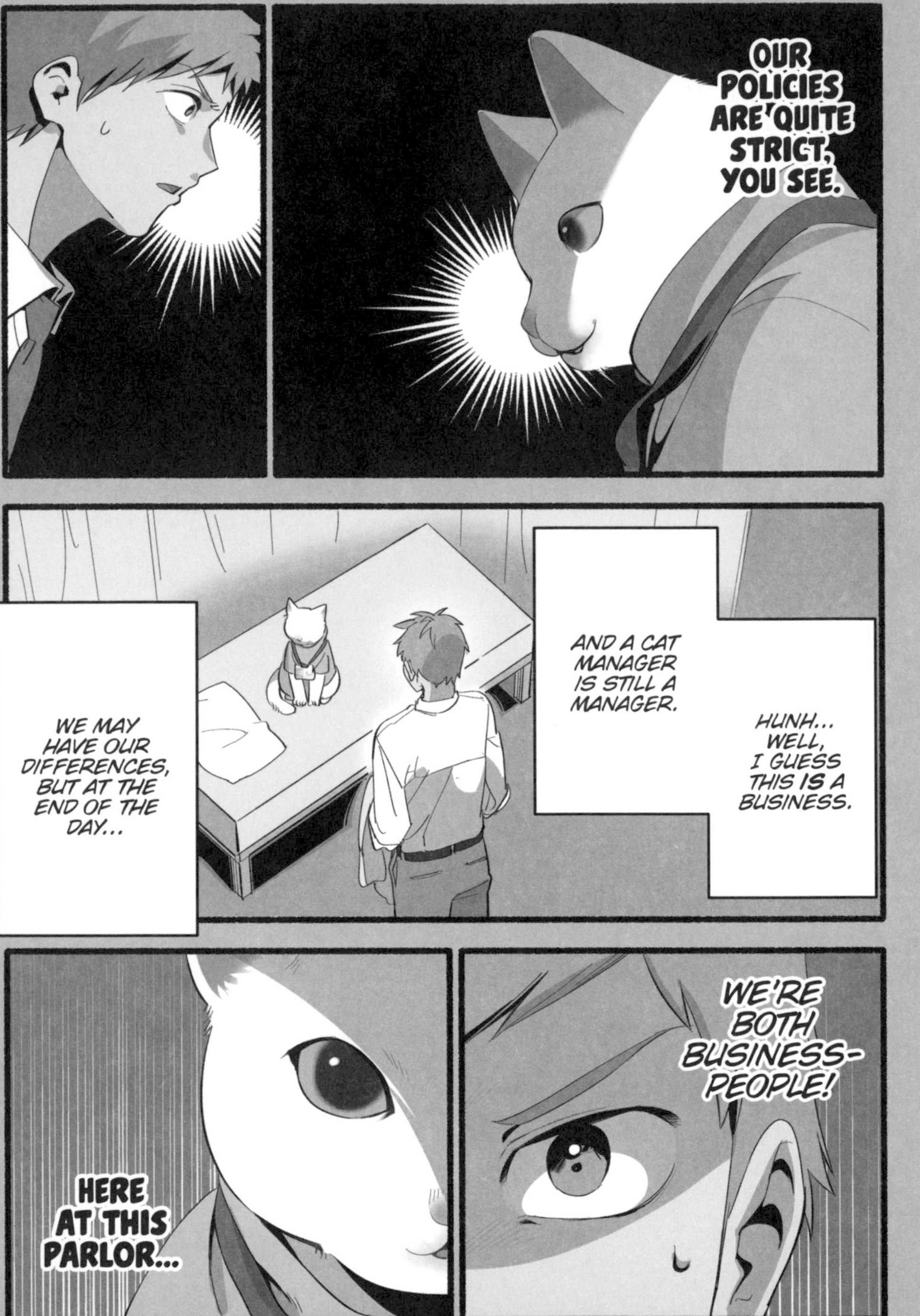
OUR POLICIES ARE QUITE STRICT, YOU SEE.
HUNH... WELL, I GUESS THIS IS A BUSINESS.
AND A CAT MANAGER IS STILL A MANAGER.
WE MAY HAVE OUR DIFFERENCES, BUT AT THE END OF THE DAY...
WE'RE BOTH BUSINESS-PEOPLE!
HERE AT THIS PARLOR...

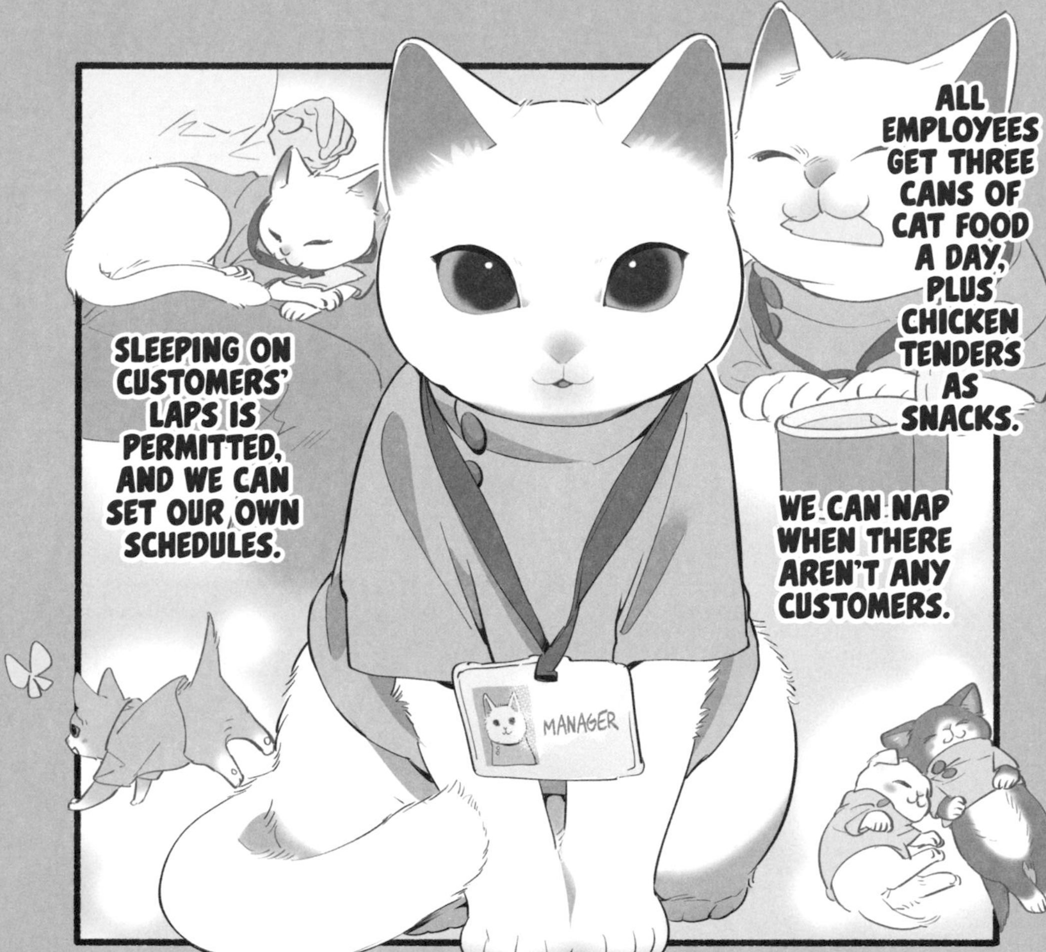
ALL EMPLOYEES GET THREE CANS OF CAT FOOD A DAY, PLUS CHICKEN TENDERS AS SNACKS.
SLEEPING ON CUSTOMERS' LAPS IS PERMITTED, AND WE CAN SET OUR OWN SCHEDULES.
WE CAN NAP WHEN THERE AREN'T ANY CUSTOMERS.
MANAGER
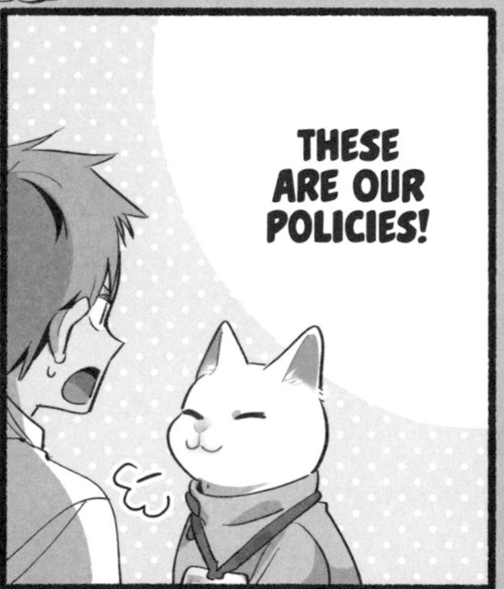
THESE ARE OUR POLICIES!
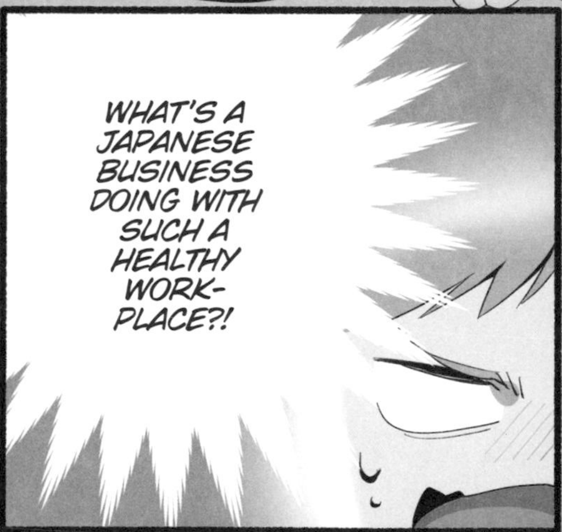
WHAT'S A JAPANESE BUSINESS DOING WITH SUCH A HEALTHY WORK-PLACE?!

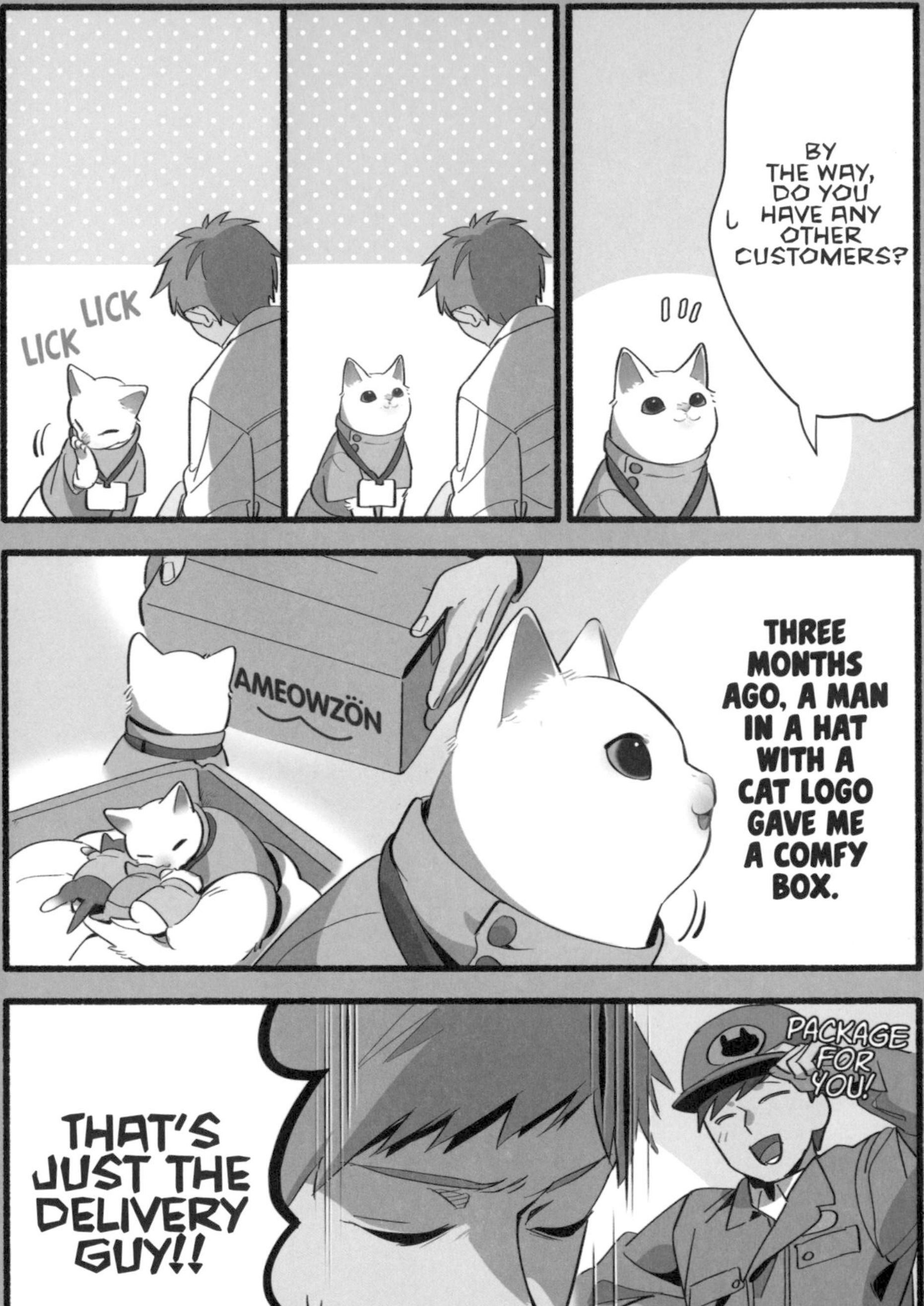
BY THE WAY, DO YOU HAVE ANY OTHER CUSTOMERS?
LICK LICK
AMEOWZÖN
THREE MONTHS AGO, A MAN IN A HAT WITH A CAT LOGO GAVE ME A COMFY BOX.
PACKAGE FOR YOU!
THAT'S JUST THE DELIVERY GUY!!

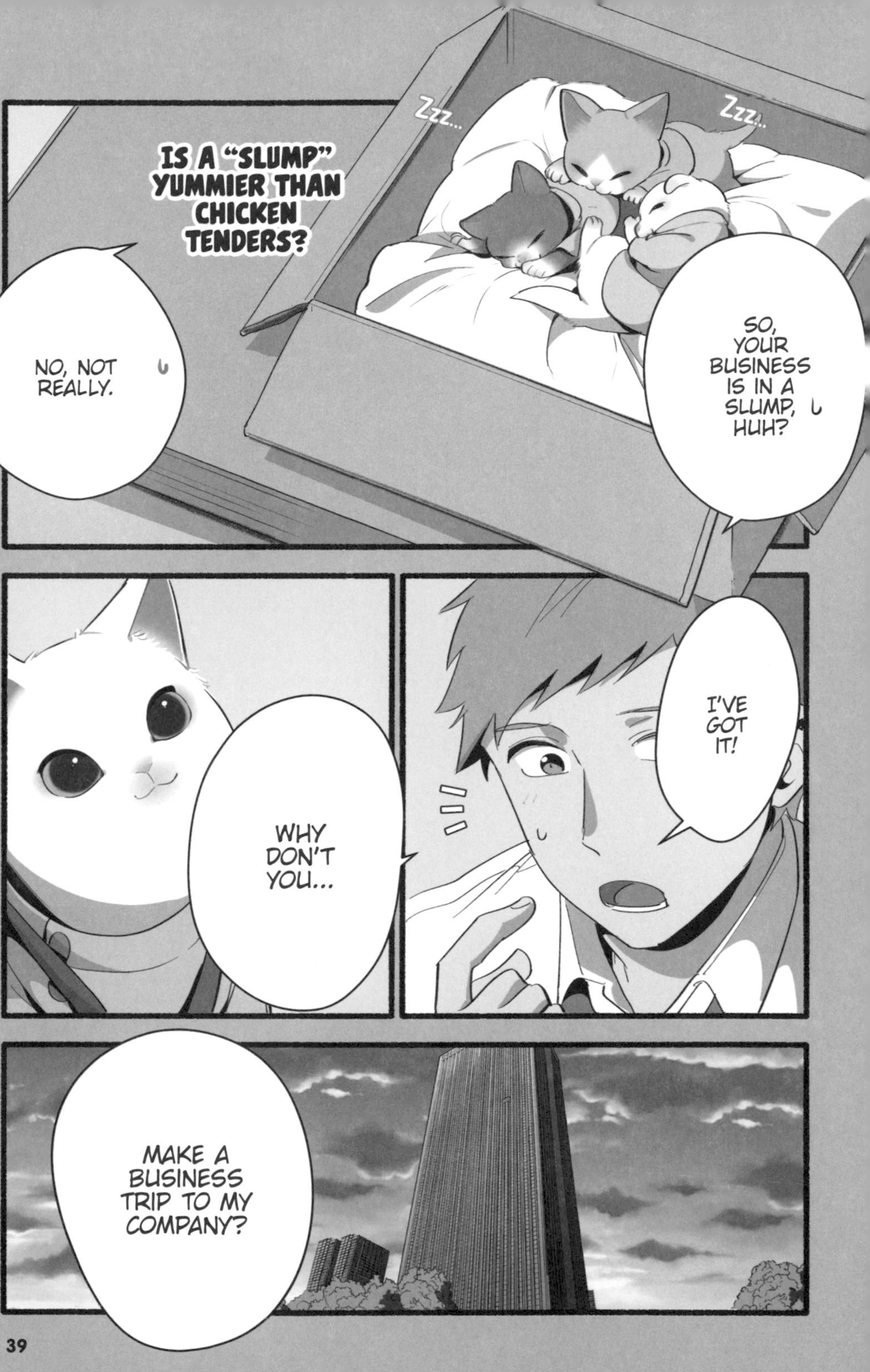
Zzz...
Zzz...
IS A "SLUMP" YUMMIER THAN CHICKEN TENDERS?
SO, YOUR BUSINESS IS IN A SLUMP, HUH?
NO, NOT REALLY.
I'VE GOT IT!
WHY DON'T YOU...
MAKE A BUSINESS TRIP TO MY COMPANY?

Q7. Can You Resist the Power of the Toe Beans?

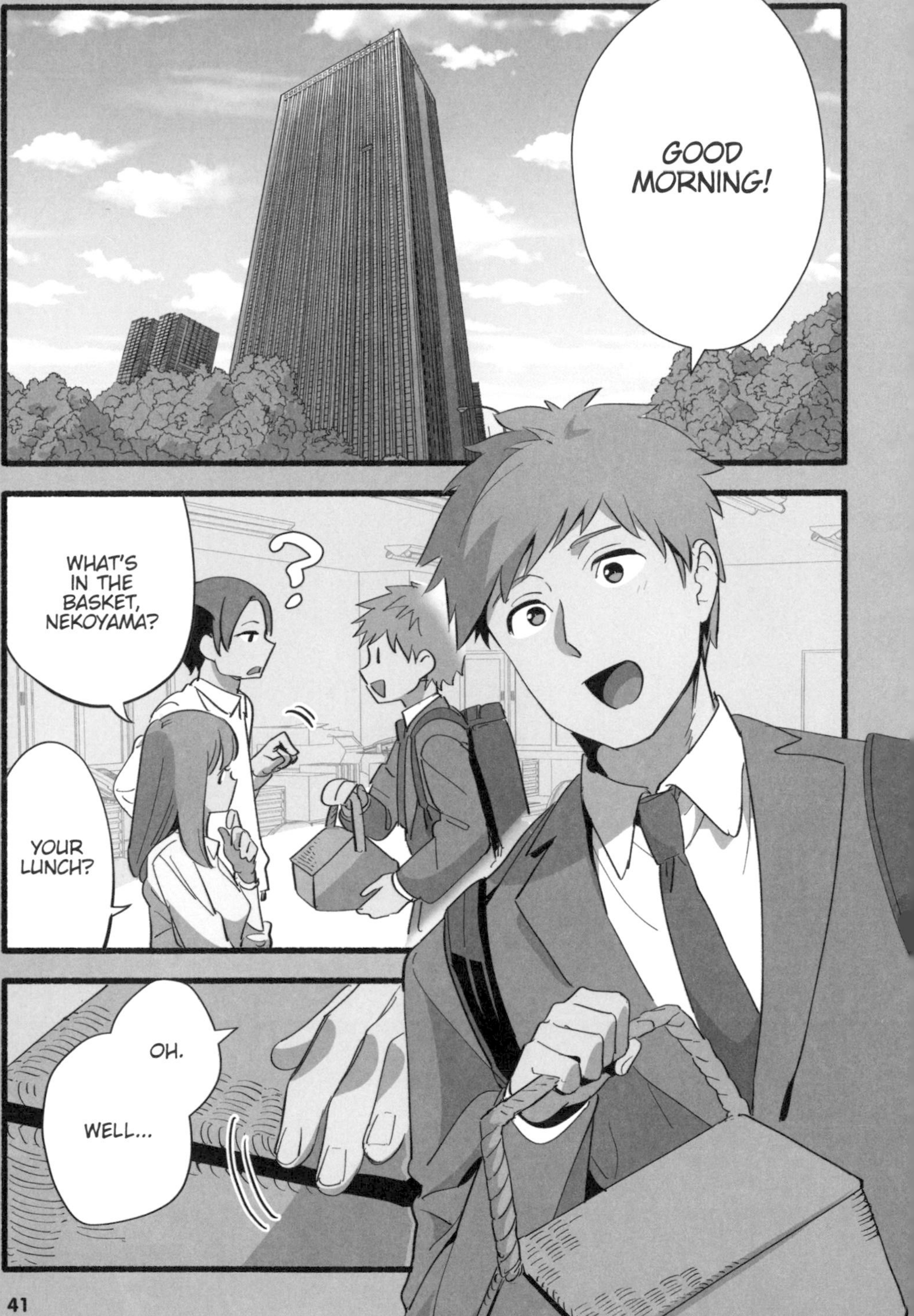
GOOD MORNING!
WHAT'S IN THE BASKET, NEKOYAMA?
YOUR LUNCH?
OH.
WELL...

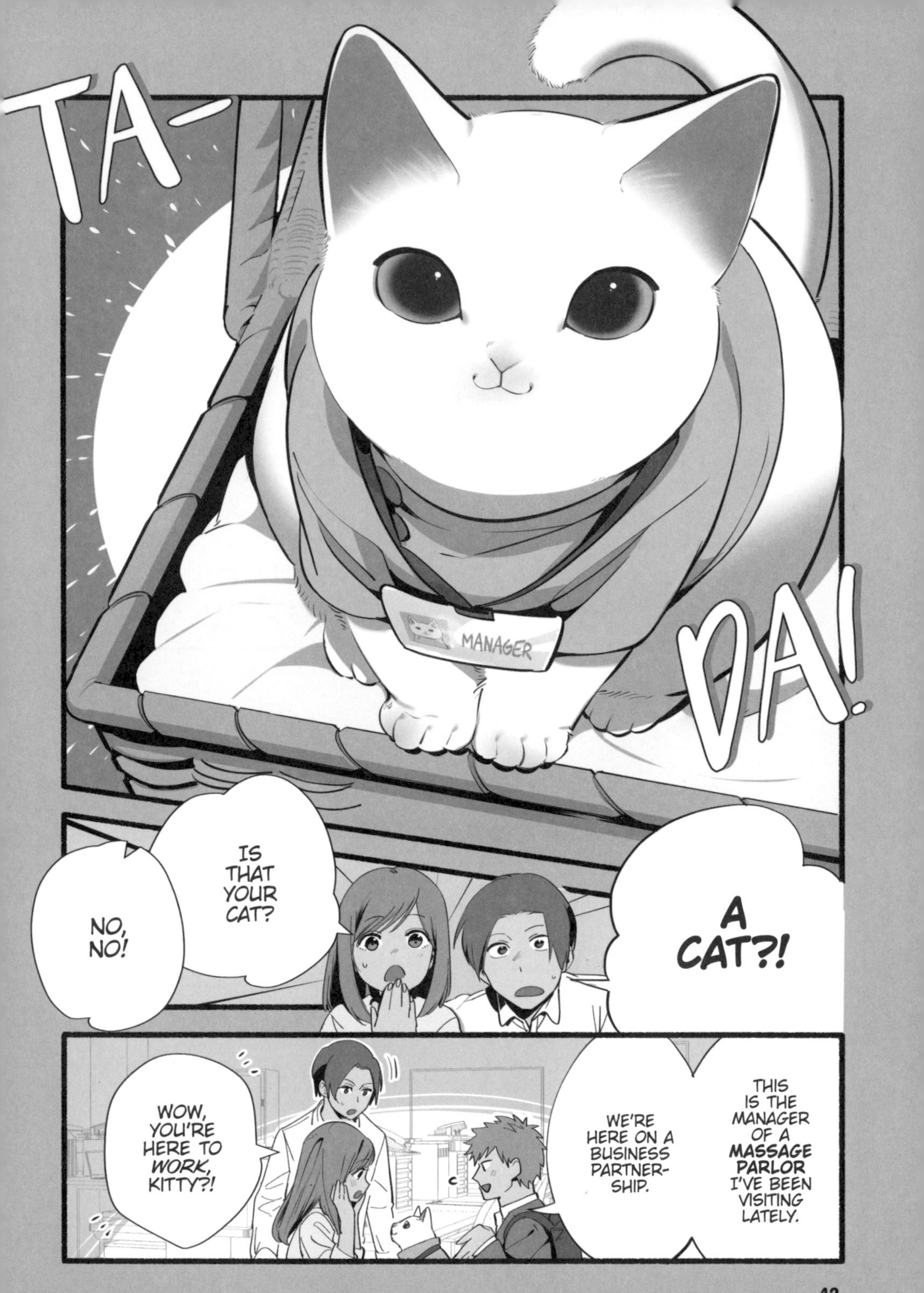
TA-
DA!
MANAGER
A CAT?!
IS THAT YOUR CAT?
NO, NO!
THIS IS THE MANAGER OF A MASSAGE PARLOR I'VE BEEN VISITING LATELY.
WE'RE HERE ON A BUSINESS PARTNER-SHIP.
WOW, YOU'RE HERE TO *WORK*, KITTY?!

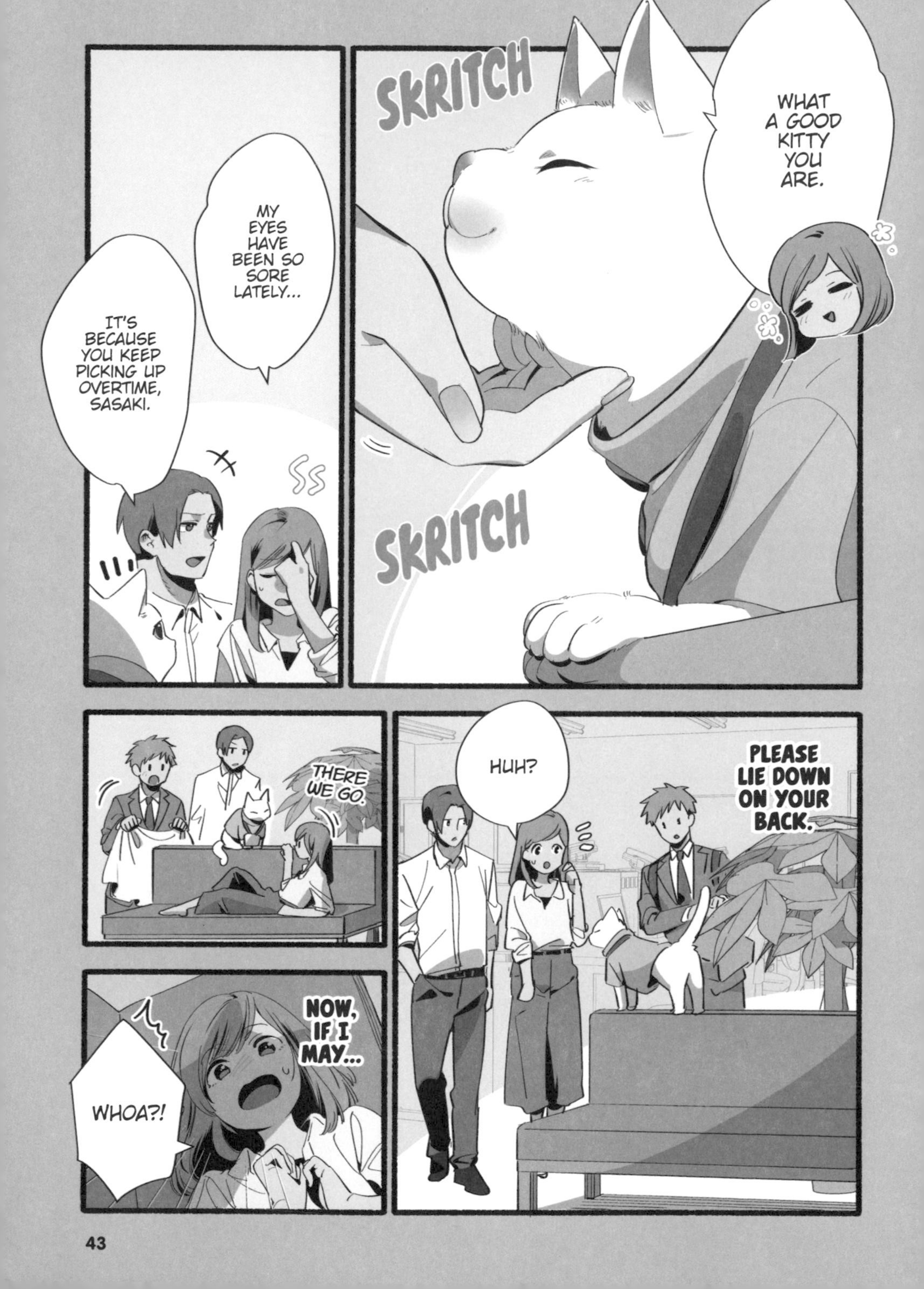
SKRITCH
WHAT A GOOD KITTY YOU ARE.
SKRITCH
MY EYES HAVE BEEN SO SORE LATELY...
IT'S BECAUSE YOU KEEP PICKING UP OVERTIME, SASAKI.
PLEASE LIE DOWN ON YOUR BACK.
HUH?
THERE WE GO.
NOW, IF I MAY...
WHOA?!

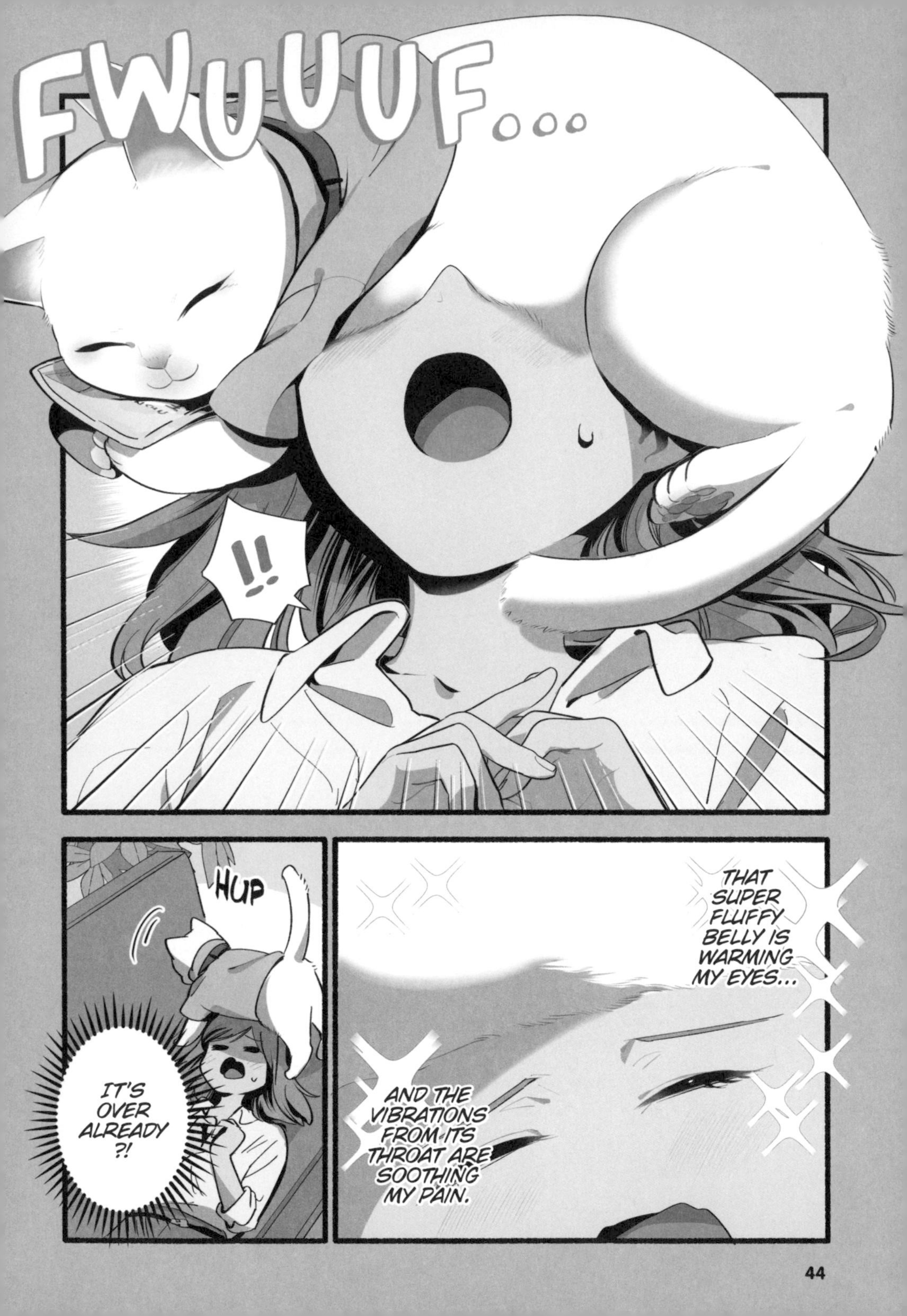
FWUUUF...
!!
THAT SUPER FLUFFY BELLY IS WARMING MY EYES...
AND THE VIBRATIONS FROM ITS THROAT ARE SOOTHING MY PAIN.
HUP
IT'S OVER ALREADY ?!

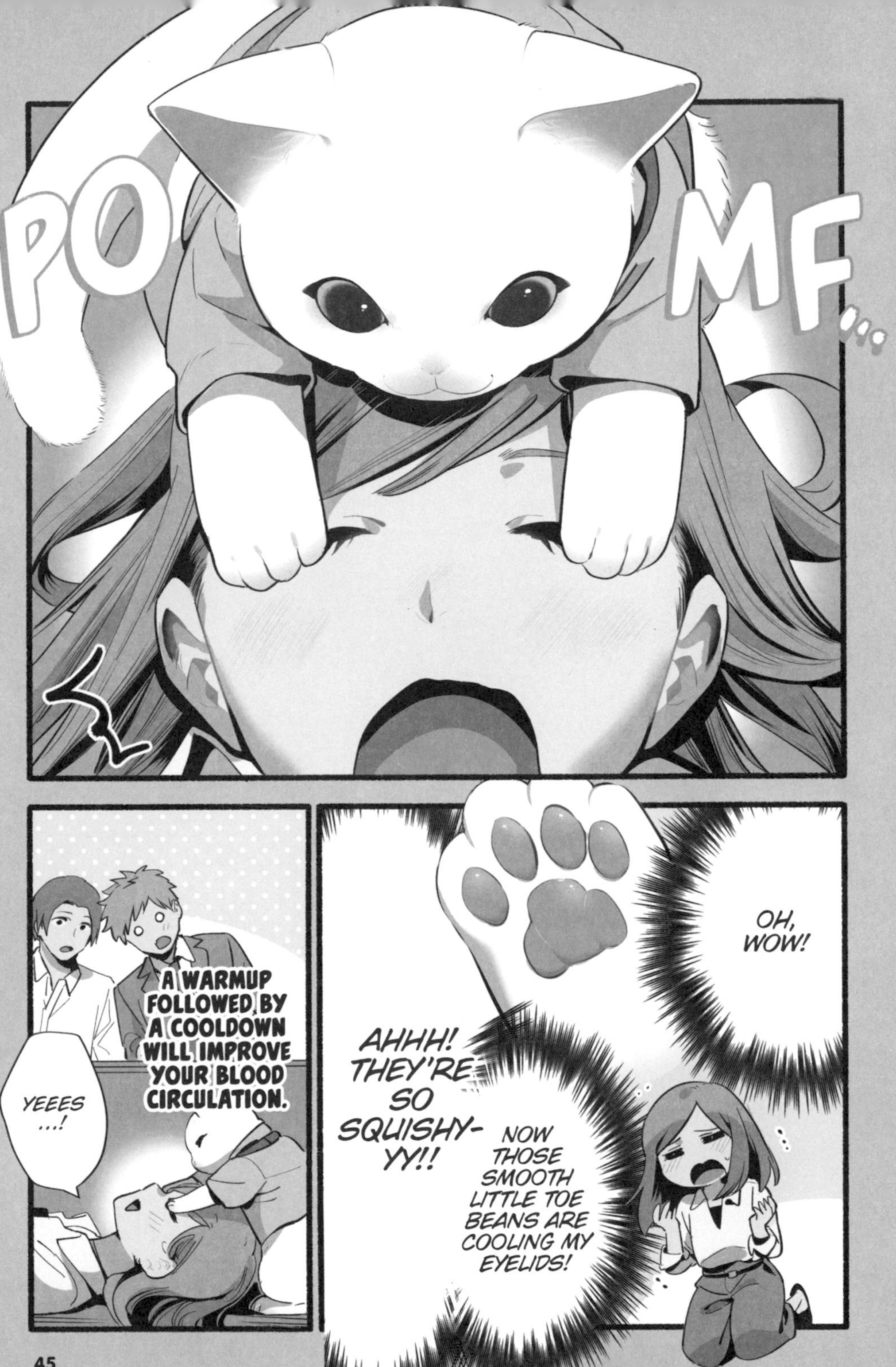
POMF...
OH, WOW!
AHHH! THEY'RE SO SQUISHY-YY!!
NOW THOSE SMOOTH LITTLE TOE BEANS ARE COOLING MY EYELIDS!
A WARMUP FOLLOWED BY A COOLDOWN WILL IMPROVE YOUR BLOOD CIRCULATION.
YEEES ...!

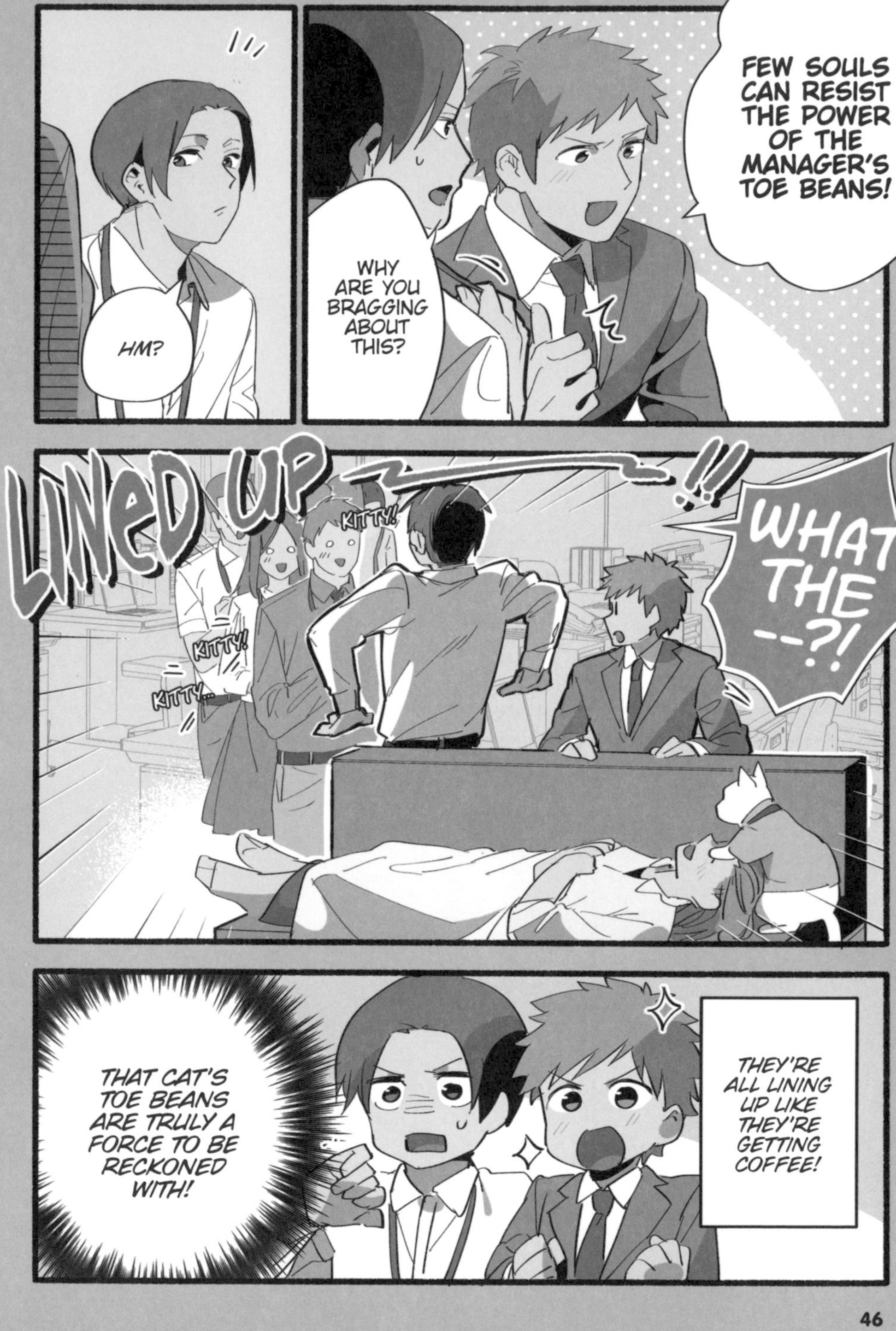
FEW SOULS CAN RESIST THE POWER OF THE MANAGER'S TOE BEANS!
WHY ARE YOU BRAGGING ABOUT THIS?
HM?
WHAT THE --?!
LINED UP!!
KITTY!
KITTY!
KITTY...
THEY'RE ALL LINING UP LIKE THEY'RE GETTING COFFEE!
THAT CAT'S TOE BEANS ARE TRULY A FORCE TO BE RECKONED WITH!

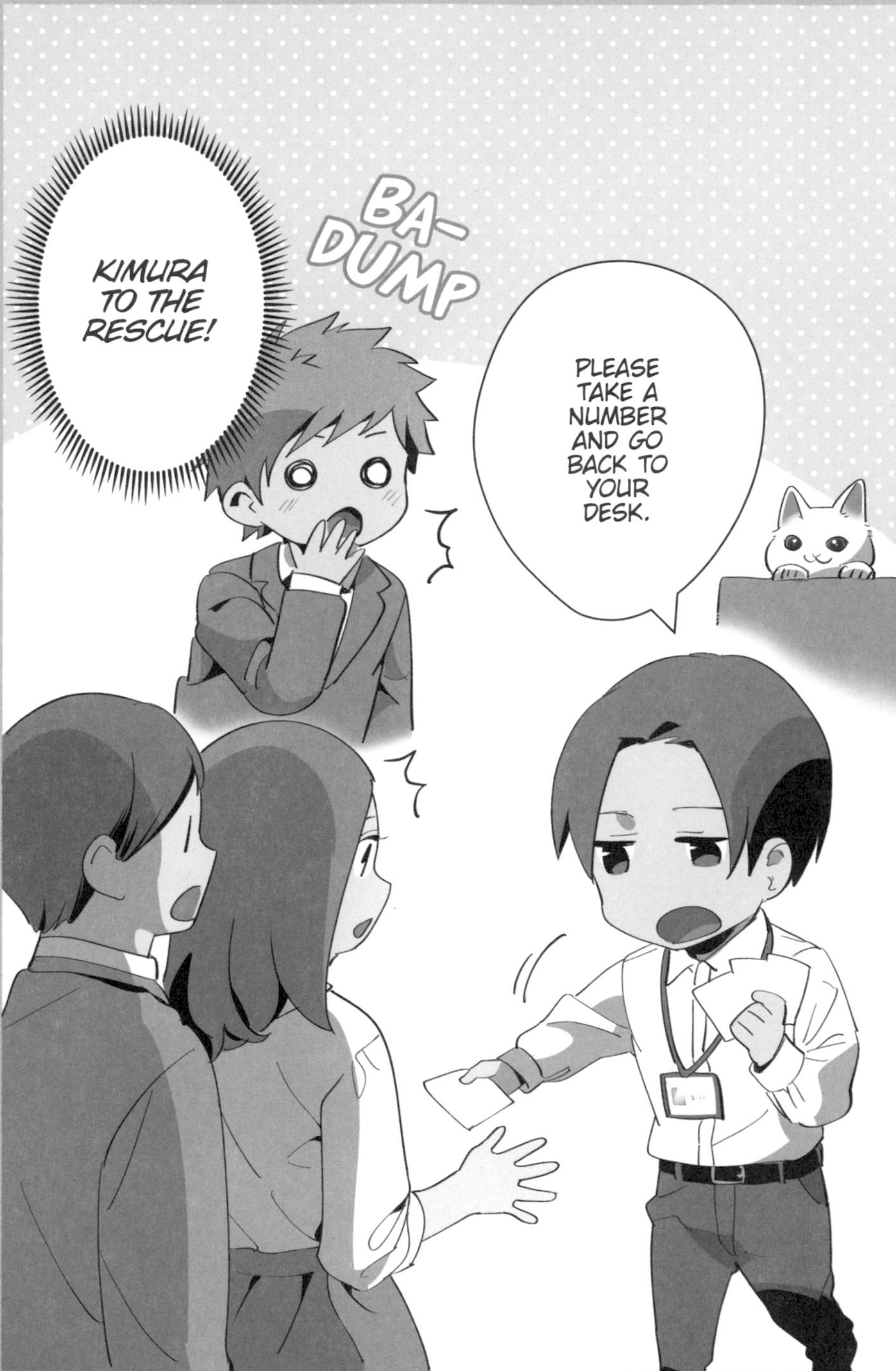
PLEASE TAKE A NUMBER AND GO BACK TO YOUR DESK.
BA-DUMP
KIMURA TO THE RESCUE!

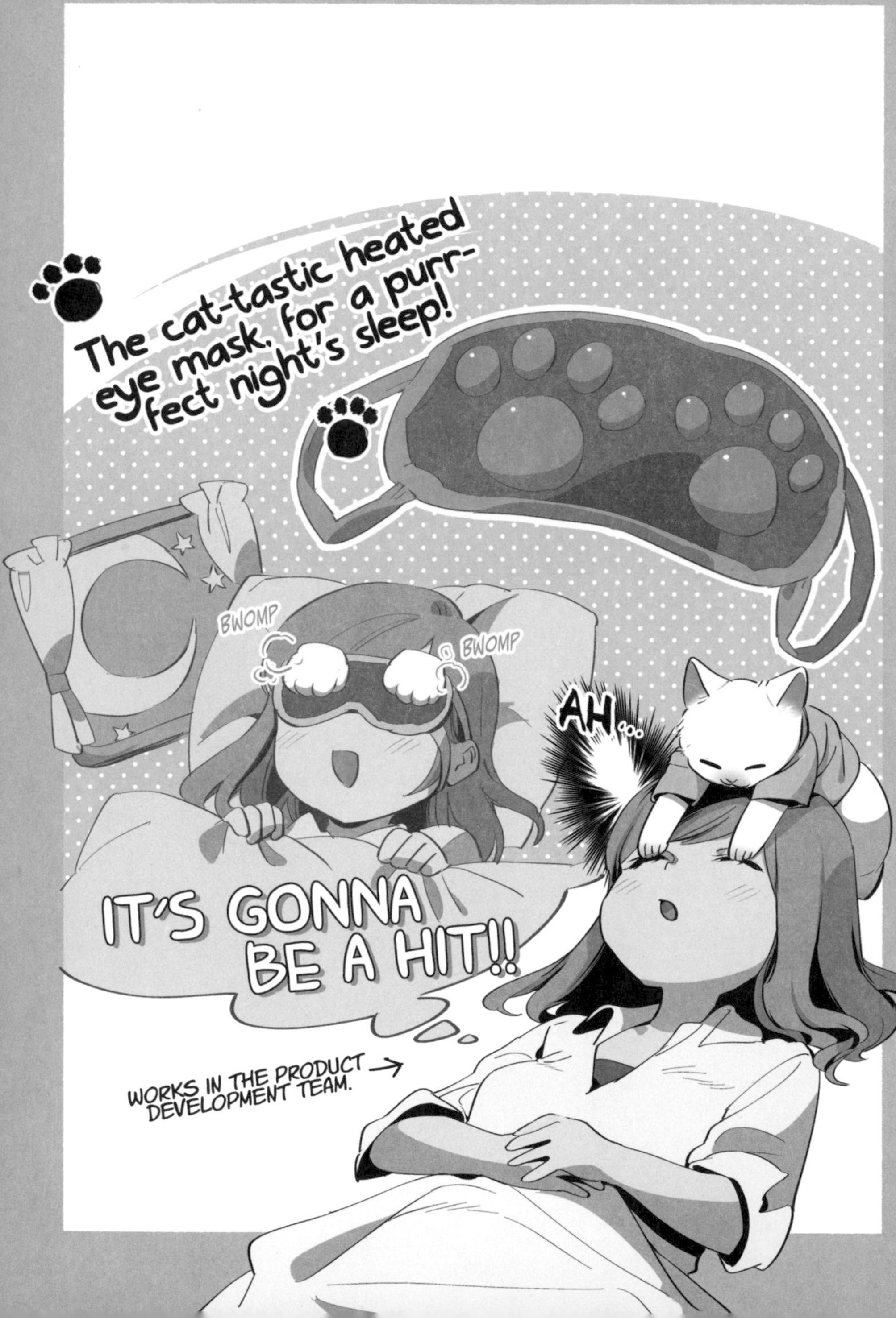
The cat-tastic heated eye mask, for a purr-fect night's sleep!
BWOMP
BWOMP
AH...
IT'S GONNA BE A HIT!!
WORKS IN THE PRODUCT DEVELOPMENT TEAM.

Q8. What's a Cat Doing in the Office?!

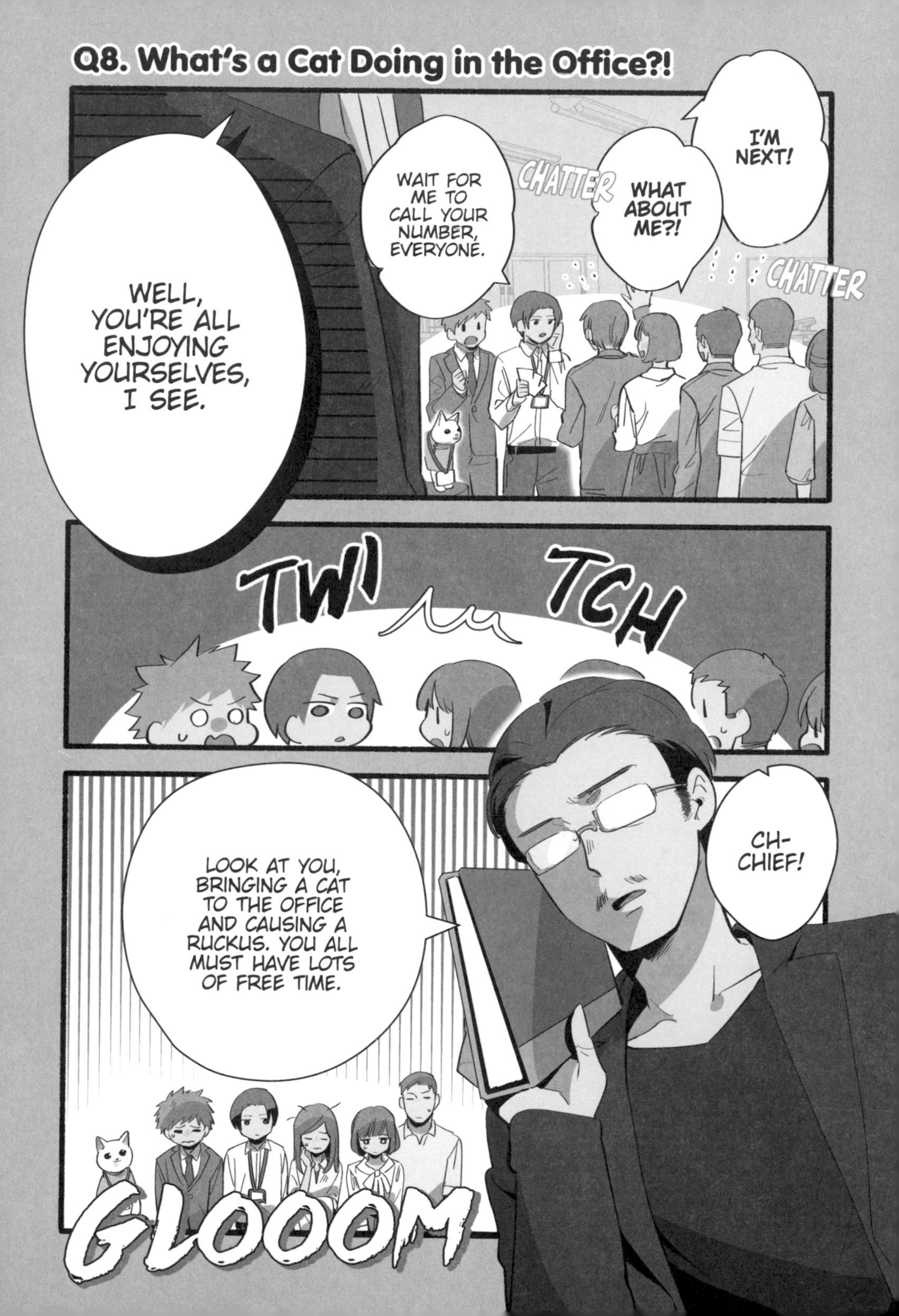
I'M NEXT!
CHATTER
WHAT ABOUT ME?!
CHATTER
WAIT FOR ME TO CALL YOUR NUMBER, EVERYONE.
WELL, YOU'RE ALL ENJOYING YOURSELVES, I SEE.
TWITCH
CH-CHIEF!
LOOK AT YOU, BRINGING A CAT TO THE OFFICE AND CAUSING A RUCKUS. YOU ALL MUST HAVE LOTS OF FREE TIME.
GLOOOM

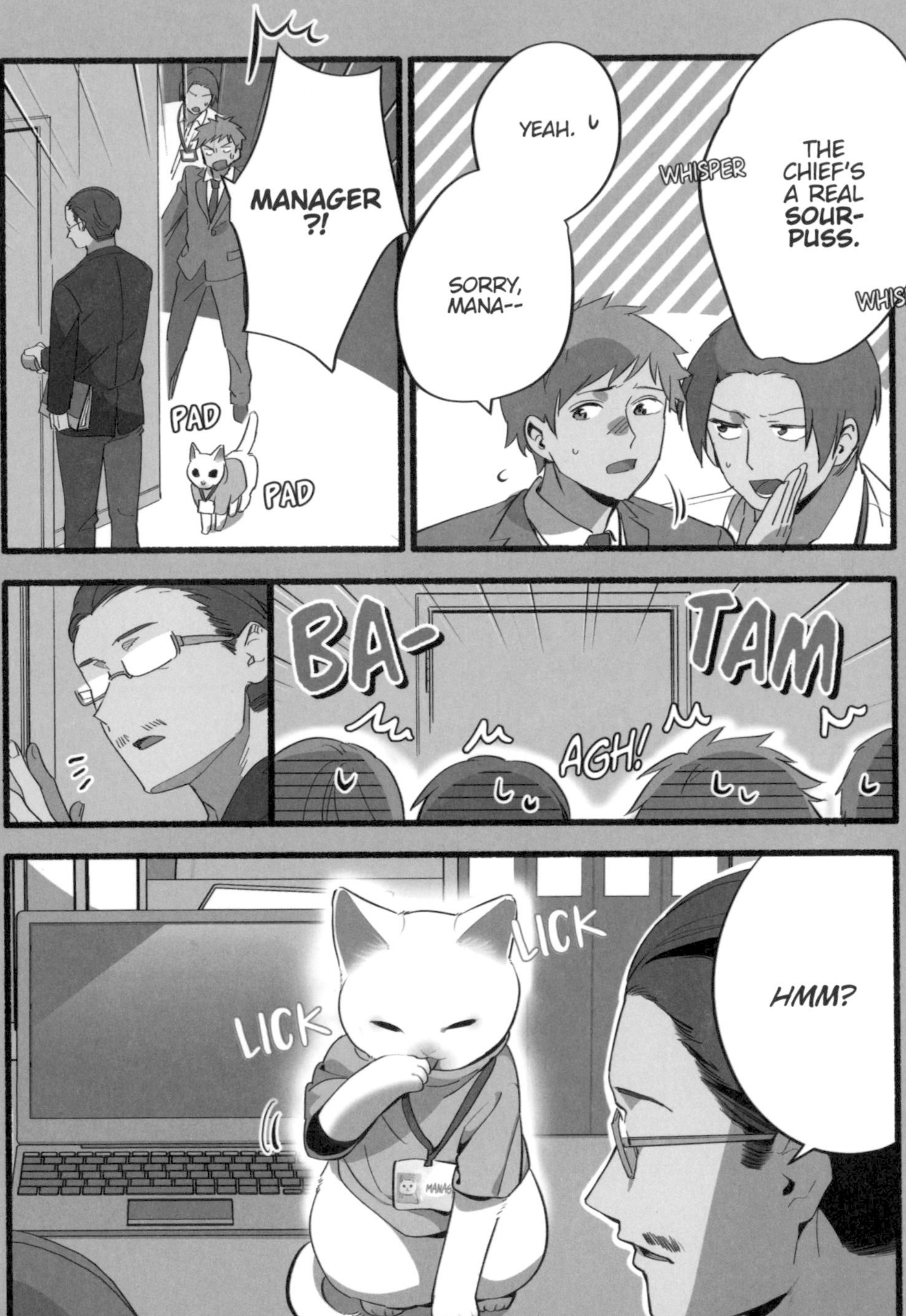
WHISPER
THE CHIEF'S A REAL SOURPUSS.
WHISPER
YEAH.
SORRY, MANA--
MANAGER?!
PAD
PAD
BA-
TAM
AGH!
LICK
LICK
HMM?

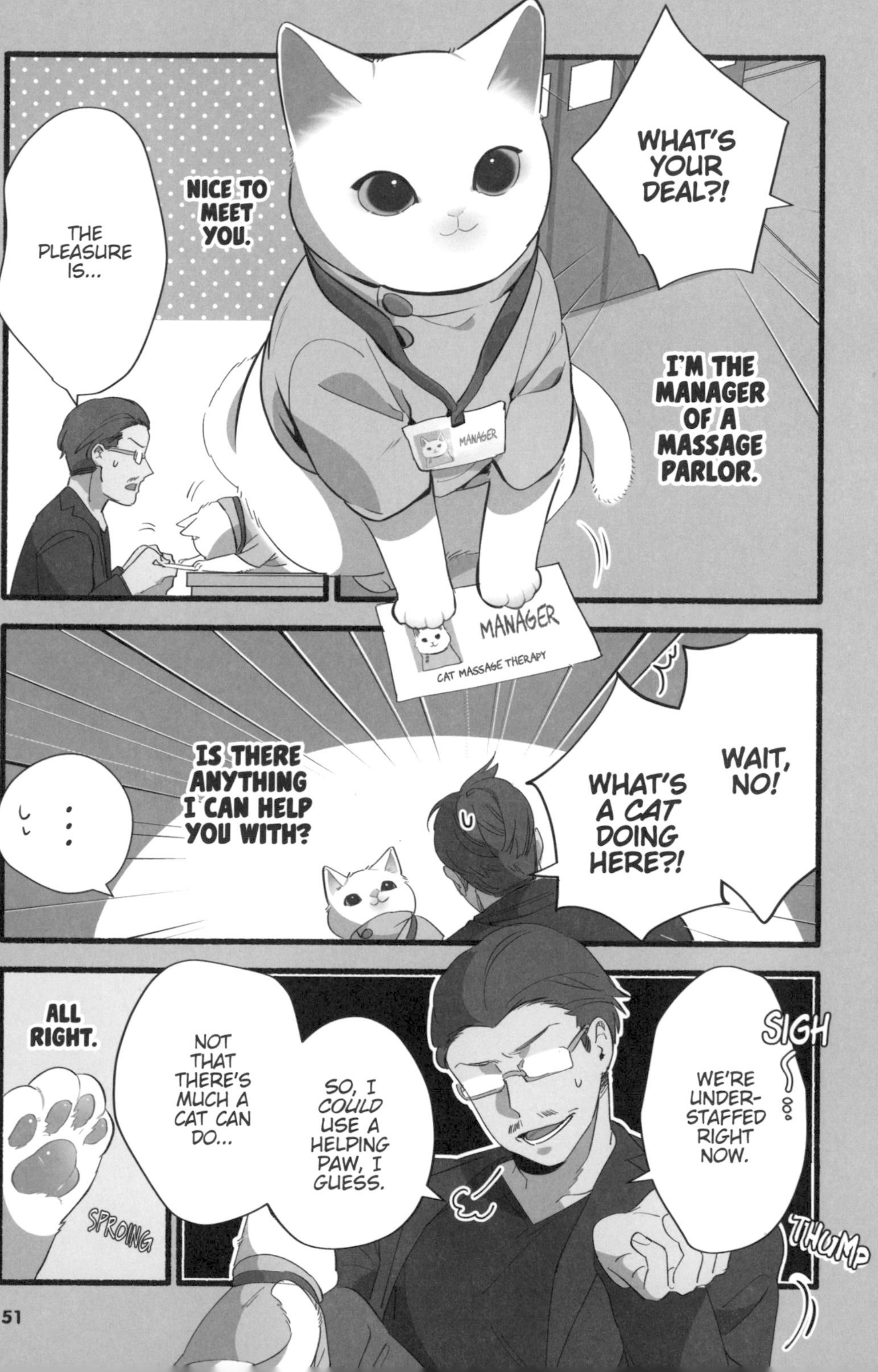
WHAT'S YOUR DEAL?!
I'M THE MANAGER OF A MASSAGE PARLOR.
NICE TO MEET YOU.
THE PLEASURE IS...
MANAGER
MANAGER
CAT MASSAGE THERAPY
WAIT, NO!
WHAT'S A CAT DOING HERE?!
IS THERE ANYTHING I CAN HELP YOU WITH?
SIGH
WE'RE UNDER-STAFFED RIGHT NOW.
THUMP
SO, I COULD USE A HELPING PAW, I GUESS.
NOT THAT THERE'S MUCH A CAT CAN DO...
ALL RIGHT.
SPROING

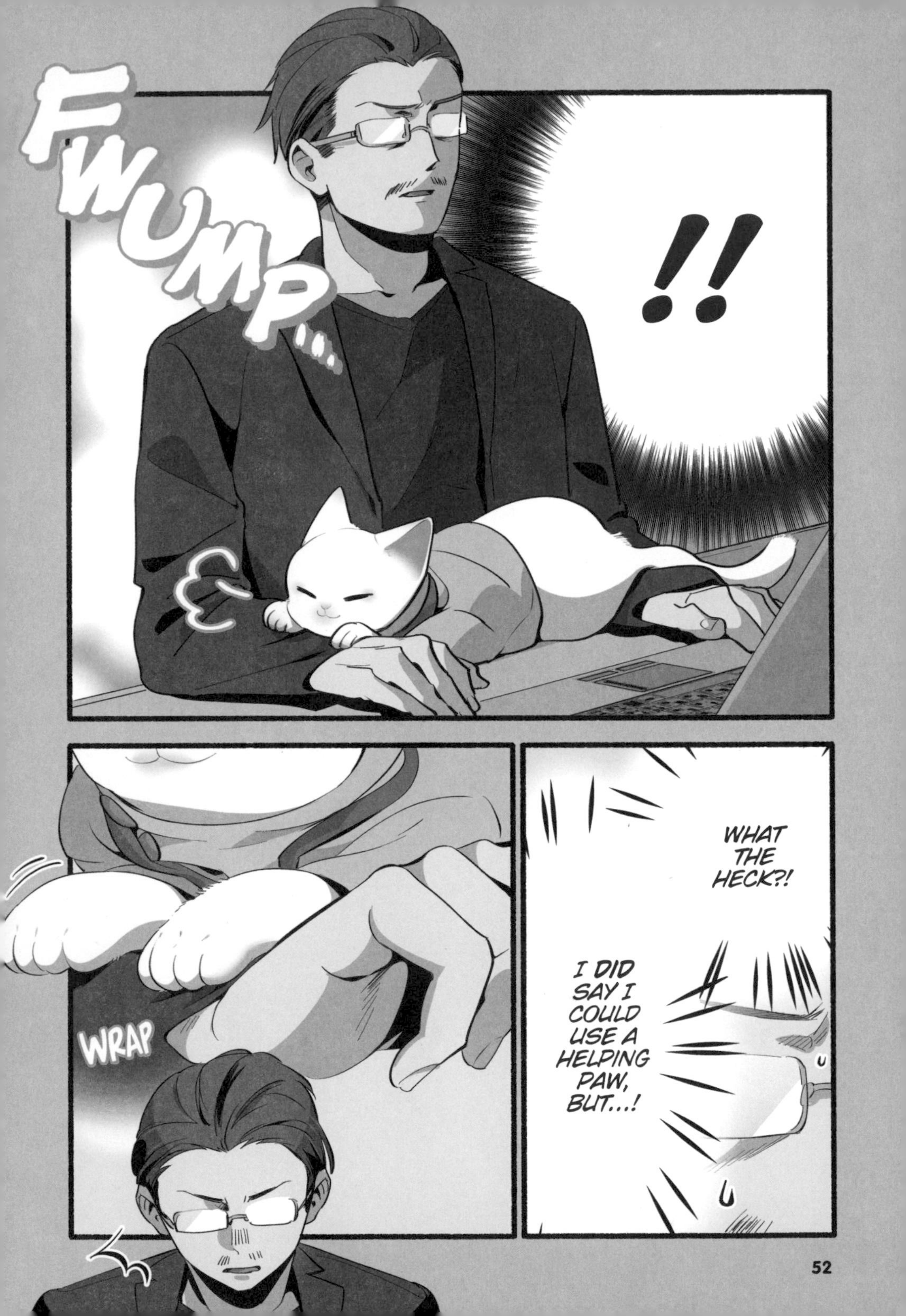
FWUMP...
!!
WHAT THE HECK?!
I DID SAY I COULD USE A HELPING PAW, BUT...!
WRAP

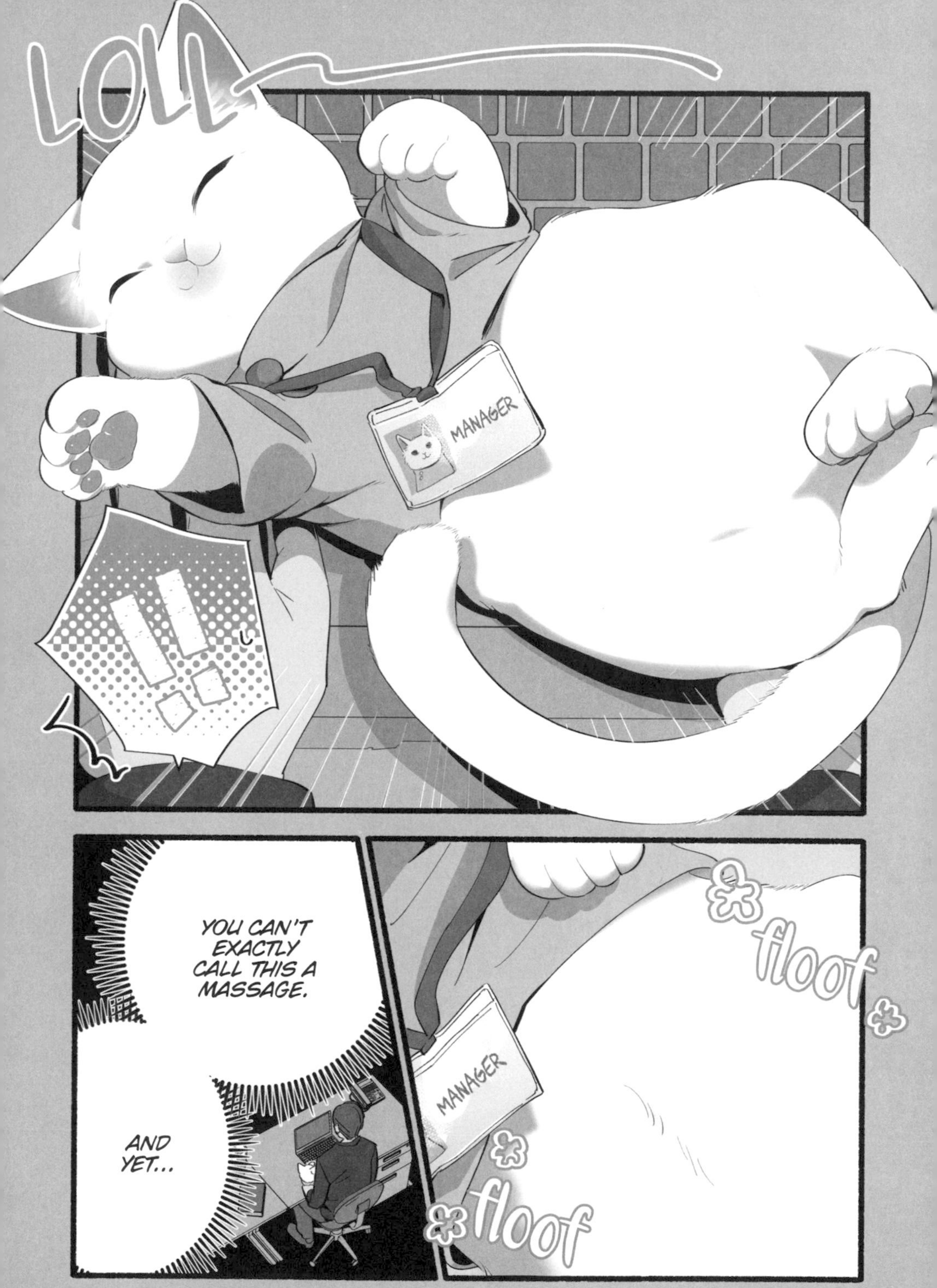
LOLL
MANAGER
MANAGER
floof
floof
YOU CAN'T EXACTLY CALL THIS A MASSAGE.
AND YET...

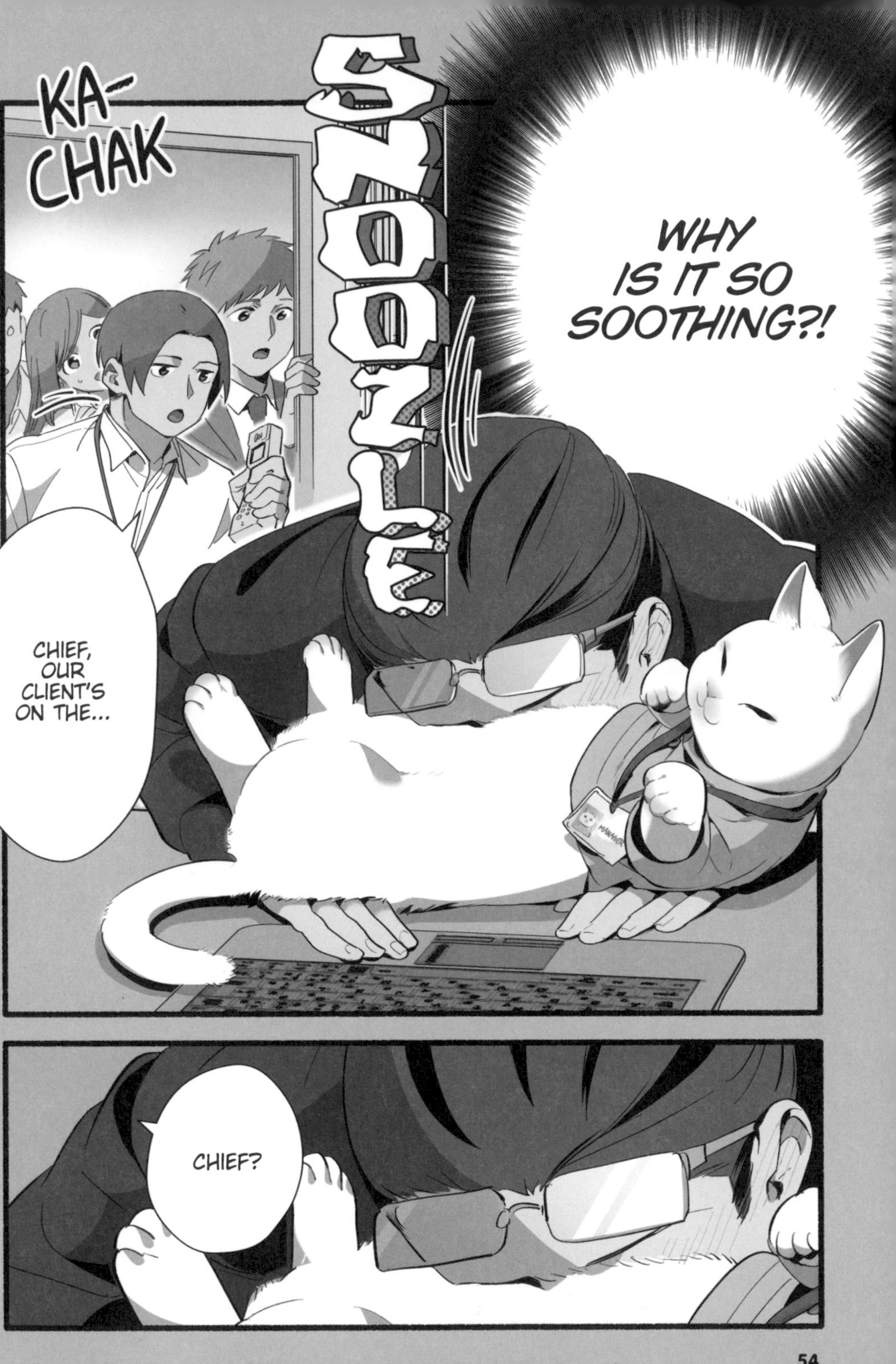
WHY IS IT SO SOOTHING?!
SNOOZLE
KA-CHAK
CHIEF, OUR CLIENT'S ON THE...
CHIEF?

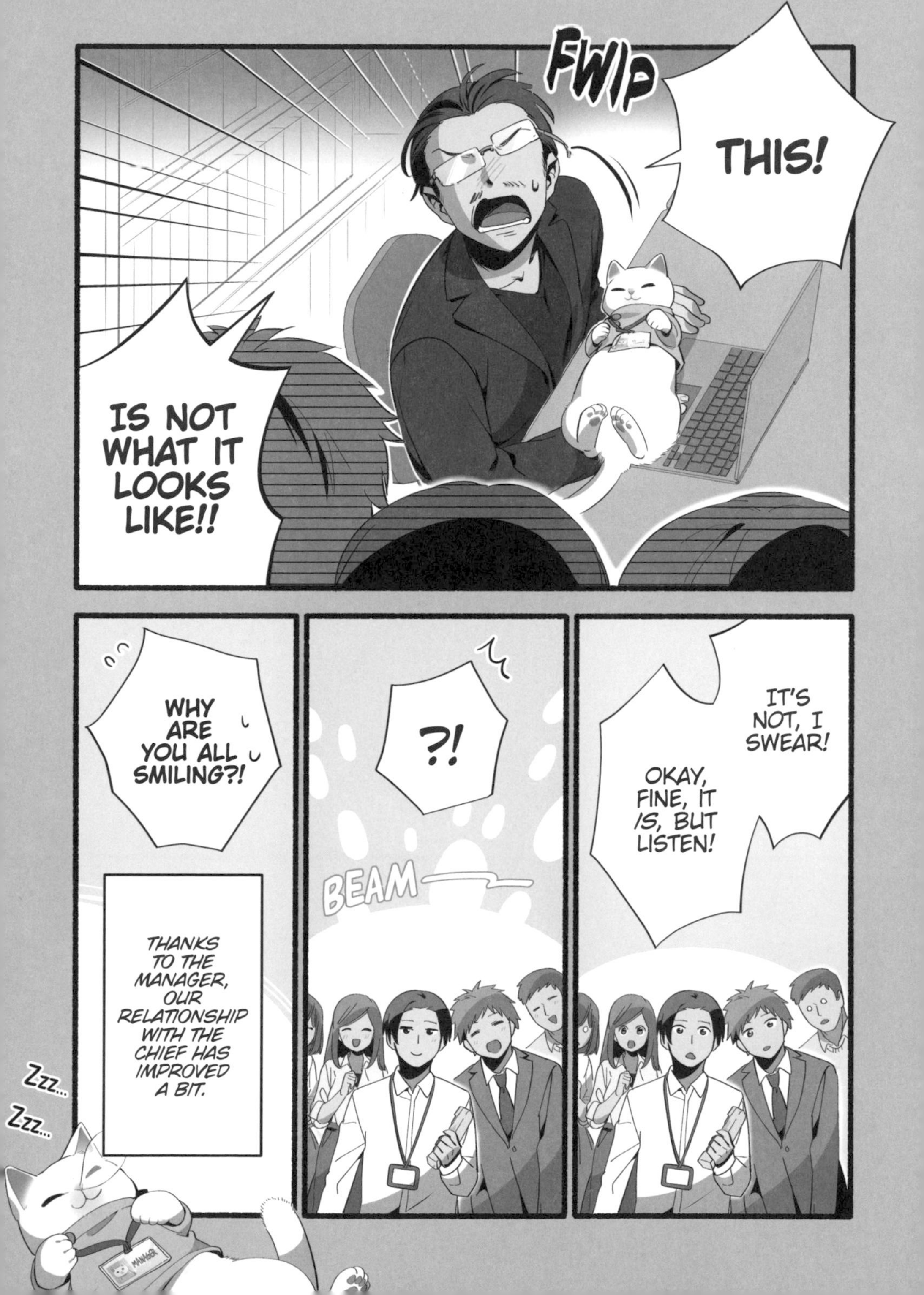
FWIP
THIS!
IS NOT WHAT IT LOOKS LIKE!!
IT'S NOT, I SWEAR!
OKAY, FINE, IT *IS*, BUT LISTEN!
?!
BEAM
WHY ARE YOU ALL SMILING?!
THANKS TO THE MANAGER, OUR RELATIONSHIP WITH THE CHIEF HAS IMPROVED A BIT.
Zzz...
Zzz...
MANAGER

Shopping Patterns

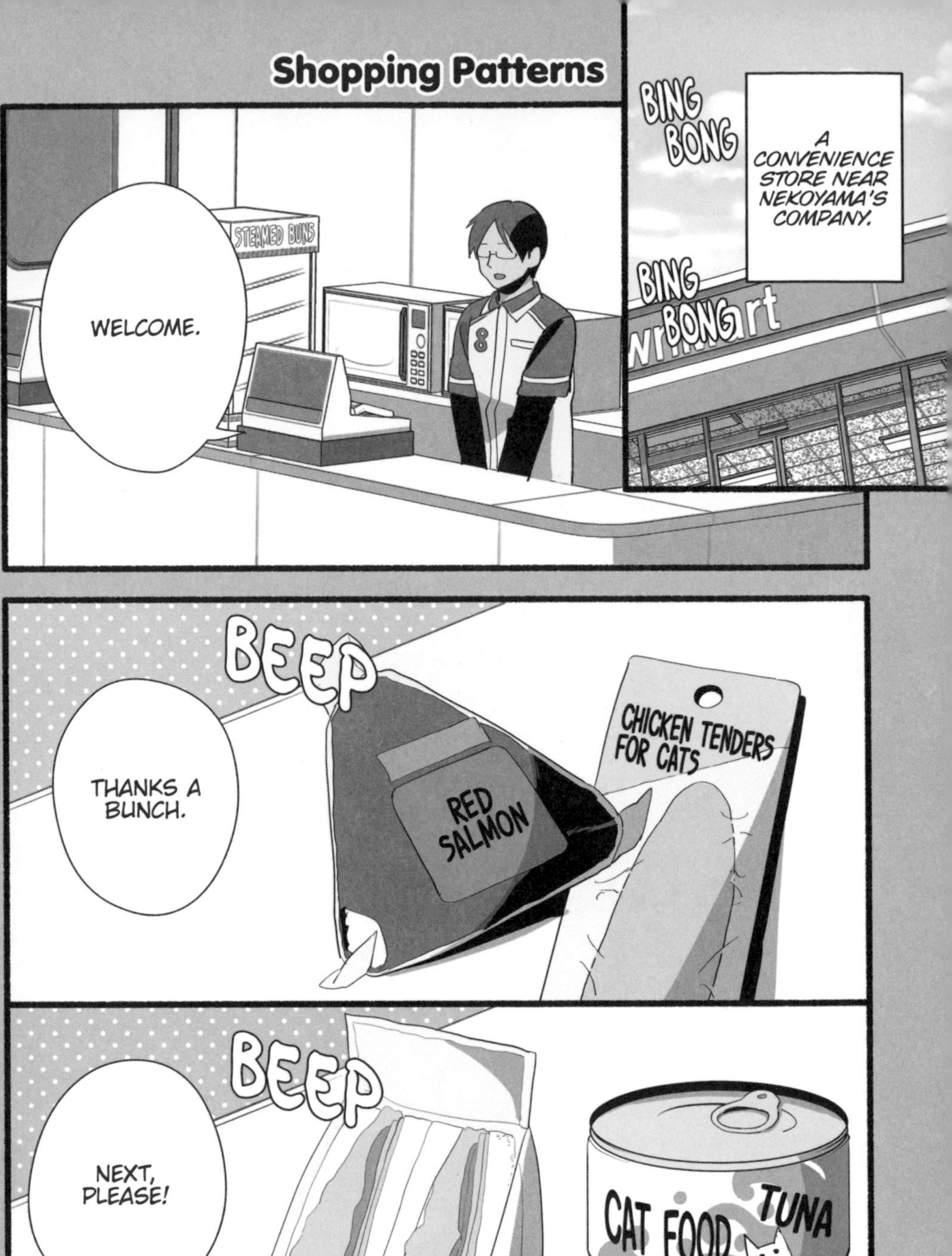

A CONVENIENCE STORE NEAR NEKOYAMA'S COMPANY.
BING BONG
BING BONG
STEAMED BUNS
WELCOME.
BEEP
CHICKEN TENDERS FOR CATS
RED SALMON
THANKS A BUNCH.
BEEP
CAT FOOD
TUNA
NEXT, PLEASE!

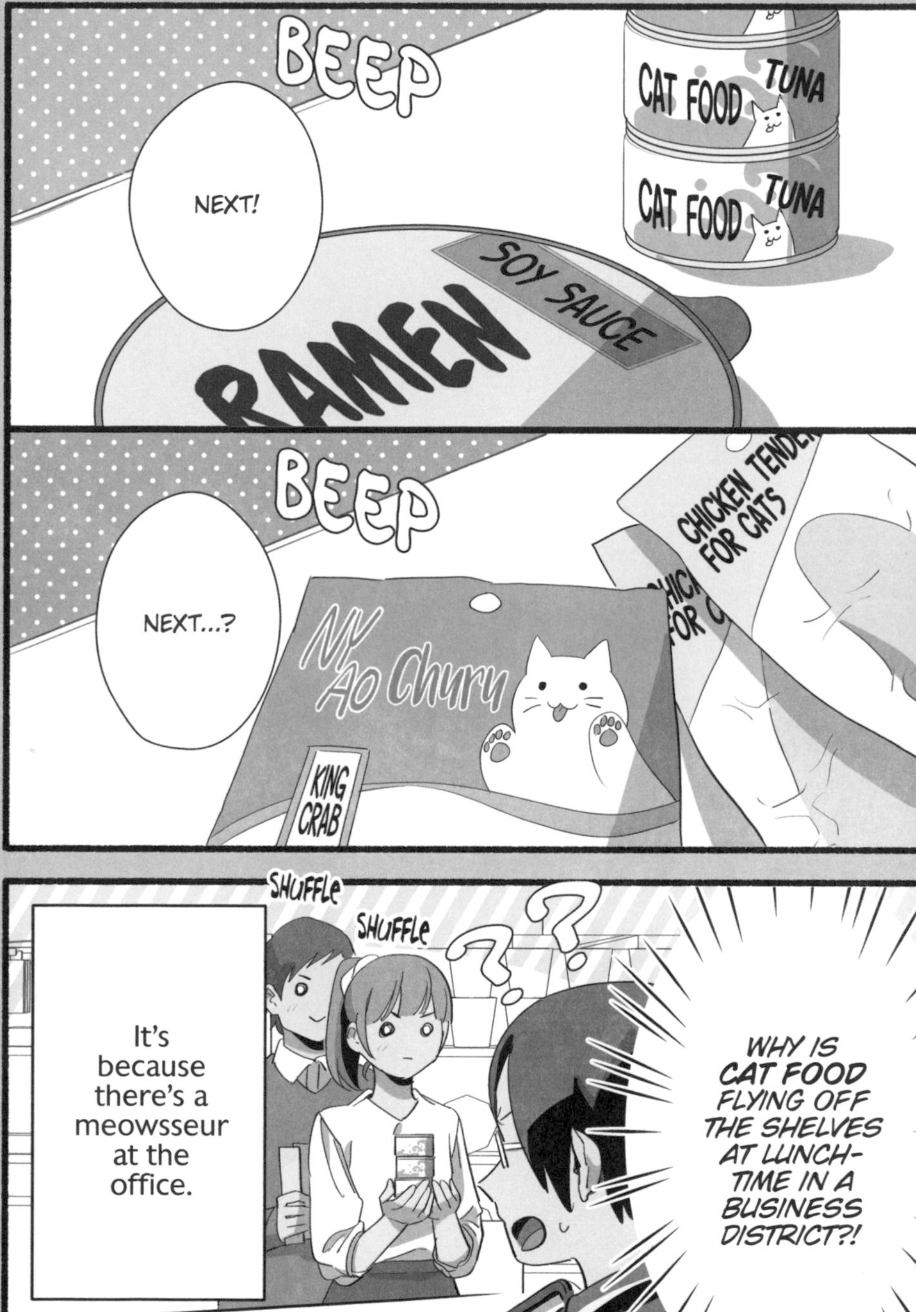
BEEP
NEXT!
CAT FOOD
TUNA
CAT FOOD
TUNA
SOY SAUCE
RAMEN
BEEP
NEXT...?
CHICKEN TENDER
FOR CATS
NY AO Churu
KING CRAB
SHUFFLE
SHUFFLE
WHY IS CAT FOOD FLYING OFF THE SHELVES AT LUNCH-TIME IN A BUSINESS DISTRICT?!
It's because there's a meowsseur at the office.

What the Manager Can't Tolerate

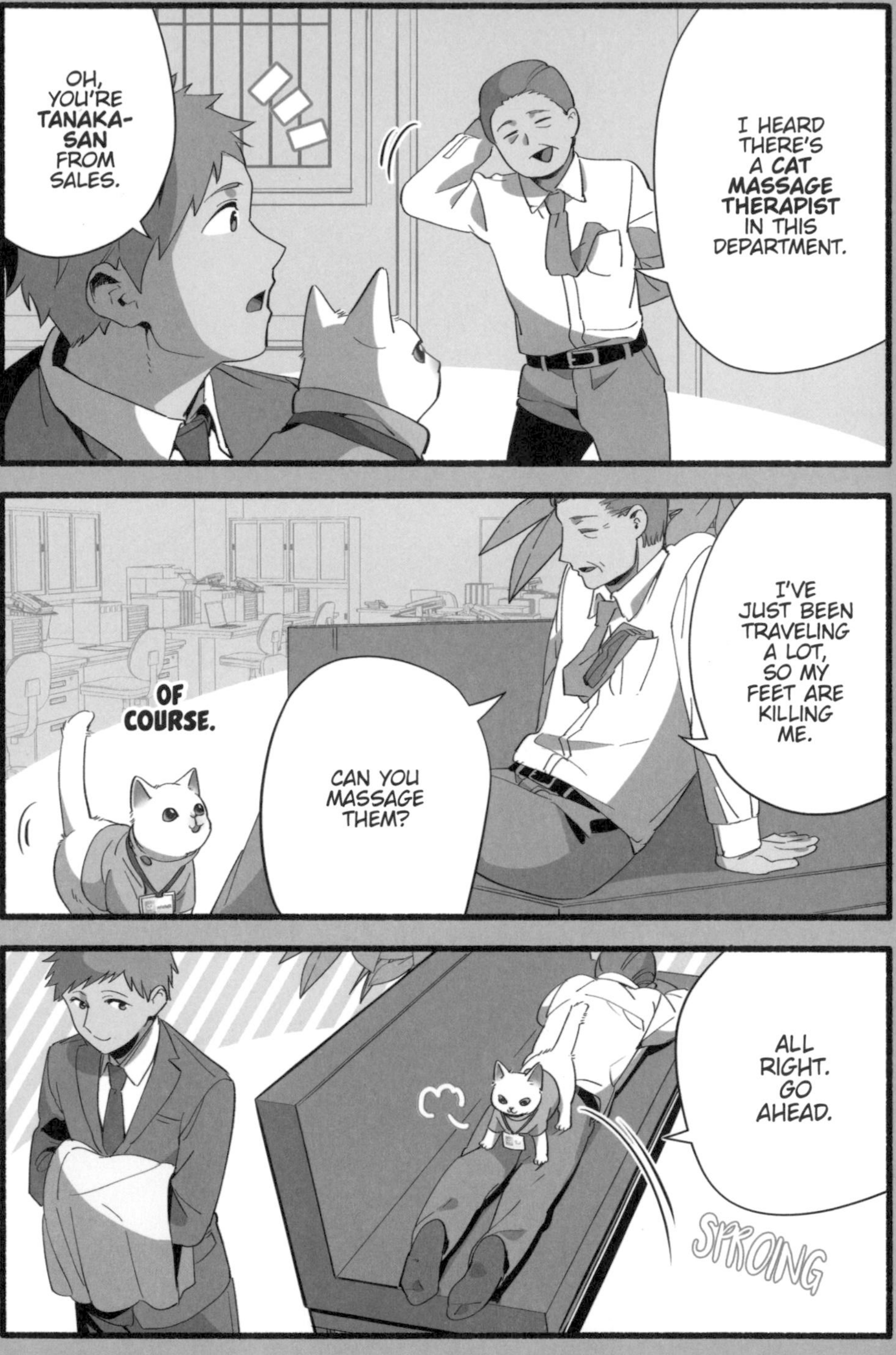
I HEARD THERE'S A CAT MASSAGE THERAPIST IN THIS DEPARTMENT.
OH, YOU'RE TANAKA-SAN FROM SALES.
I'VE JUST BEEN TRAVELING A LOT, SO MY FEET ARE KILLING ME.
CAN YOU MASSAGE THEM?
OF COURSE.
ALL RIGHT. GO AHEAD.
SPROING

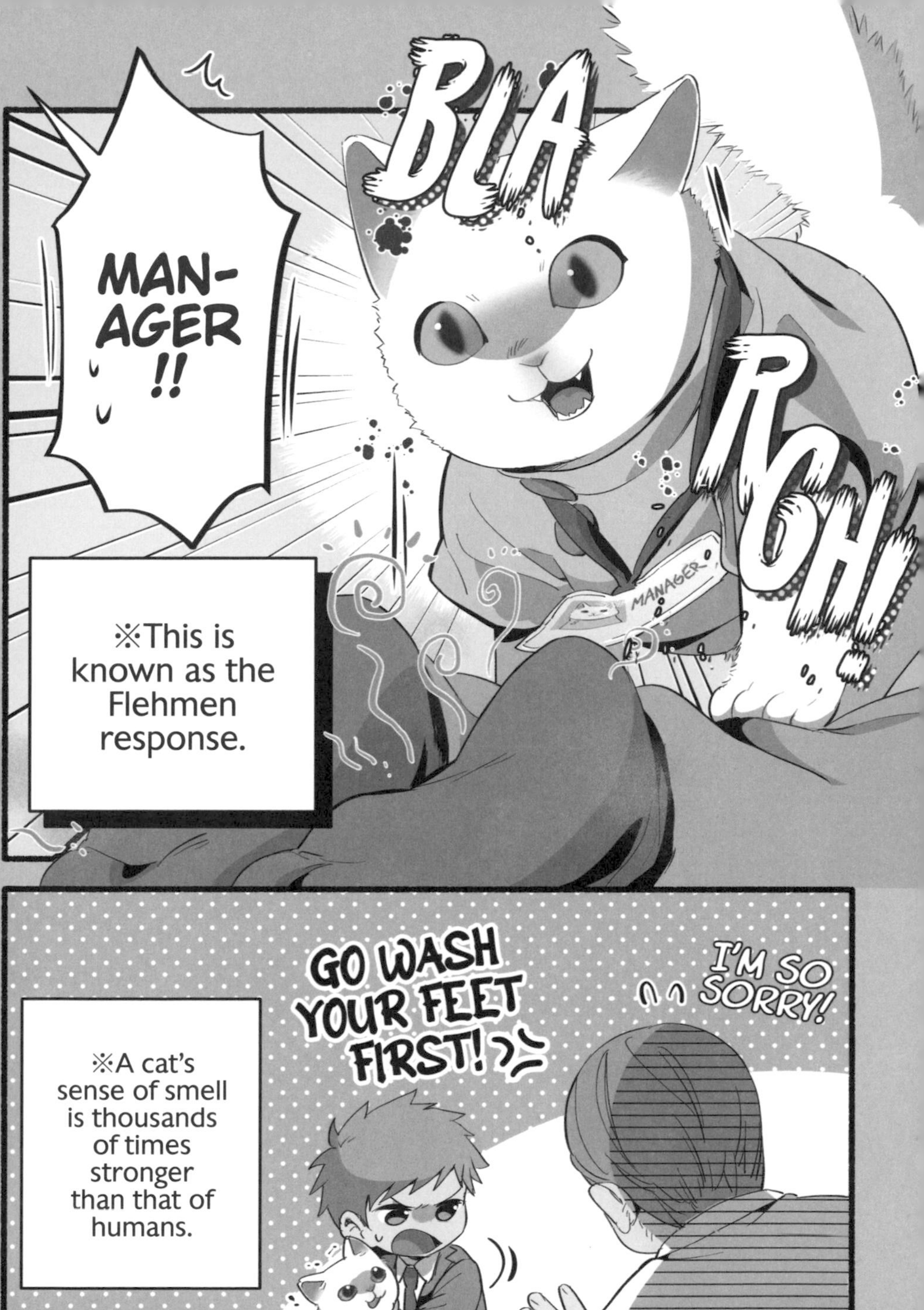
BLA
ROCH!
MANAGER
MAN-AGER!!
※This is known as the Flehmen response.
I'M SO SORRY!
GO WASH YOUR FEET FIRST!
※A cat's sense of smell is thousands of times stronger than that of humans.

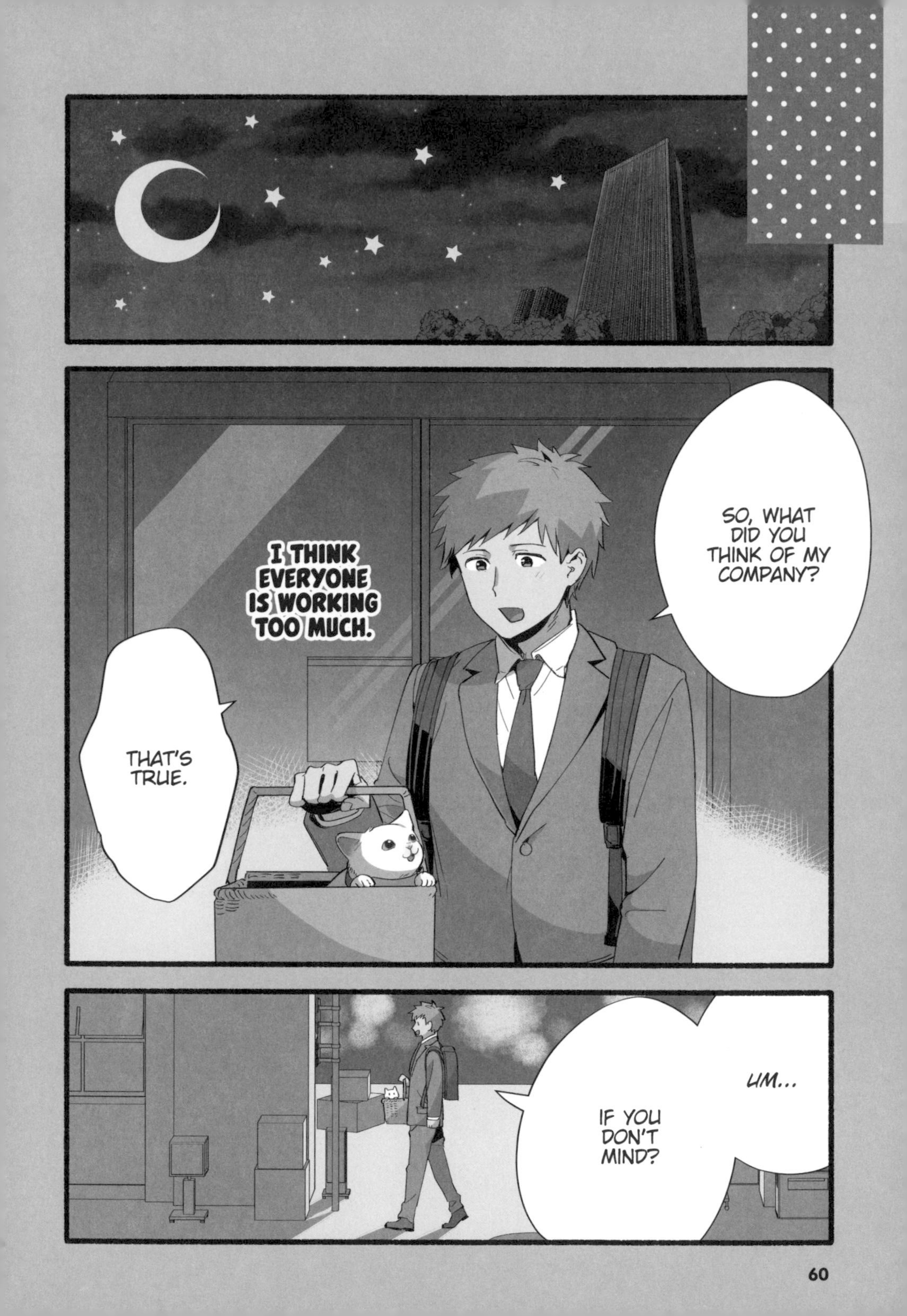
SO, WHAT DID YOU THINK OF MY COMPANY?
I THINK EVERYONE IS WORKING TOO MUCH.
THAT'S TRUE.
UM...
IF YOU DON'T MIND?

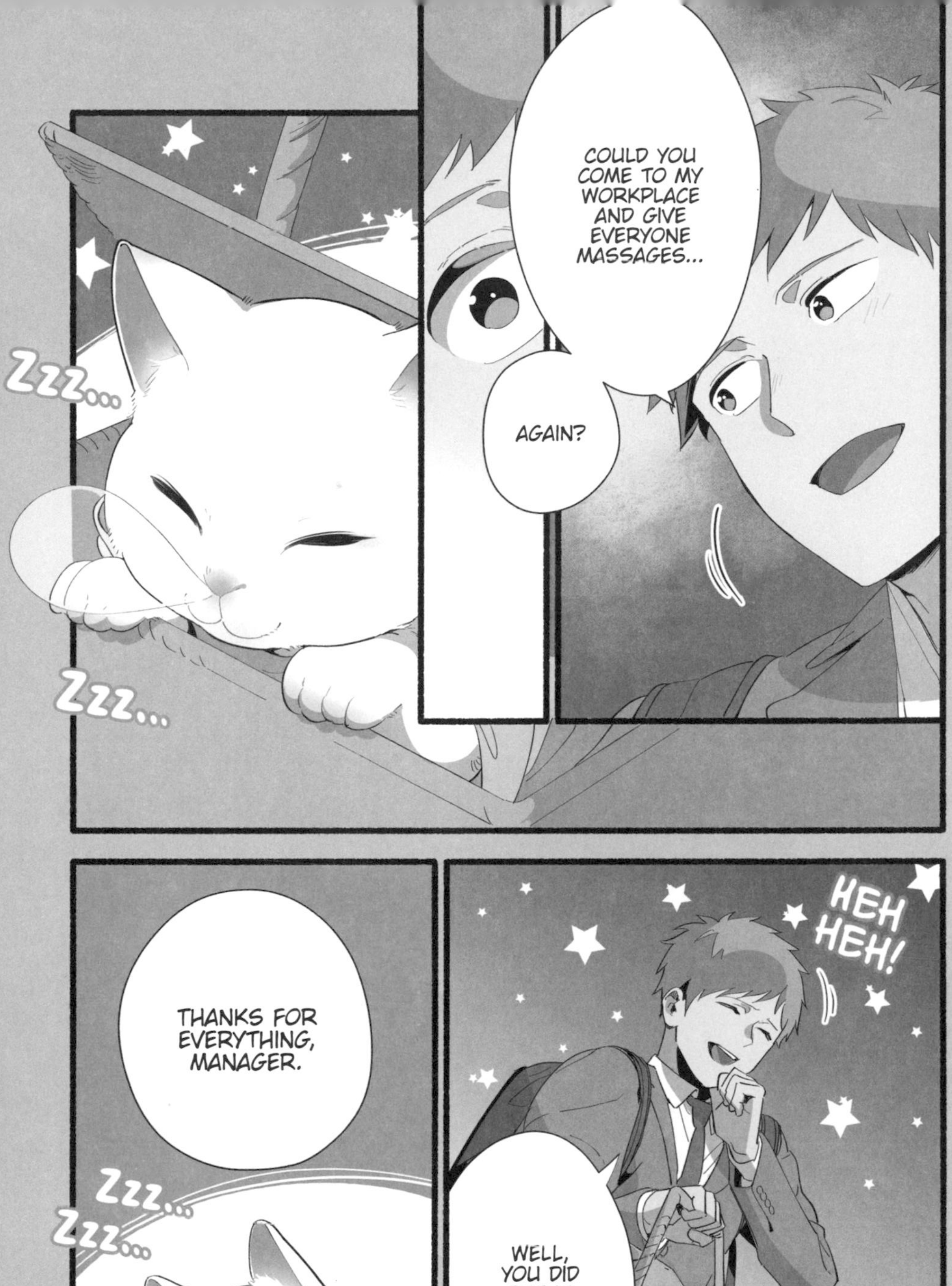
COULD YOU COME TO MY WORKPLACE AND GIVE EVERYONE MASSAGES...
AGAIN?
ZZZ...
ZZZ...
HEH HEH!
WELL, YOU DID PUT IN A LONG DAY.
THANKS FOR EVERYTHING, MANAGER.
ZZZ...
ZZZ...

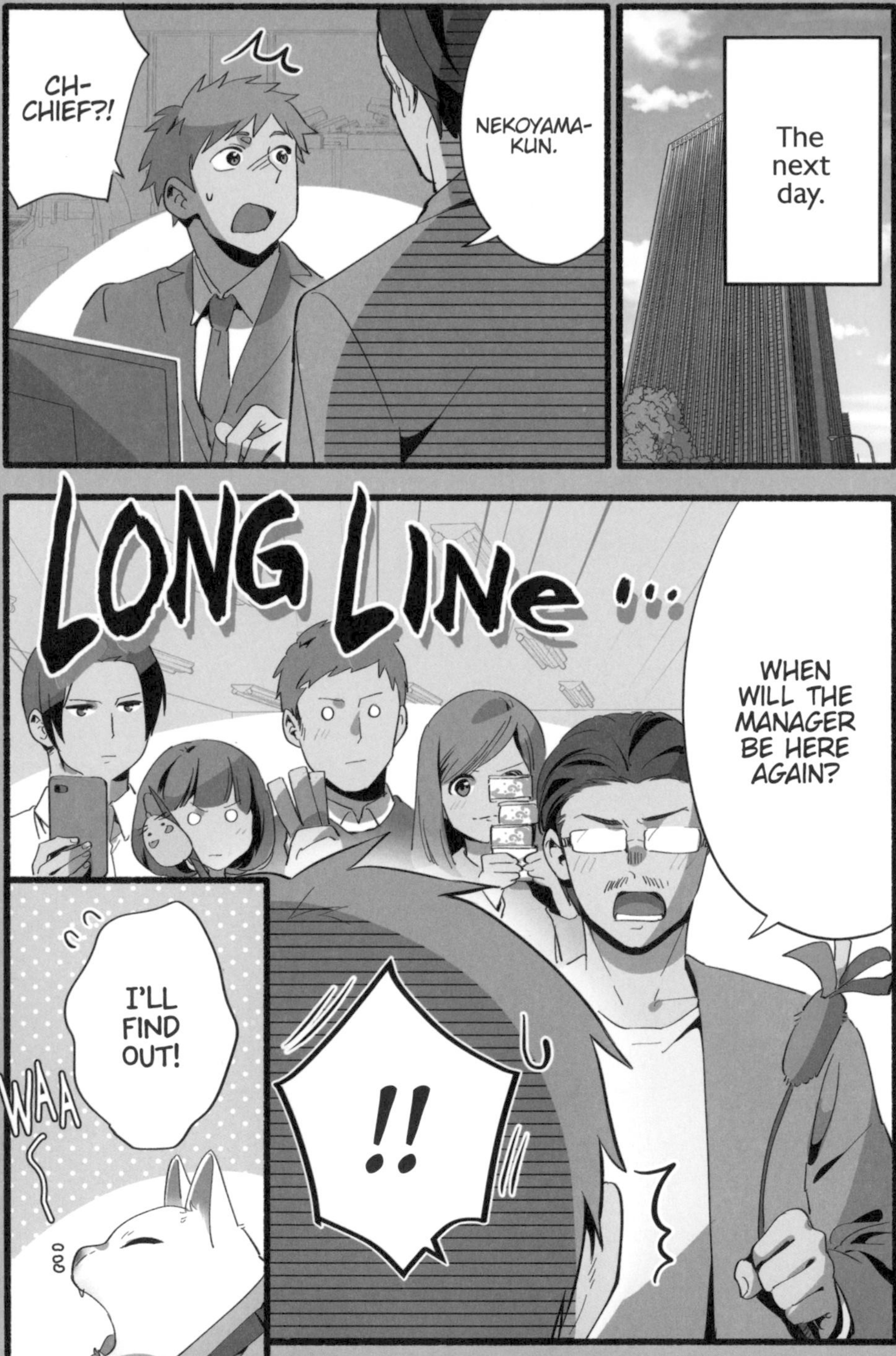
The next day.
NEKOYAMA-KUN.
CH-CHIEF?!
WHEN WILL THE MANAGER BE HERE AGAIN?
LONG LINE...
!!
I'LL FIND OUT!
FWAA

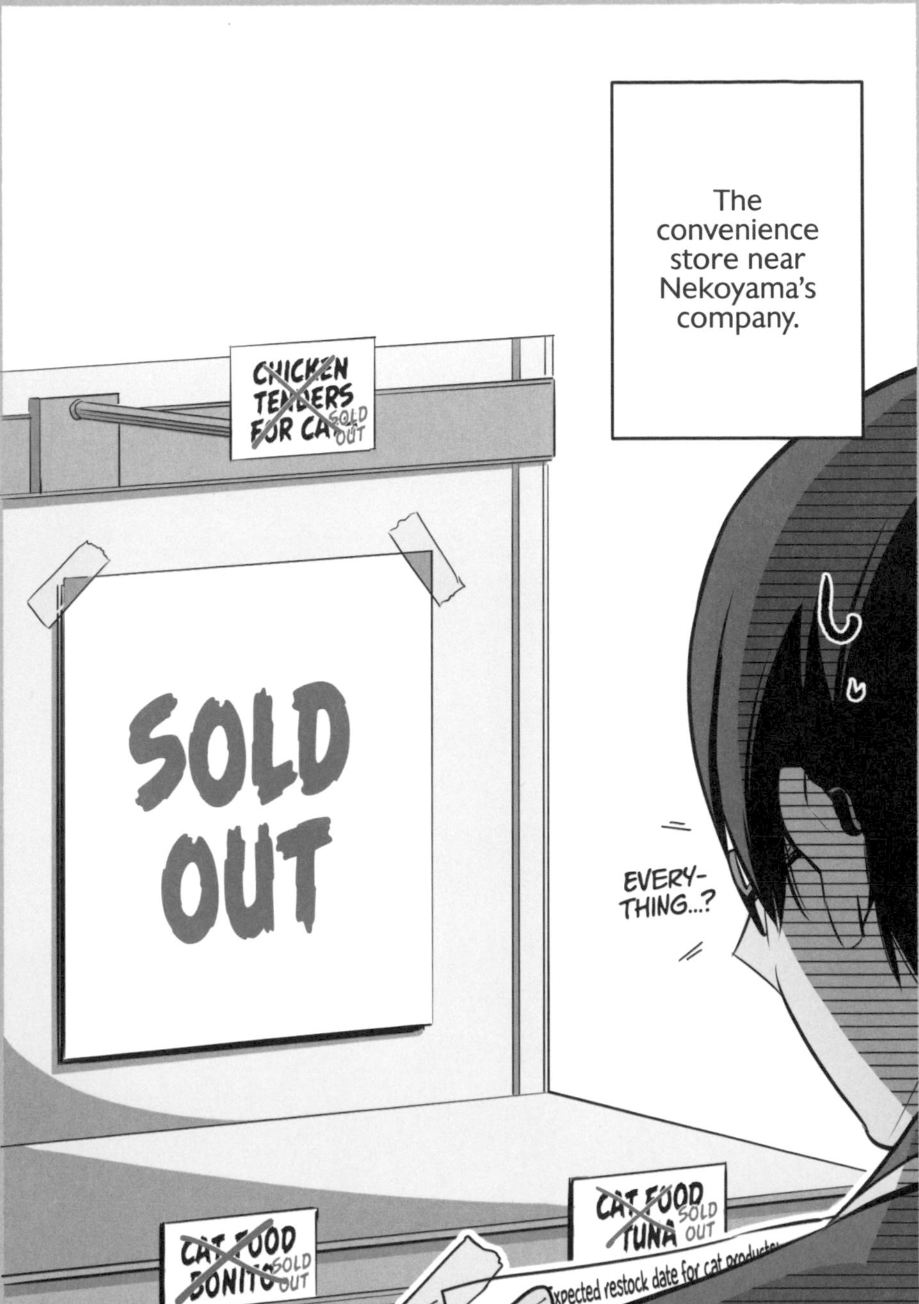

The convenience store near Nekoyama's company.
CHICKEN TENDERS FOR CAT
SOLD OUT
SOLD OUT
EVERY-THING...?
CAT FOOD TUNA
SOLD OUT
CAT FOOD BONITO
SOLD OUT
Expected restock date for cat

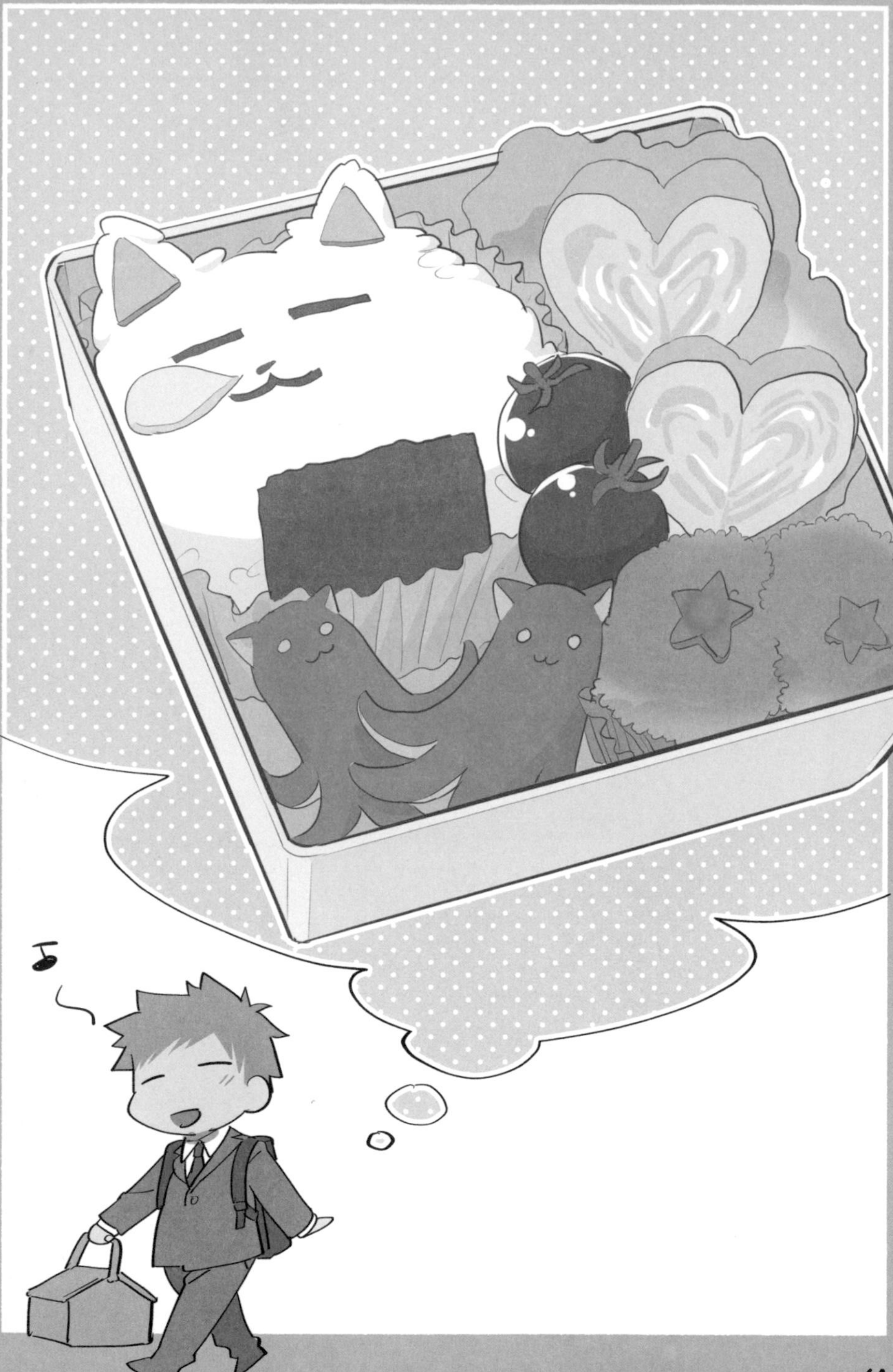

Q9. Can the Trainees Come, Too?

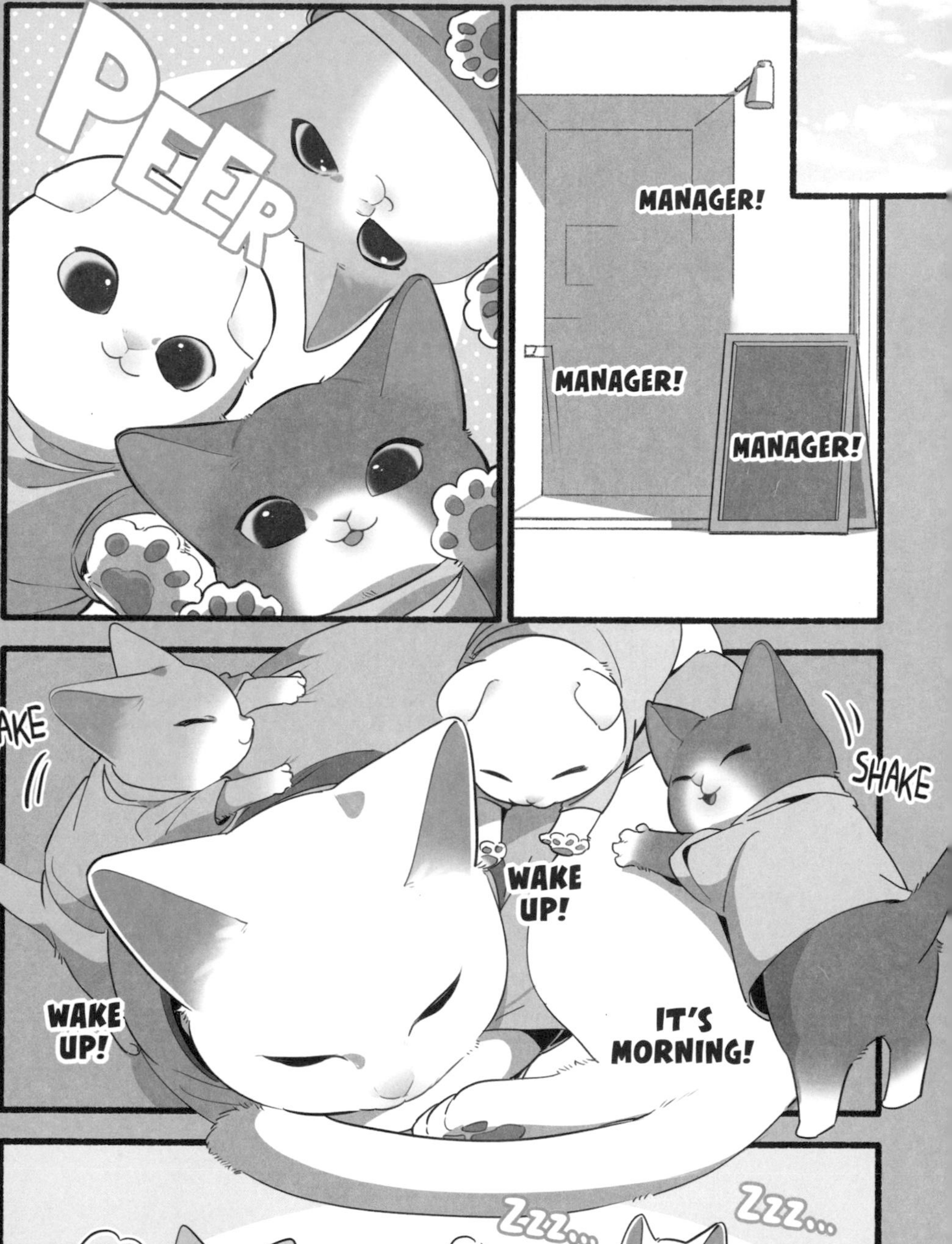

MANAGER!
MANAGER!
MANAGER!
PEER
SHAKE
WAKE UP!
IT'S MORNING!
SHAKE
WAKE UP!
ZZZ...
ZZZ...

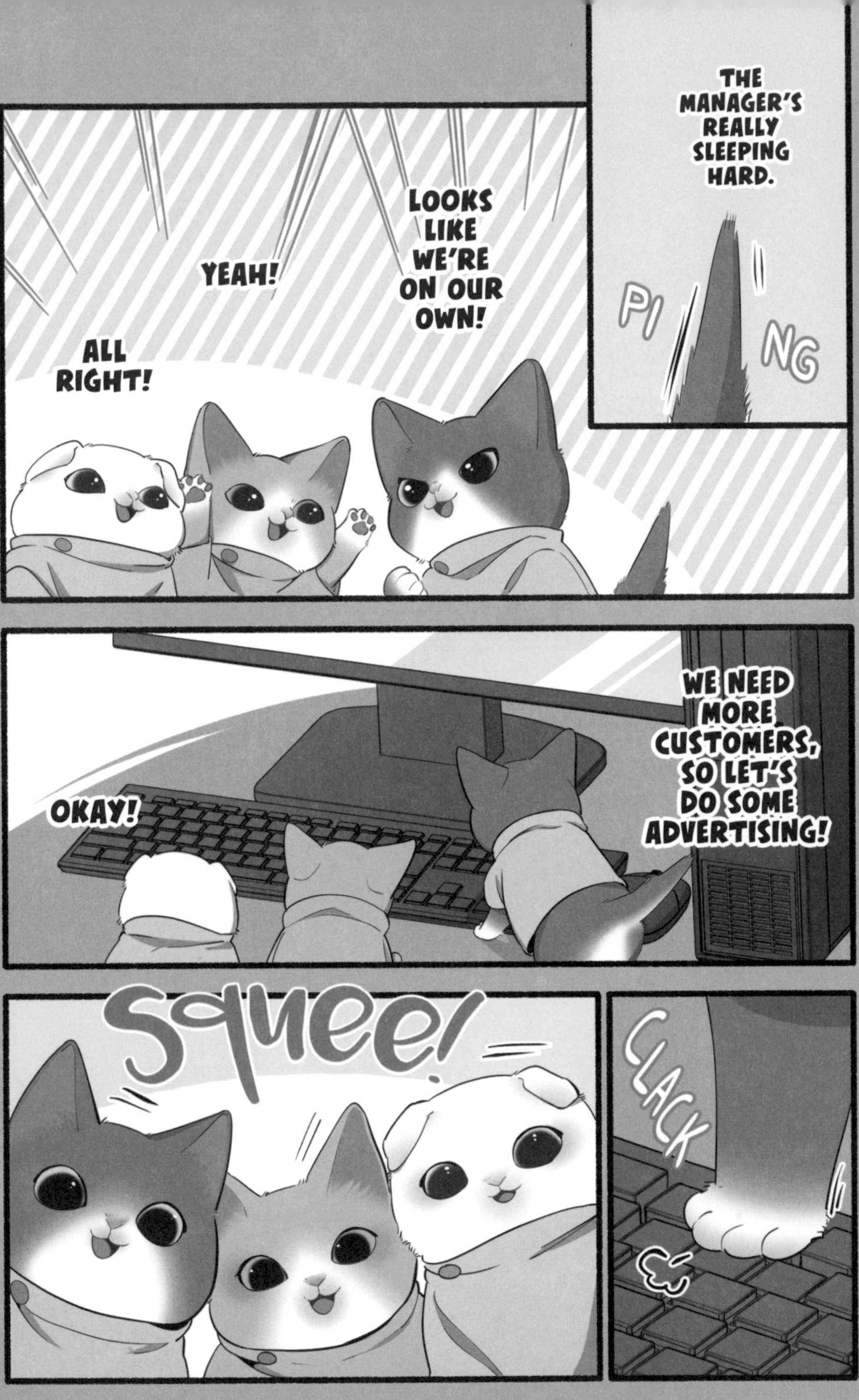
THE MANAGER'S REALLY SLEEPING HARD.
PING
LOOKS LIKE WE'RE ON OUR OWN!
YEAH!
ALL RIGHT!
WE NEED MORE CUSTOMERS, SO LET'S DO SOME ADVERTISING!
OKAY!
CLACK
Squee!

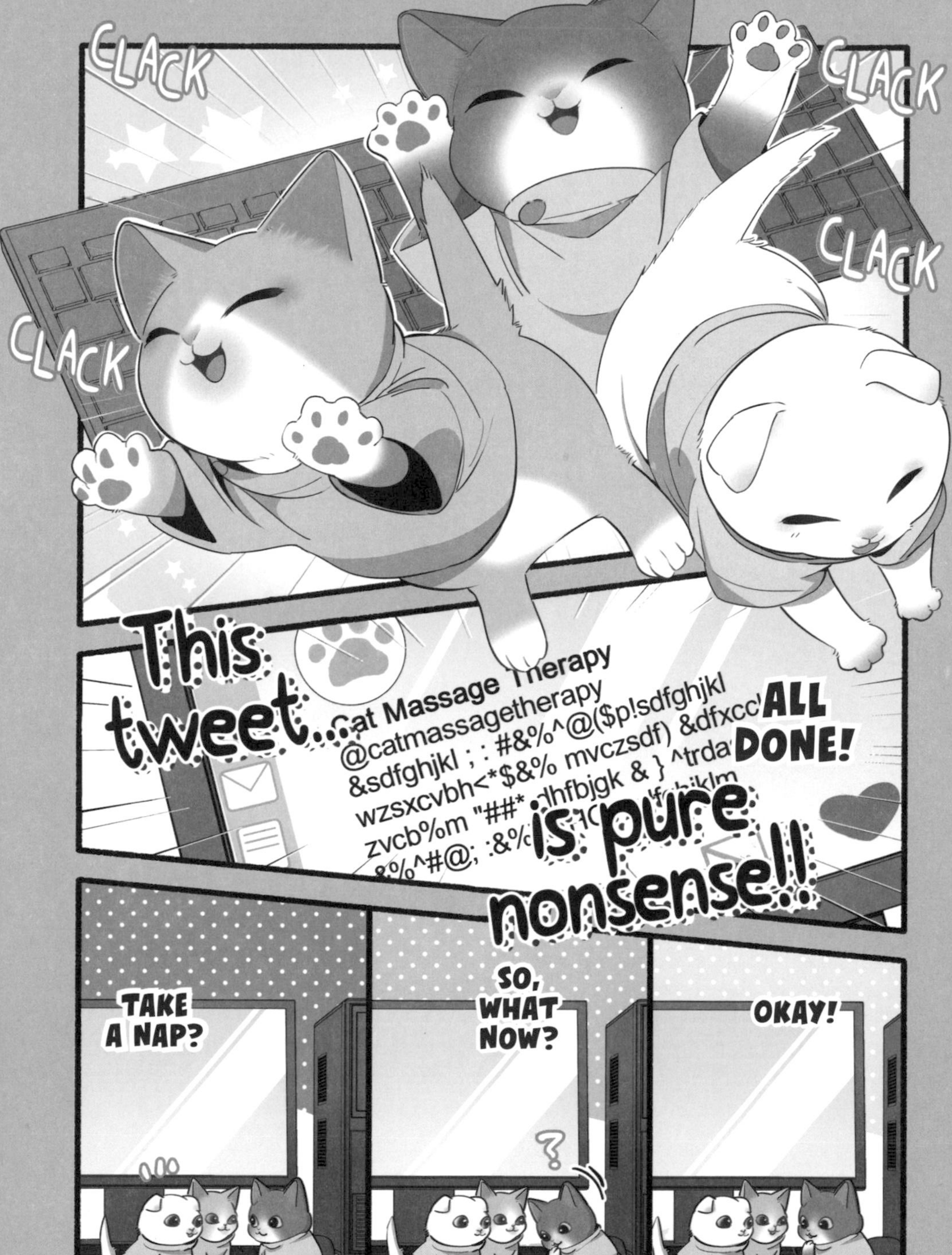
CLACK
CLACK
CLACK
CLACK
ALL DONE!
Cat Massage Therapy
@catmassagetherapy
&sdfghjkl ; : #&%^@($p!sdfghjkl
wzsxcvbh<*$&% mvczsdf) &dfxcc
This tweet... is pure nonsense!!
OKAY!
SO, WHAT NOW?
TAKE A NAP?

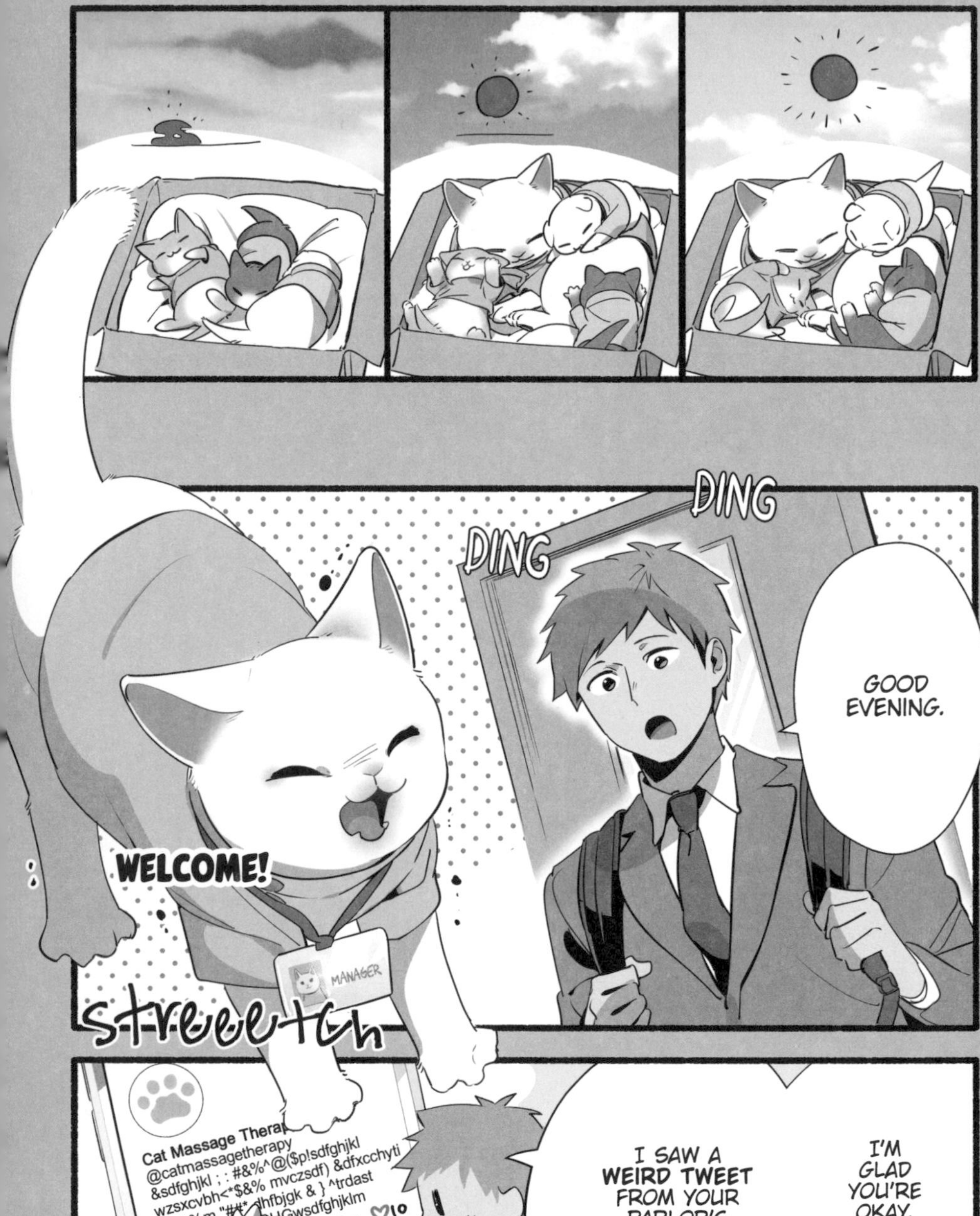
DING
DING
GOOD EVENING.
WELCOME!
MANAGER
streeetch
I'M GLAD YOU'RE OKAY, MANAGER!
I SAW A **WEIRD TWEET** FROM YOUR PARLOR'S ACCOUNT, SO I WAS KIND OF CONCERNED.
Cat Massage Therap
@catmassagetherapy

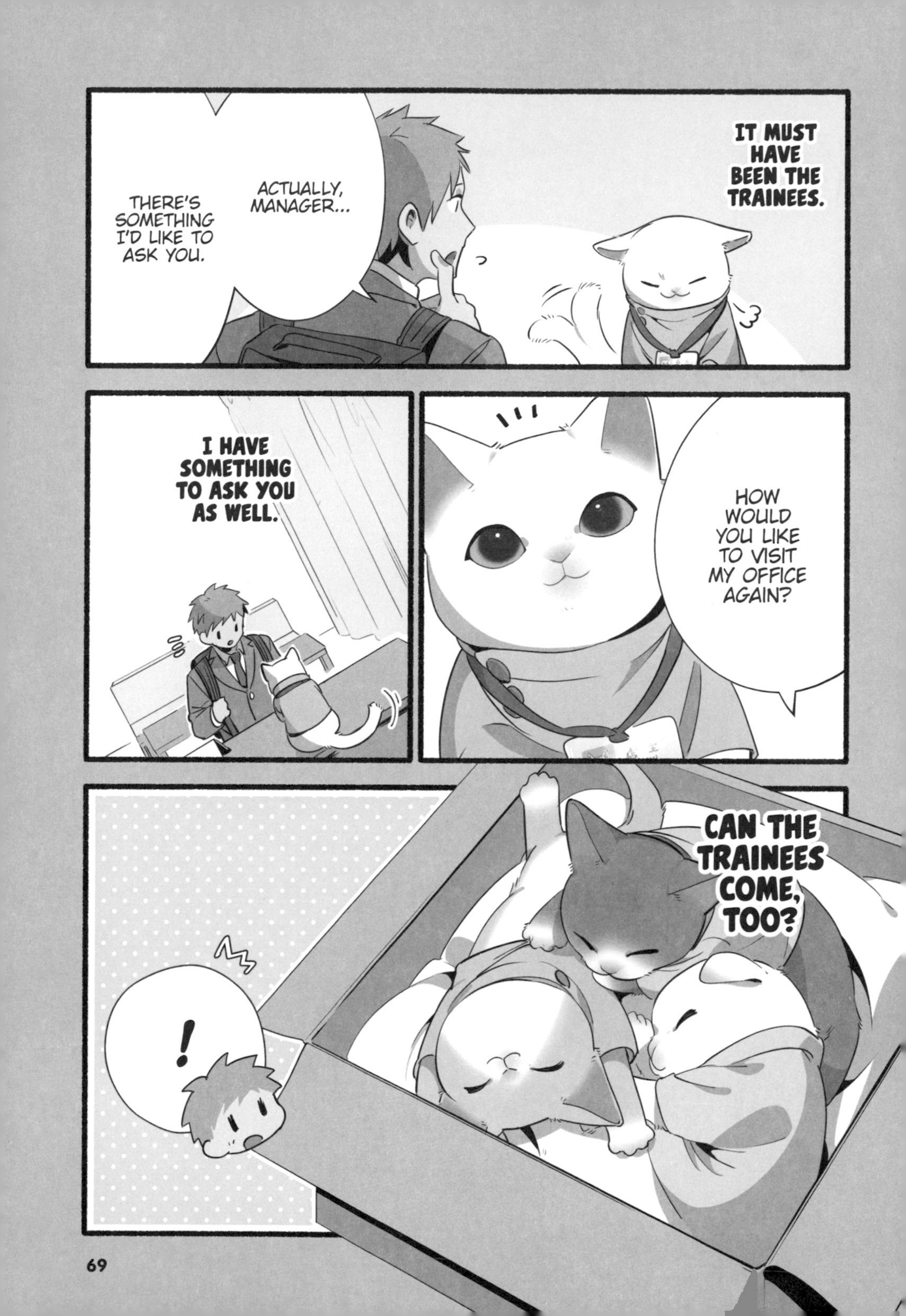
IT MUST HAVE BEEN THE TRAINEES.
ACTUALLY, MANAGER...
THERE'S SOMETHING I'D LIKE TO ASK YOU.
HOW WOULD YOU LIKE TO VISIT MY OFFICE AGAIN?
I HAVE SOMETHING TO ASK YOU AS WELL.
CAN THE TRAINEES COME, TOO?
!

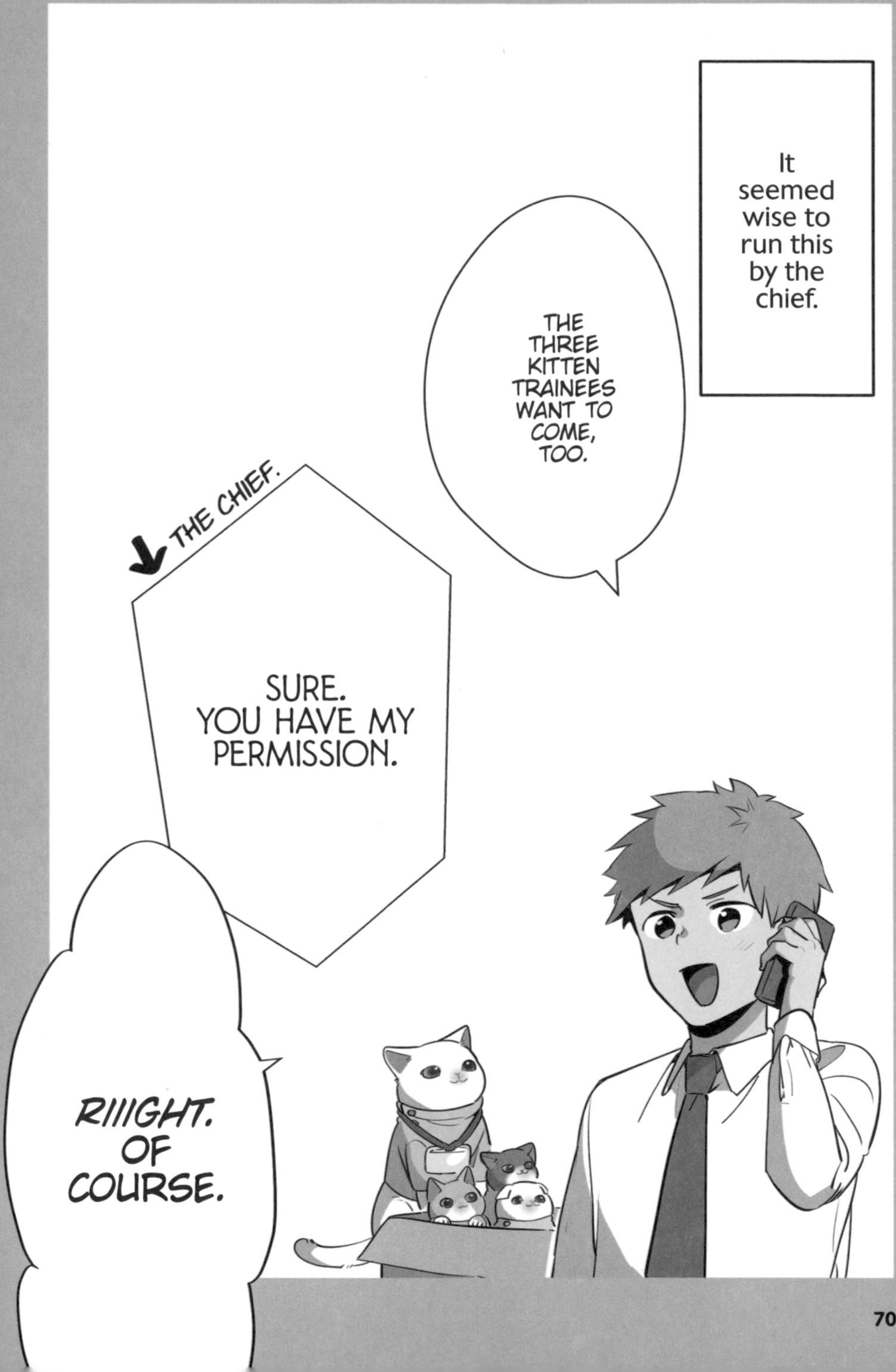
It seemed wise to run this by the chief.
THE THREE KITTEN TRAINEES WANT TO COME, TOO.
THE CHIEF.
SURE. YOU HAVE MY PERMISSION.
RIIIGHT. OF COURSE.

Q10. Give It a Rest, Will You?!

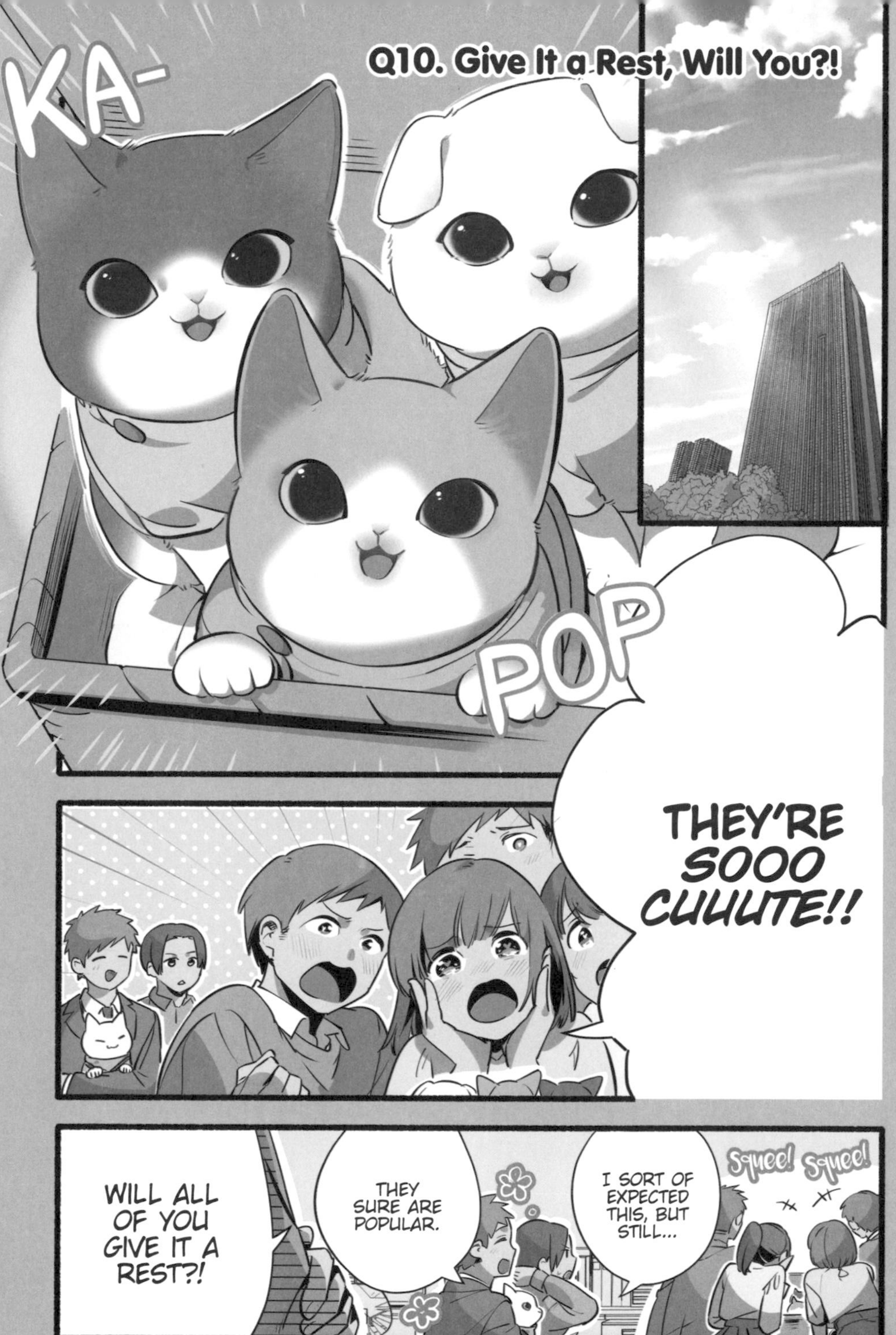
KA-
POP
THEY'RE SOOO CUUUTE!!
Squee! Squee!
I SORT OF EXPECTED THIS, BUT STILL...
THEY SURE ARE POPULAR.
WILL ALL OF YOU GIVE IT A REST?!

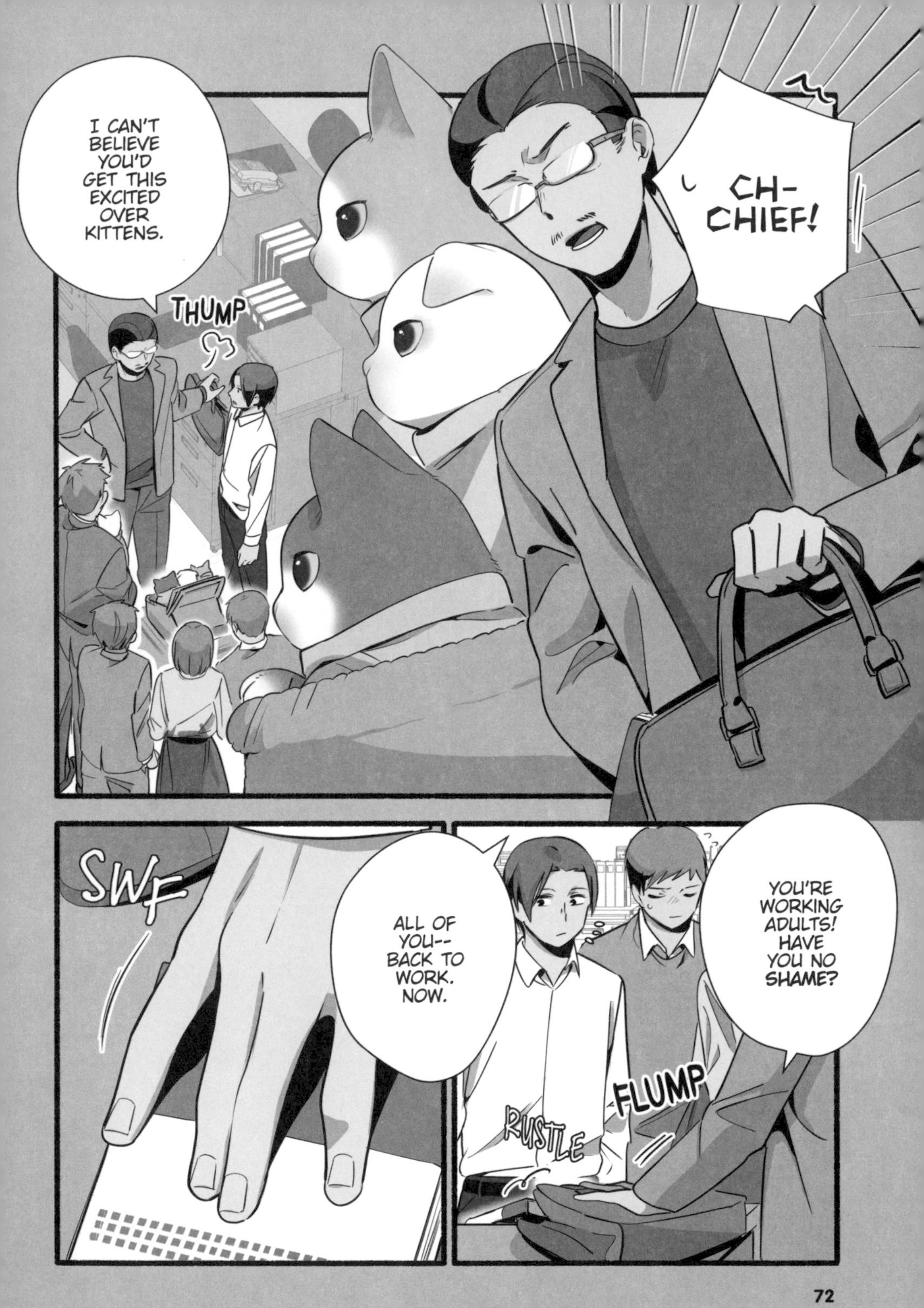

CH- CHIEF!
I CAN'T BELIEVE YOU'D GET THIS EXCITED OVER KITTENS.
THUMP
YOU'RE WORKING ADULTS! HAVE YOU NO SHAME?
ALL OF YOU-- BACK TO WORK. NOW.
FLUMP
RUSTLE
SWF

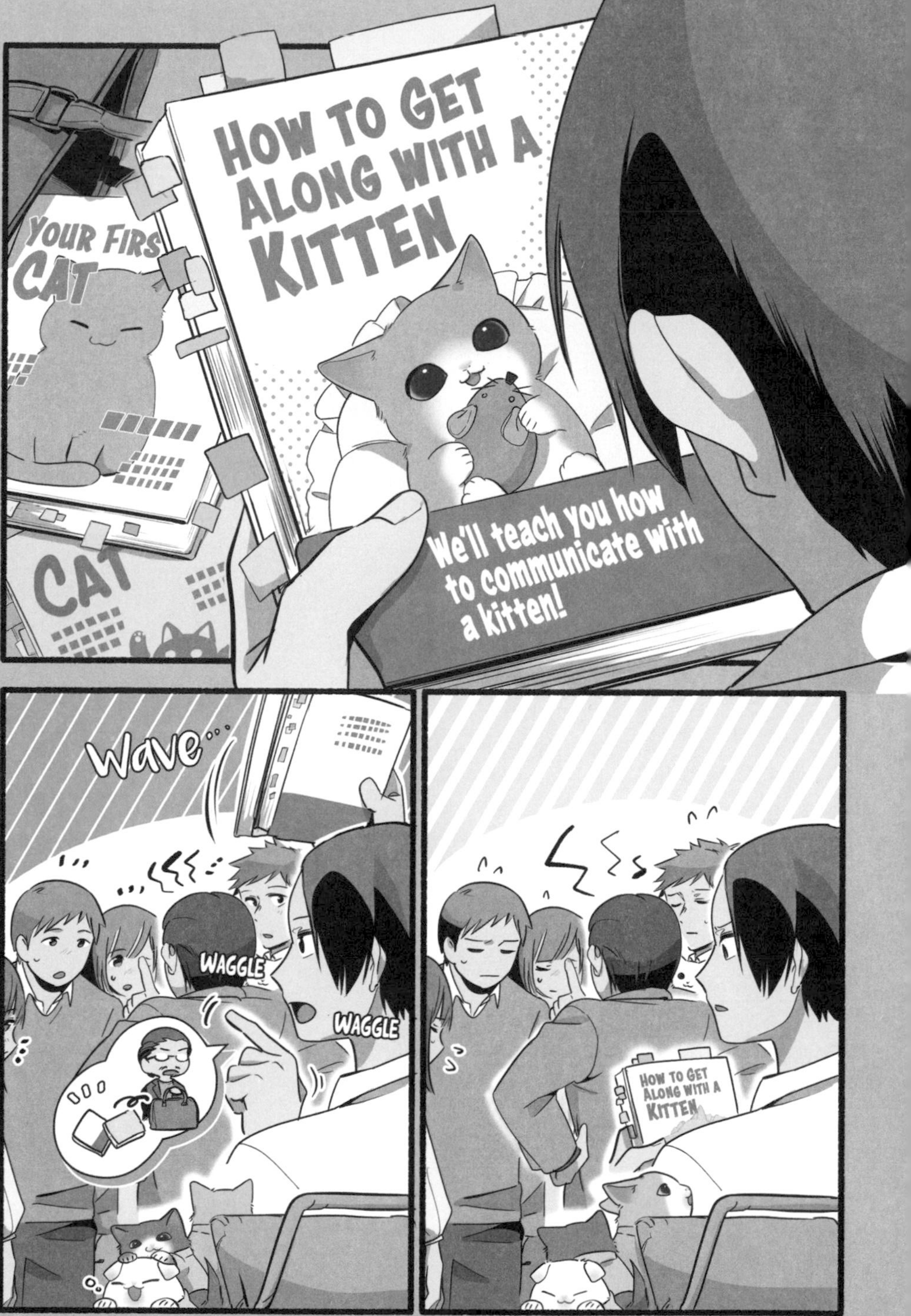
HOW TO GET ALONG WITH A KITTEN
YOUR FIRS
CAT
CAT
We'll teach you how to communicate with a kitten!
HOW TO GET ALONG WITH A KITTEN
Wave...
WAGGLE
WAGGLE

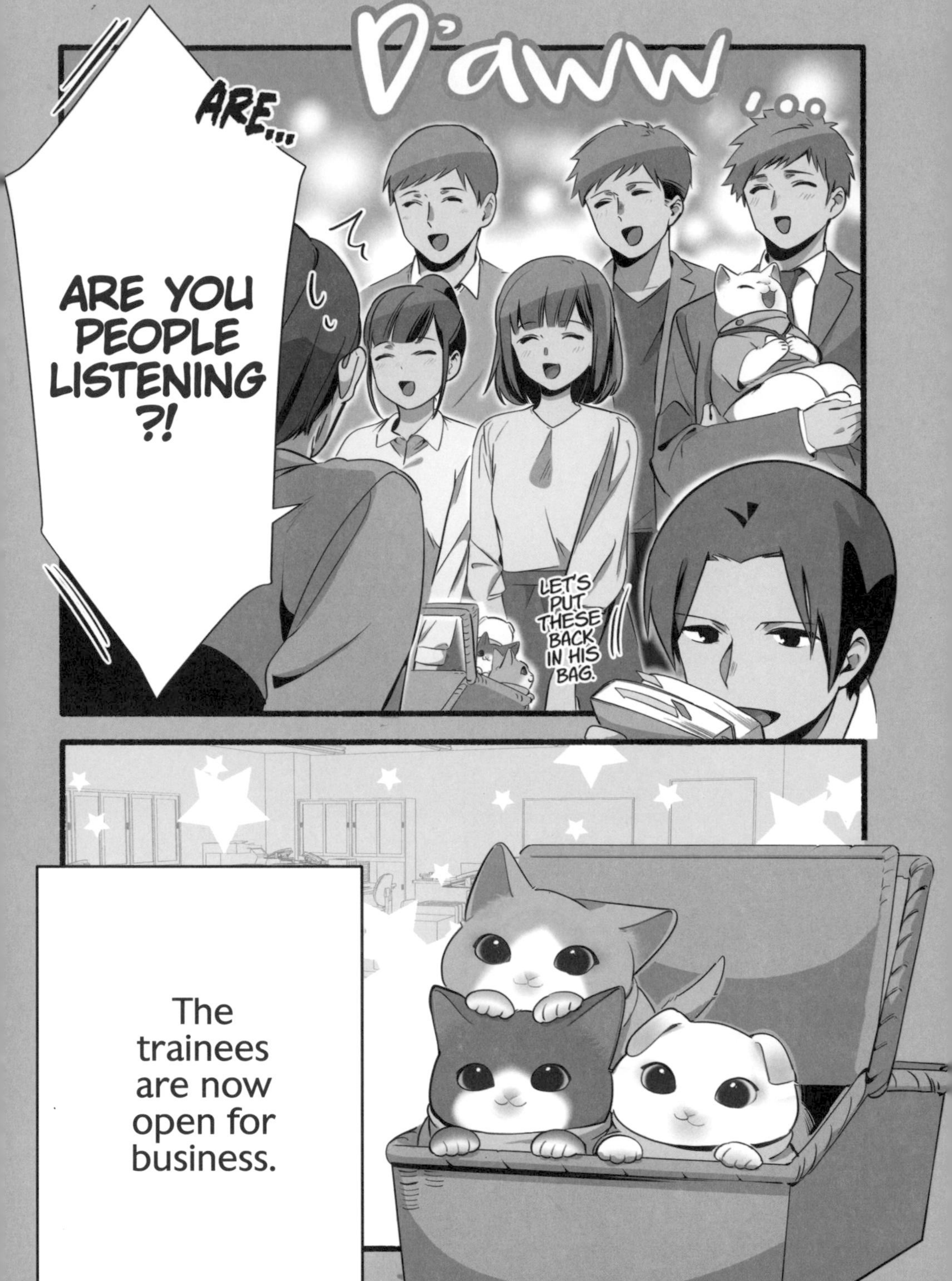
D'aww...
ARE...
ARE YOU PEOPLE LISTENING?!
LET'S PUT THESE BACK IN HIS BAG.
The trainees are now open for business.

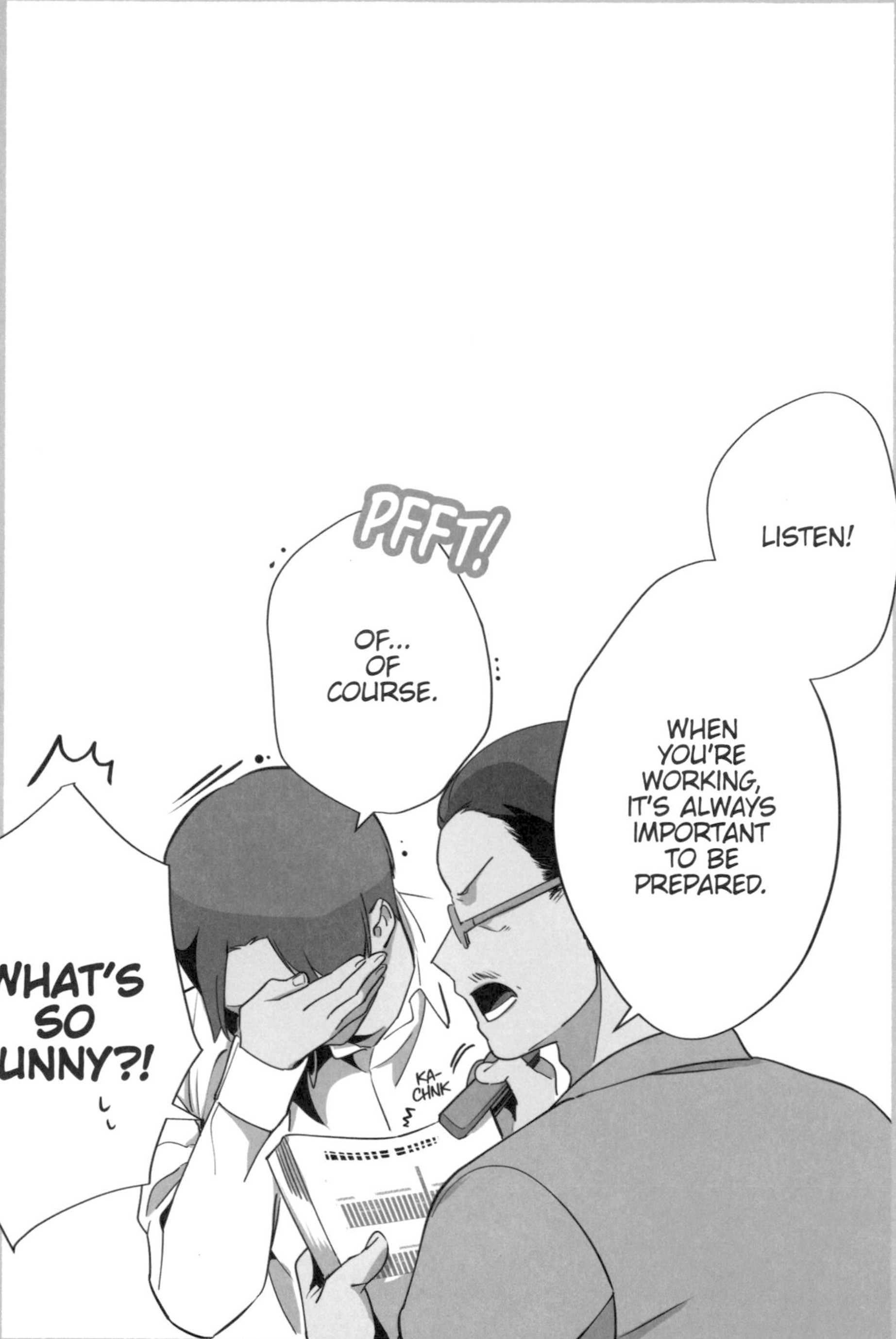
LISTEN!
WHEN YOU'RE WORKING, IT'S ALWAYS IMPORTANT TO BE PREPARED.
PFFT!
OF... OF COURSE.
KA-CHNK
WHAT'S SO FUNNY?!

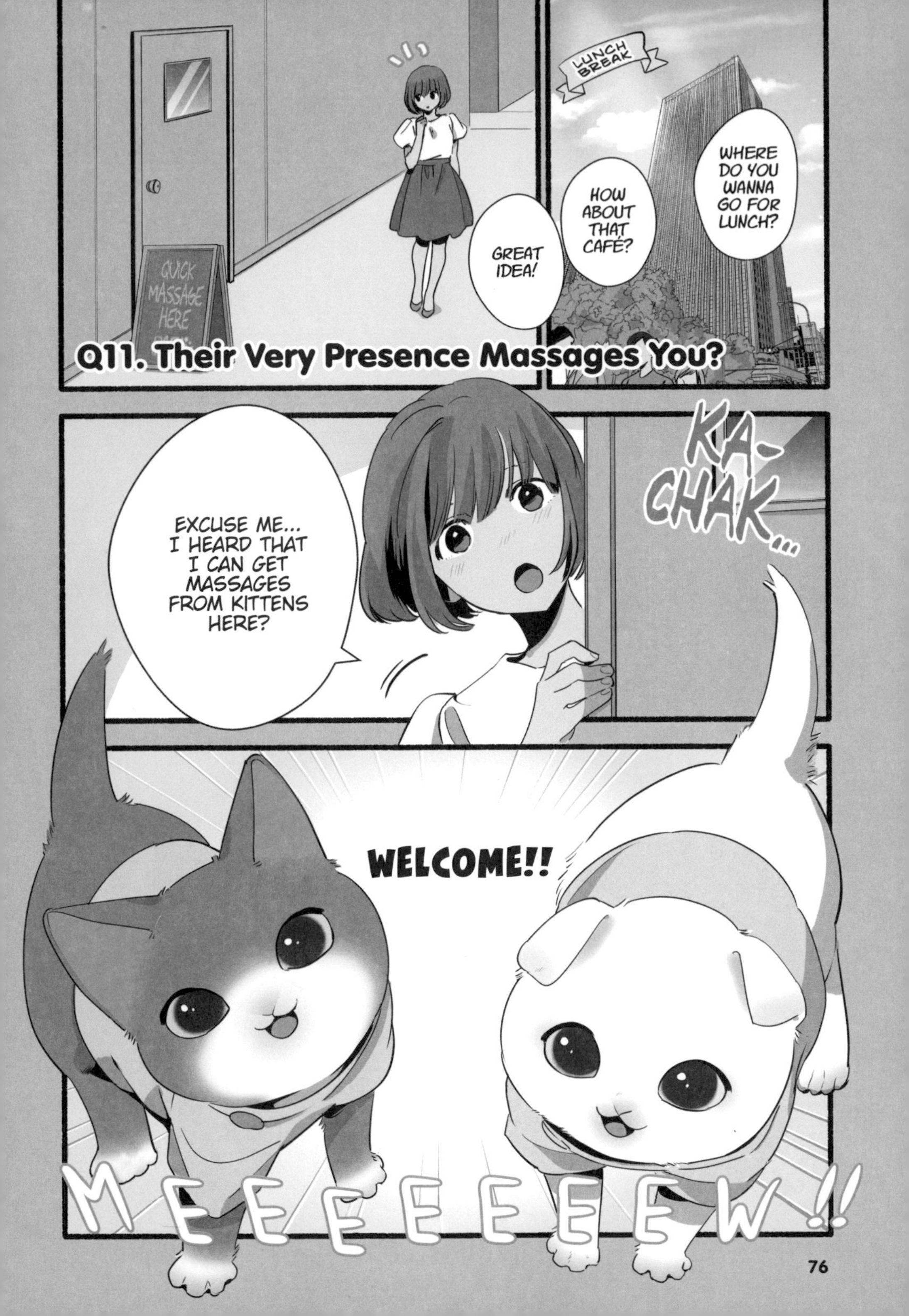
LUNCH BREAK
WHERE DO YOU WANNA GO FOR LUNCH?
HOW ABOUT THAT CAFÉ?
GREAT IDEA!
QUICK MASSAGE HERE
Q11. Their Very Presence Massages You?
KA-CHAK...
EXCUSE ME... I HEARD THAT I CAN GET MASSAGES FROM KITTENS HERE?
WELCOME!!
MEEEEEEEW!!

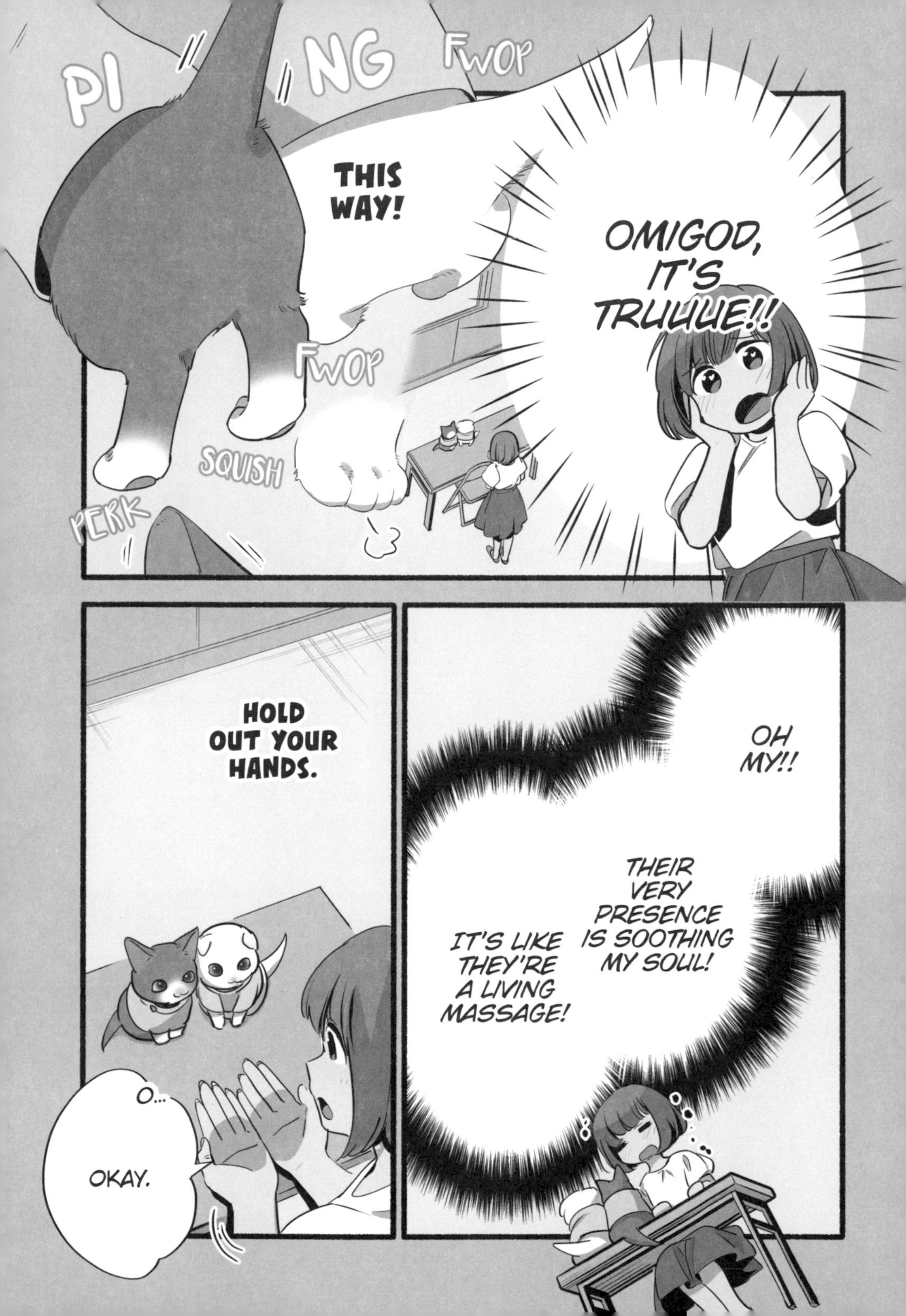
FWOP
OMIGOD, IT'S TRUUUE!!
PI NG
THIS WAY!
FWOP
SQUISH
PERK
OH MY!!
THEIR VERY PRESENCE IS SOOTHING MY SOUL!
IT'S LIKE THEY'RE A LIVING MASSAGE!
HOLD OUT YOUR HANDS.
O...
OKAY.

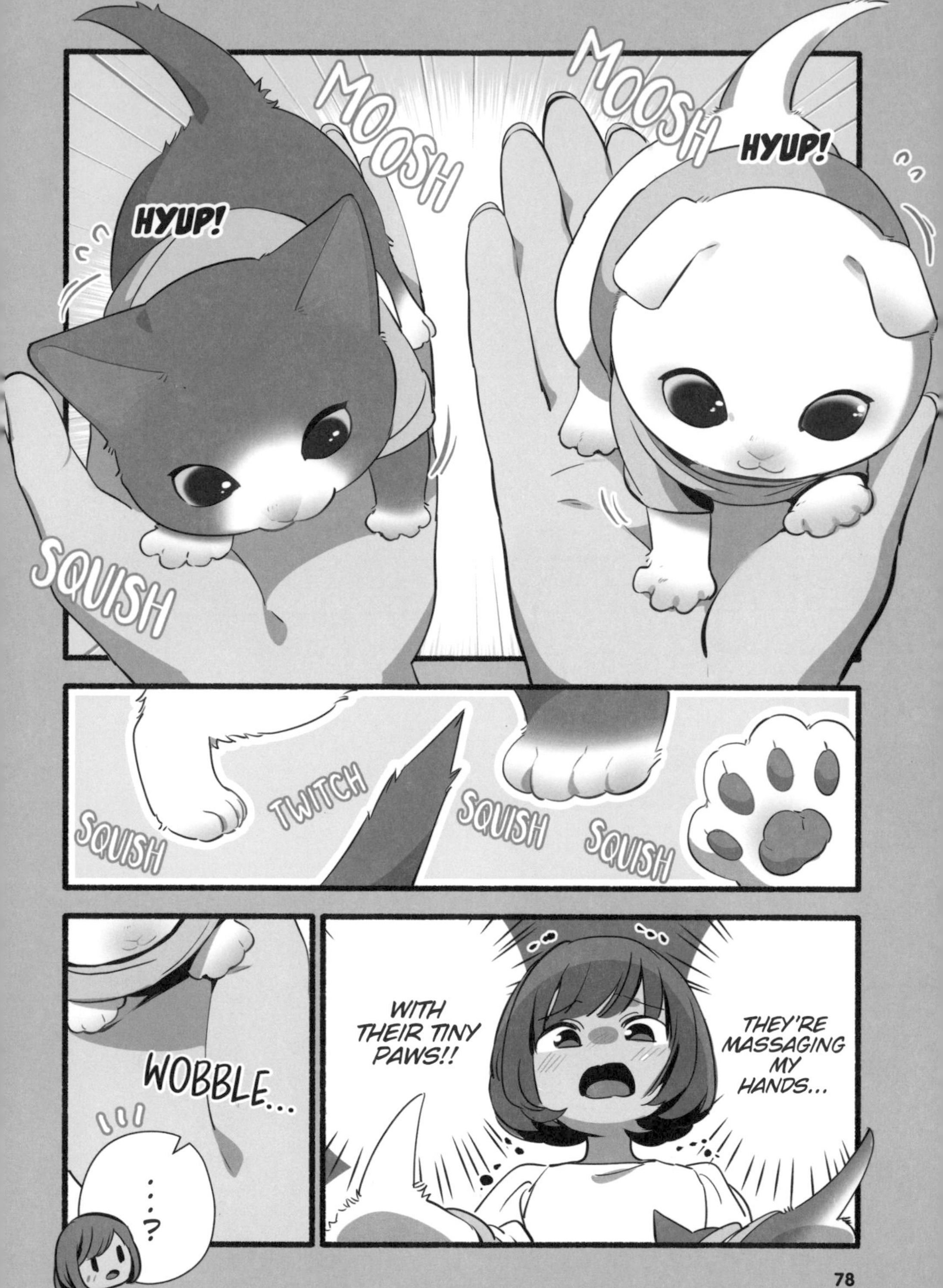
MOOSH
HYUP!
MOOSH
HYUP!
SQUISH
SQUISH
SQUISH
TWITCH
SQUISH
THEY'RE MASSAGING MY HANDS...
WITH THEIR TINY PAWS!!
WOBBLE...
...?

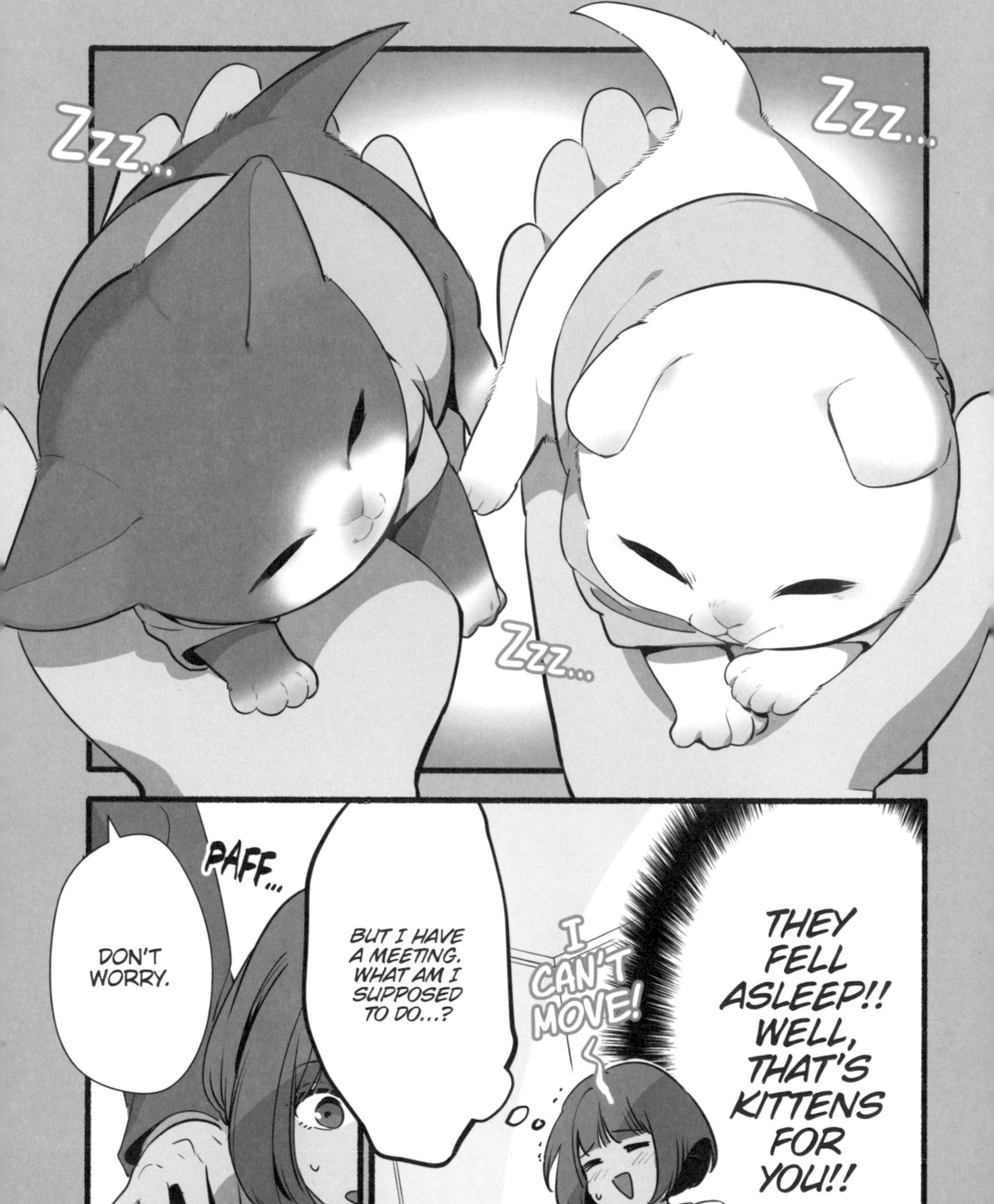
Zzz...
Zzz...
Zzz...
THEY FELL ASLEEP!! WELL, THAT'S KITTENS FOR YOU!!
I CAN'T MOVE!
BUT I HAVE A MEETING. WHAT AM I SUPPOSED TO DO...?
PAFF...
DON'T WORRY.

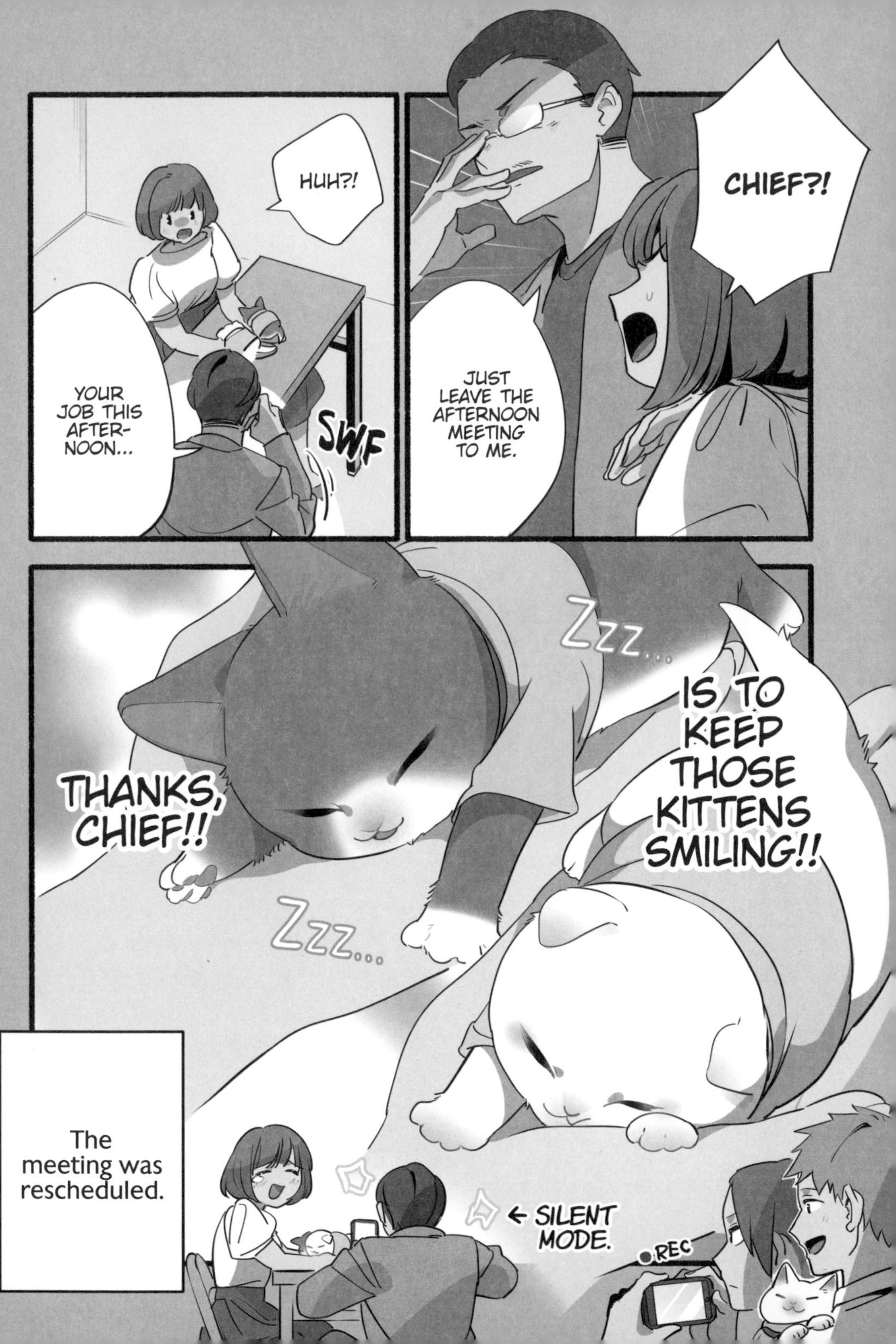
CHIEF?!
JUST LEAVE THE AFTERNOON MEETING TO ME.
HUH?!
YOUR JOB THIS AFTER-NOON...
SWF
IS TO KEEP THOSE KITTENS SMILING!!
Zzz...
THANKS, CHIEF!!
Zzz...
← SILENT MODE.
●REC
The meeting was rescheduled.

To all members of my 1PM meeting:

The trainees are sleeping on my hands,
so the meeting will be moved to 2PM

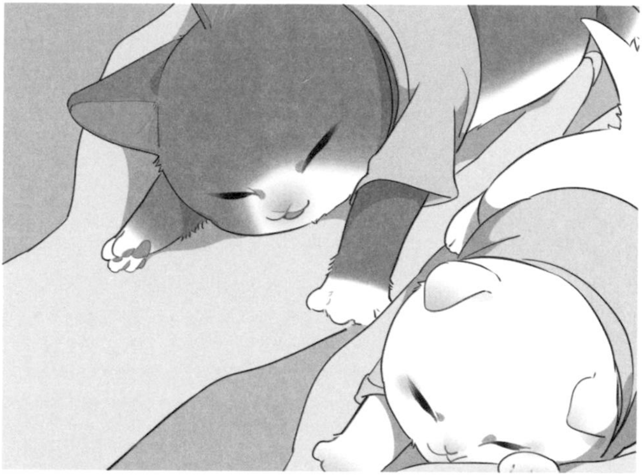

5 ok 12 3

Approved.

12 ok 15 10

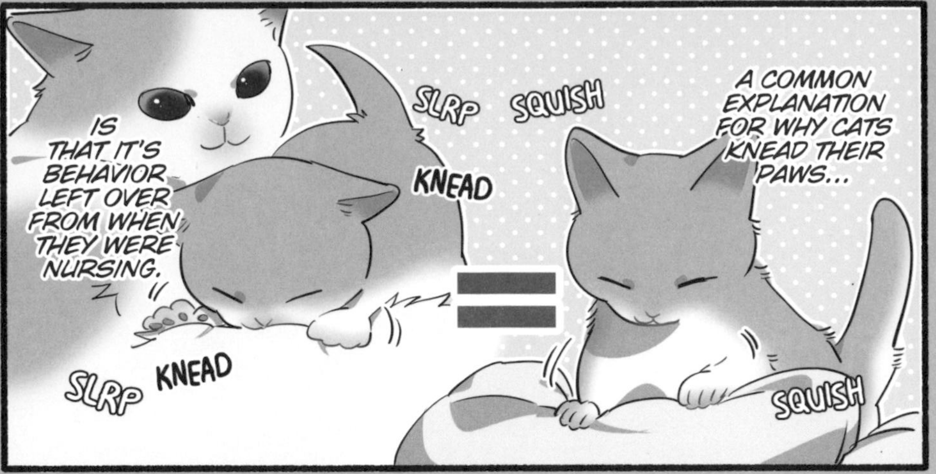
A COMMON EXPLANATION FOR WHY CATS KNEAD THEIR PAWS...
SQUISH
SLRP
KNEAD
IS THAT IT'S BEHAVIOR LEFT OVER FROM WHEN THEY WERE NURSING.
SQUISH
KNEAD
SLRP

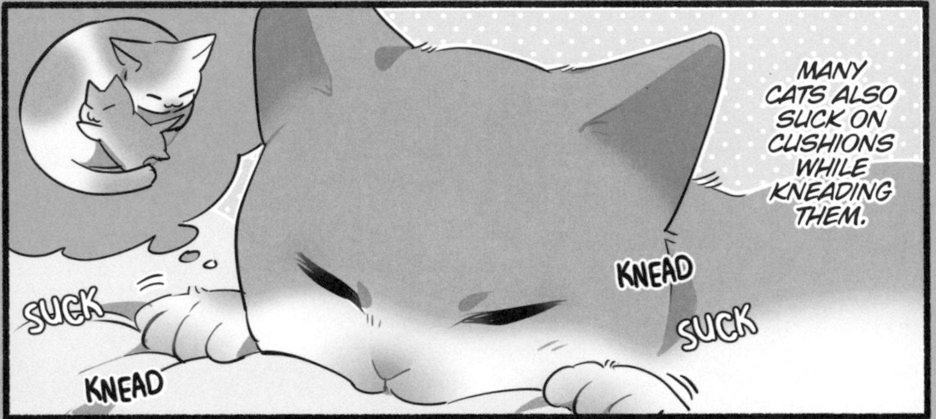
MANY CATS ALSO SUCK ON CUSHIONS WHILE KNEADING THEM.
KNEAD
SUCK
SUCK
KNEAD

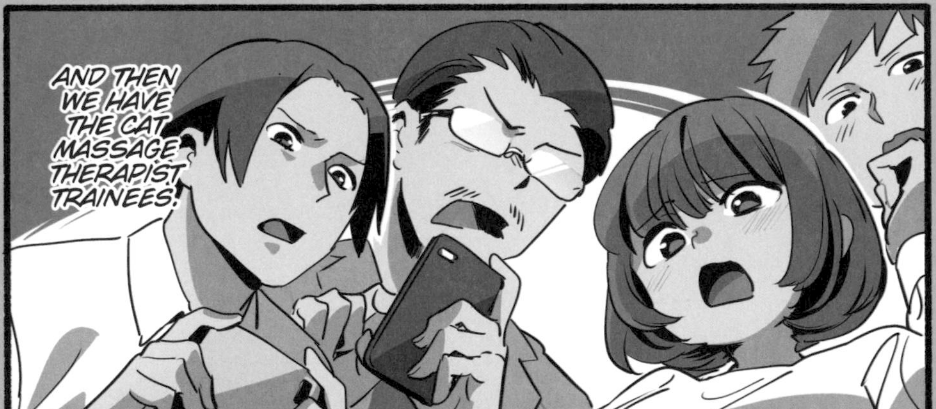
AND THEN WE HAVE THE CAT MASSAGE THERAPIST TRAINEES!

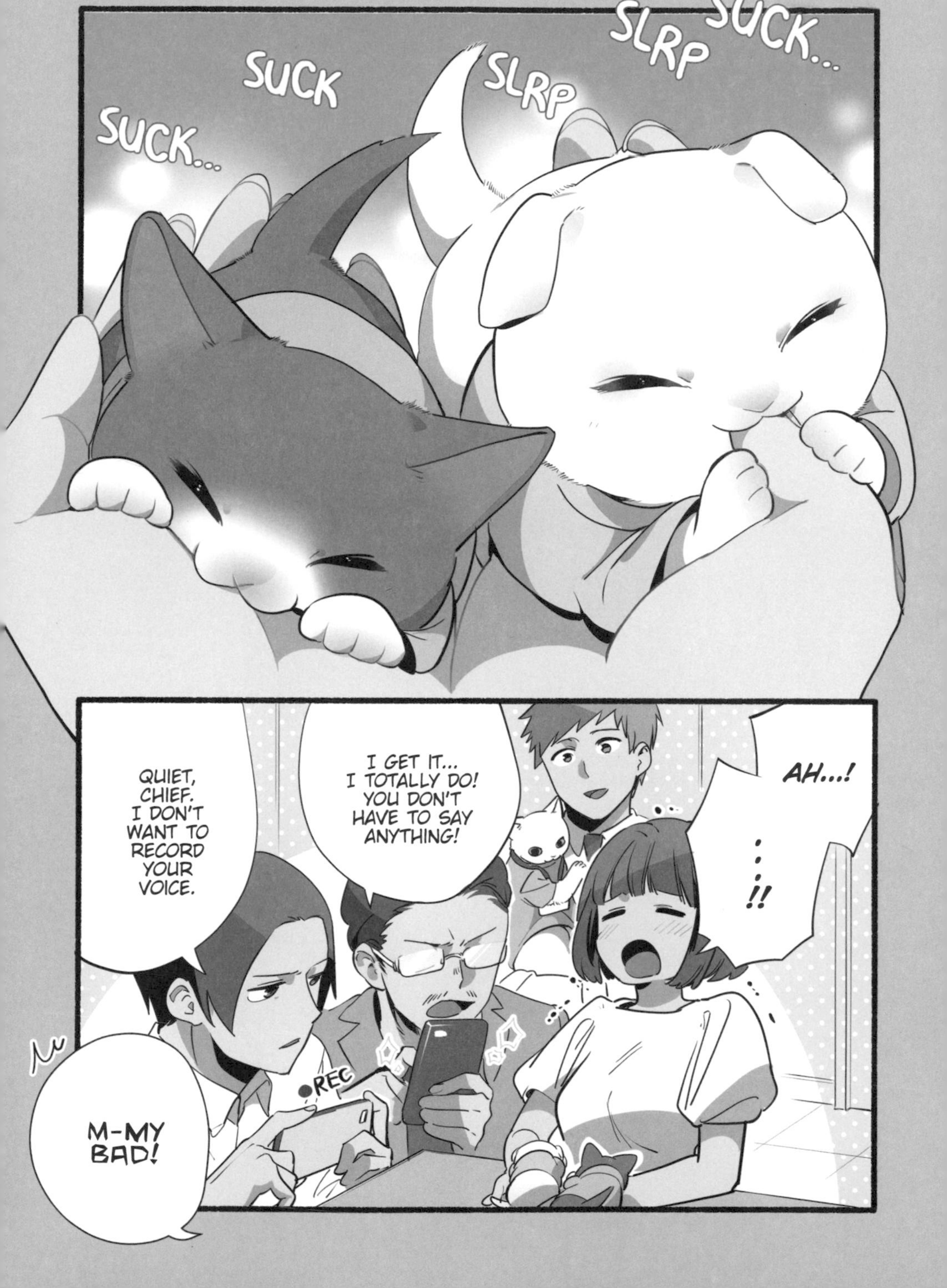
SUCK...
SLRP
SLRP
SUCK
SUCK...
AH...!
...!!
I GET IT... I TOTALLY DO! YOU DON'T HAVE TO SAY ANYTHING!
QUIET, CHIEF. I DON'T WANT TO RECORD YOUR VOICE.
REC
M-MY BAD!

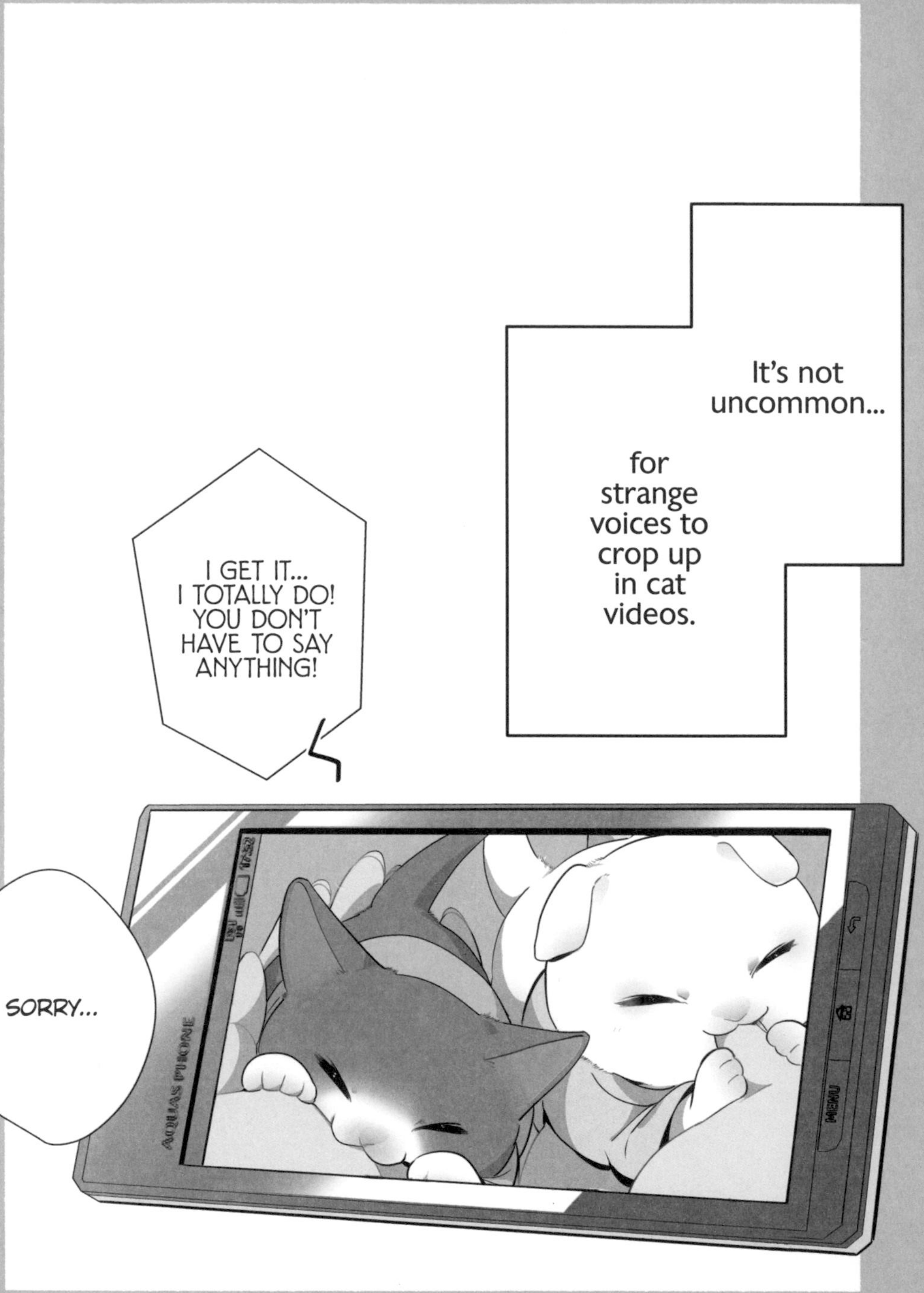
It's not uncommon...
for strange voices to crop up in cat videos.
I GET IT... I TOTALLY DO! YOU DON'T HAVE TO SAY ANYTHING!
SORRY...

Q12. Give Paws...?

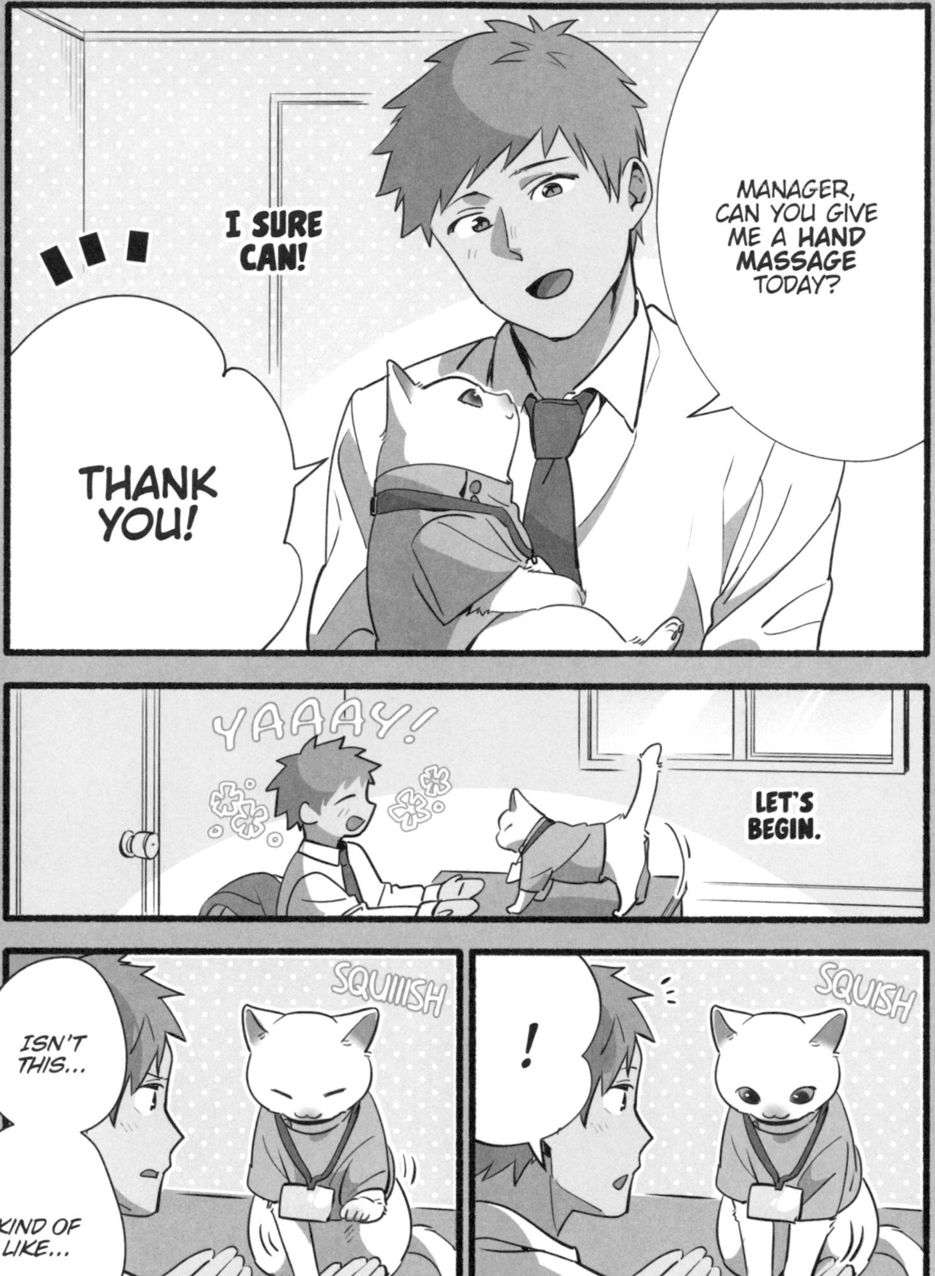
MANAGER, CAN YOU GIVE ME A HAND MASSAGE TODAY?
I SURE CAN!
...
THANK YOU!
YAAAY!
LET'S BEGIN.
SQUISH
!
SQUIIISH
ISN'T THIS...
KIND OF LIKE...

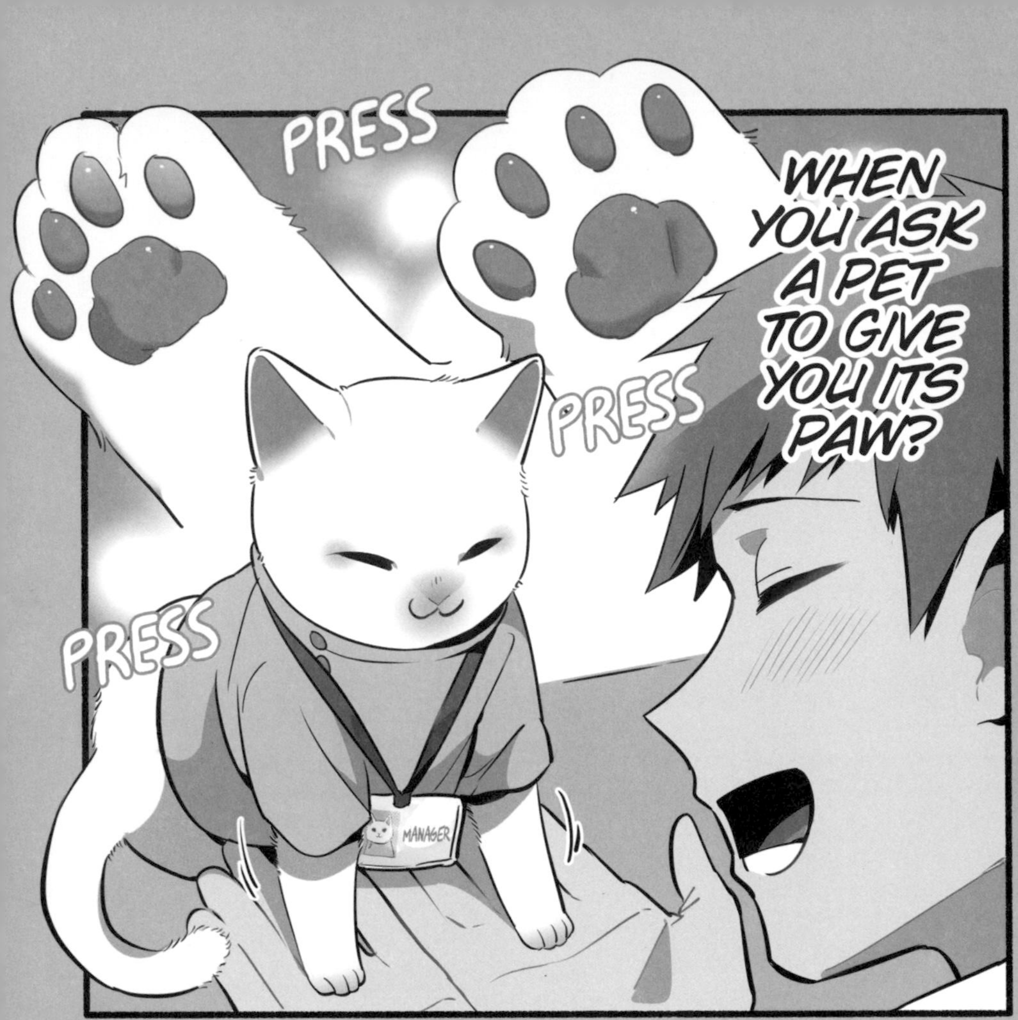
PRESS
WHEN YOU ASK A PET TO GIVE YOU ITS PAW?
PRESS
PRESS
MANAGER

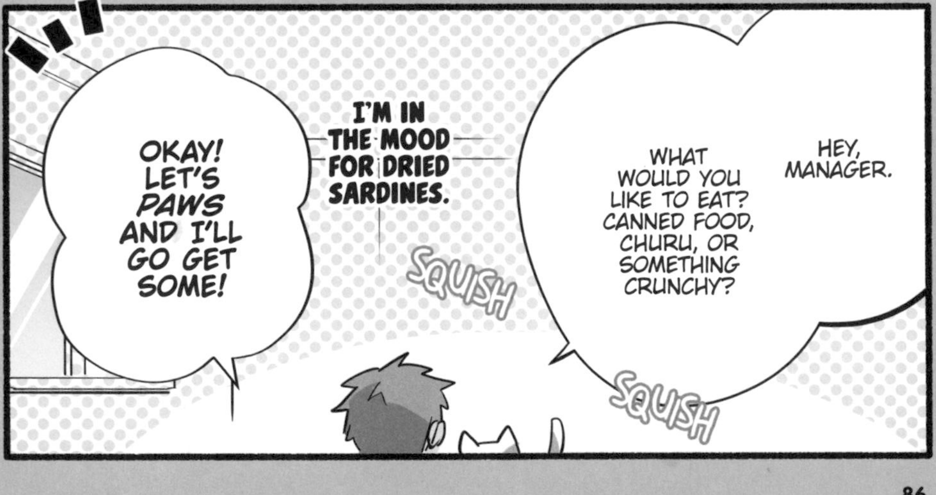
HEY, MANAGER.
WHAT WOULD YOU LIKE TO EAT? CANNED FOOD, CHURU, OR SOMETHING CRUNCHY?
SQUISH
I'M IN THE MOOD FOR DRIED SARDINES.
SQUISH
OKAY! LET'S PAWS AND I'LL GO GET SOME!

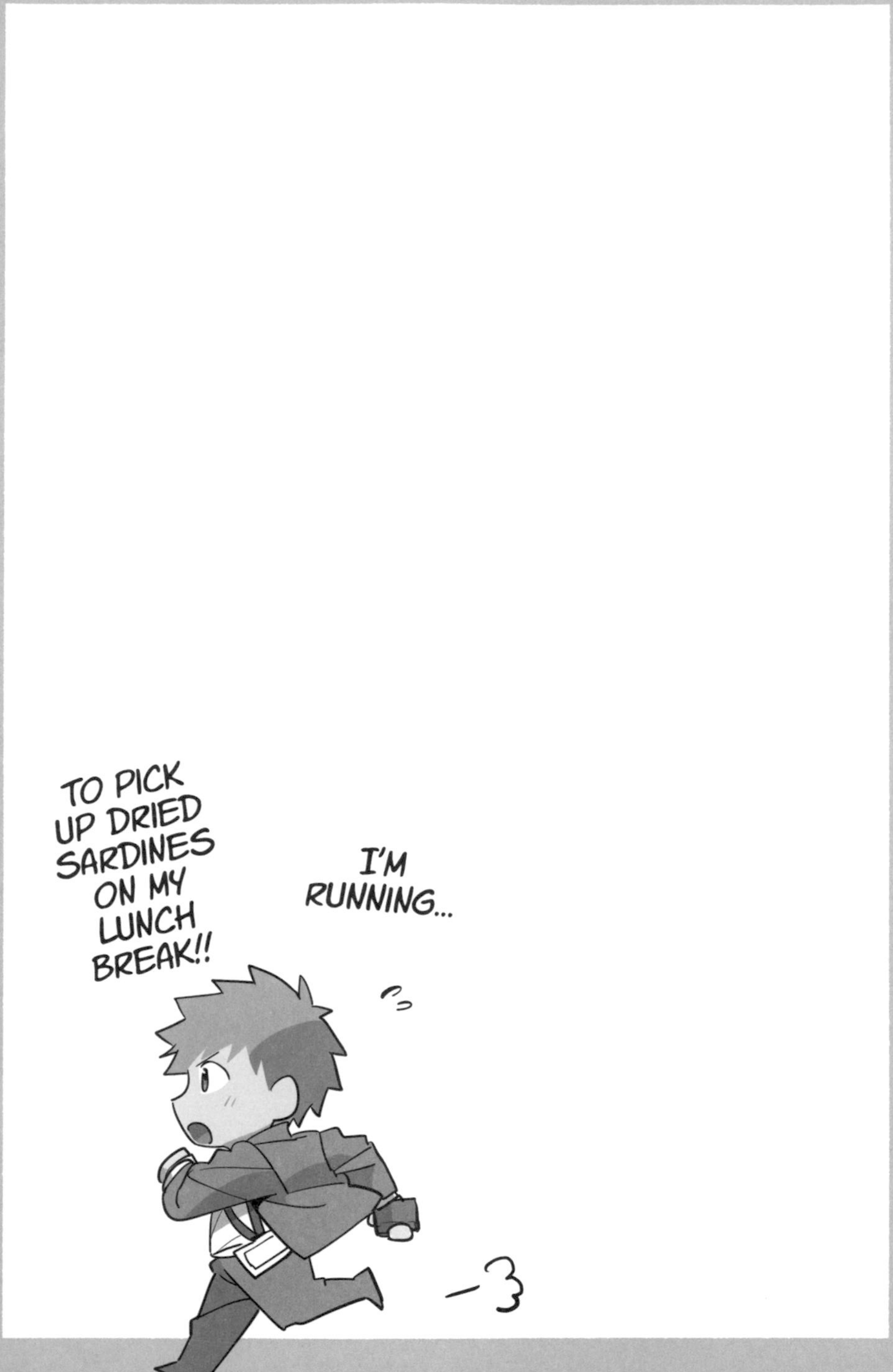
I'M RUNNING...
TO PICK UP DRIED SARDINES ON MY LUNCH BREAK!!

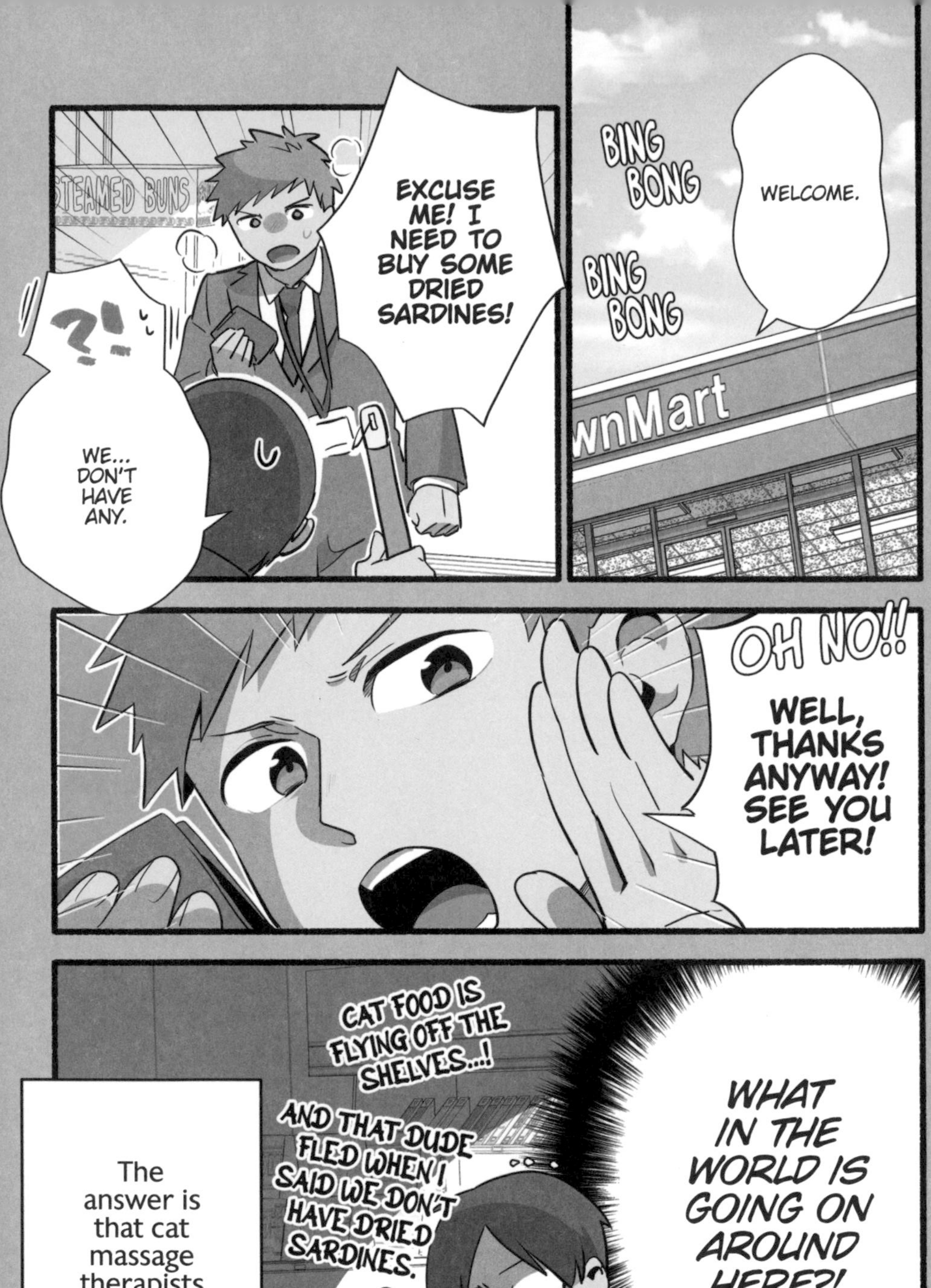
BING BONG
BING BONG
WELCOME.
wnMart
EXCUSE ME! I NEED TO BUY SOME DRIED SARDINES!
STEAMED BUNS
?!
WE... DON'T HAVE ANY.
OH NO!!
WELL, THANKS ANYWAY! SEE YOU LATER!
WHAT IN THE WORLD IS GOING ON AROUND HERE?!
CAT FOOD IS FLYING OFF THE SHELVES...!
AND THAT DUDE FLED WHEN I SAID WE DON'T HAVE DRIED SARDINES.
The answer is that cat massage therapists are providing on-site services.

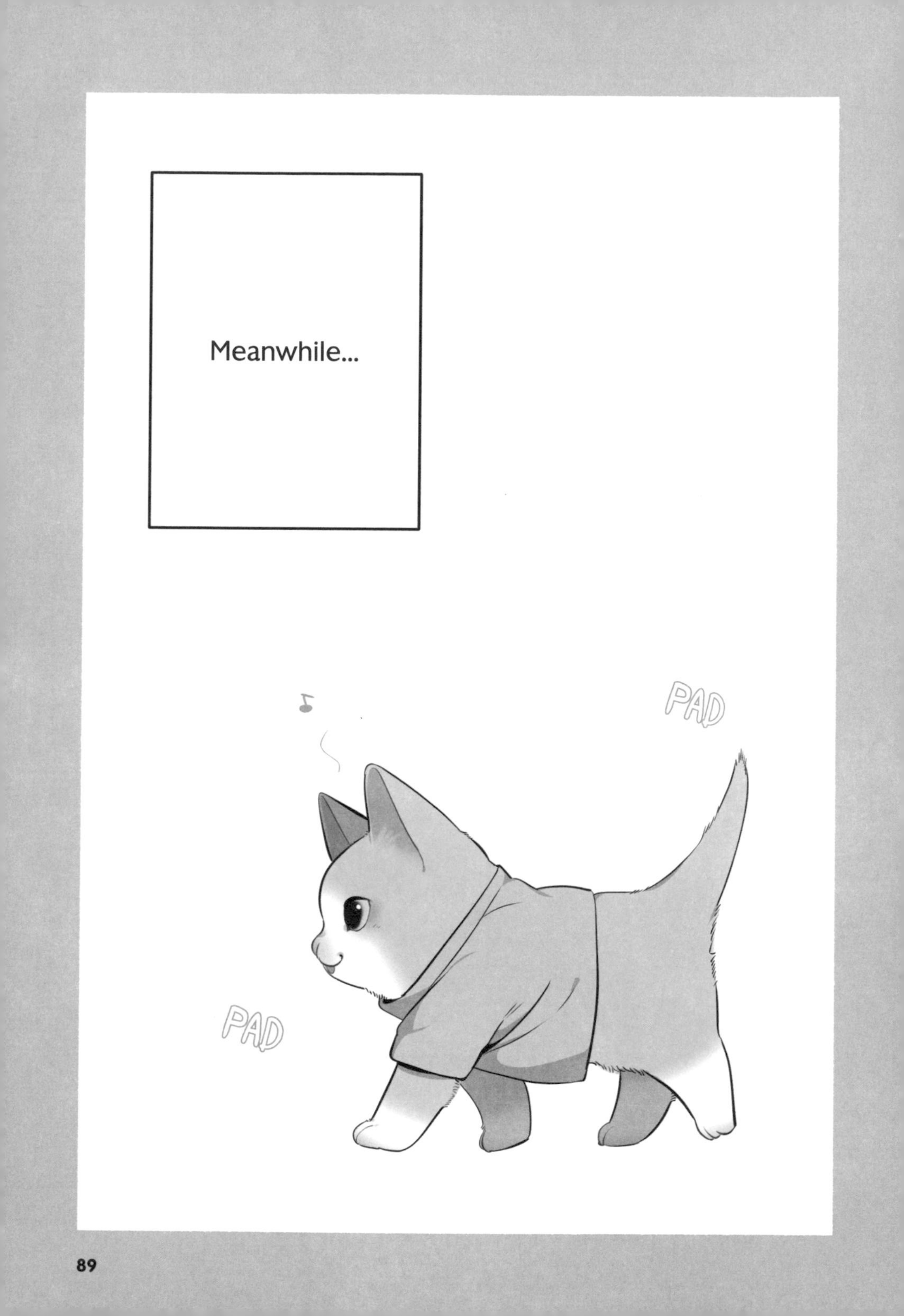
Meanwhile...
PAD
PAD

Q13. The Warmth in My Heart

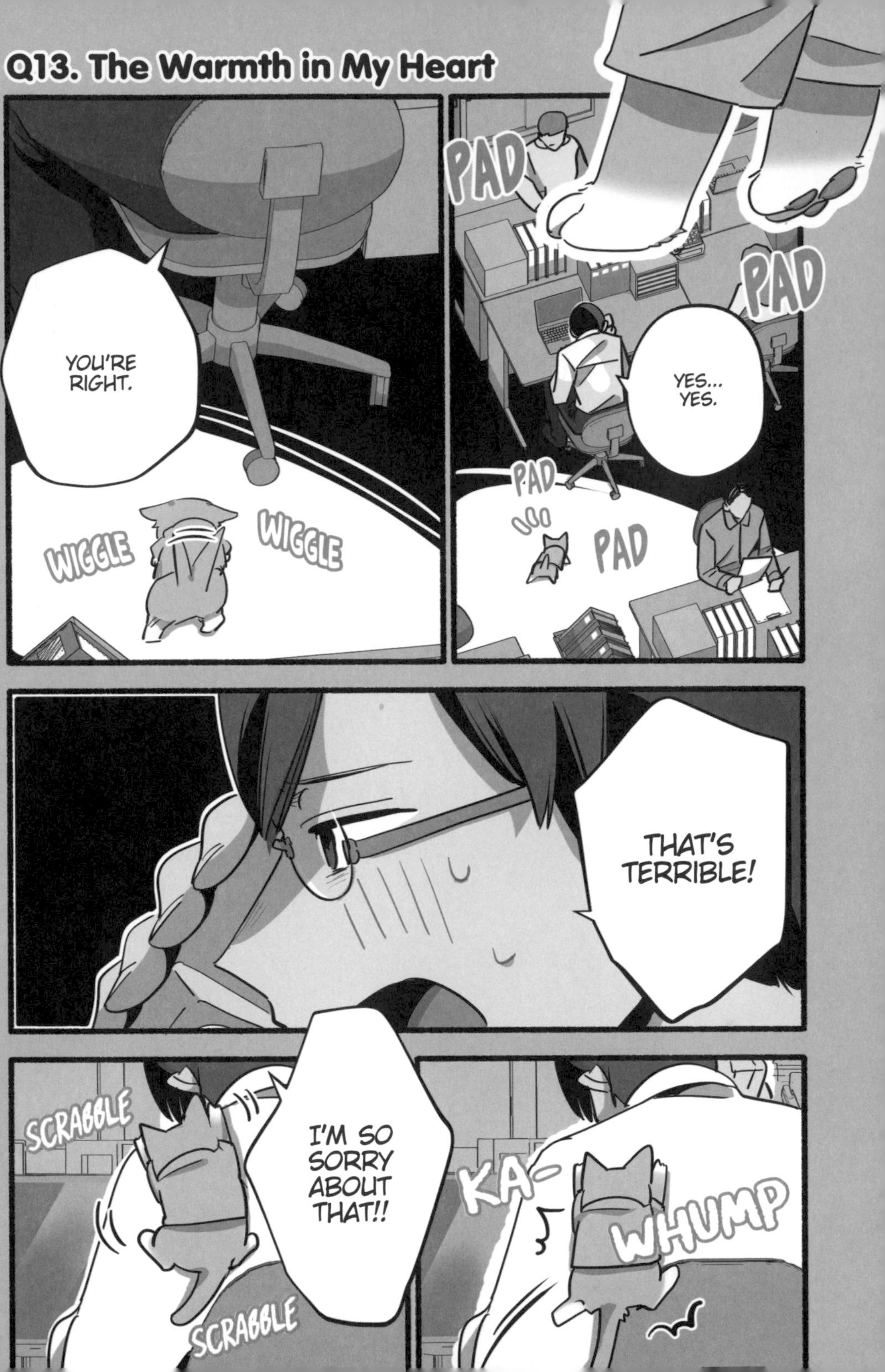
PAD
PAD
YES... YES.
PAD
PAD
YOU'RE RIGHT.
WIGGLE
WIGGLE
THAT'S TERRIBLE!
KA-
WHUMP
SCRABBLE
I'M SO SORRY ABOUT THAT!!
SCRABBLE

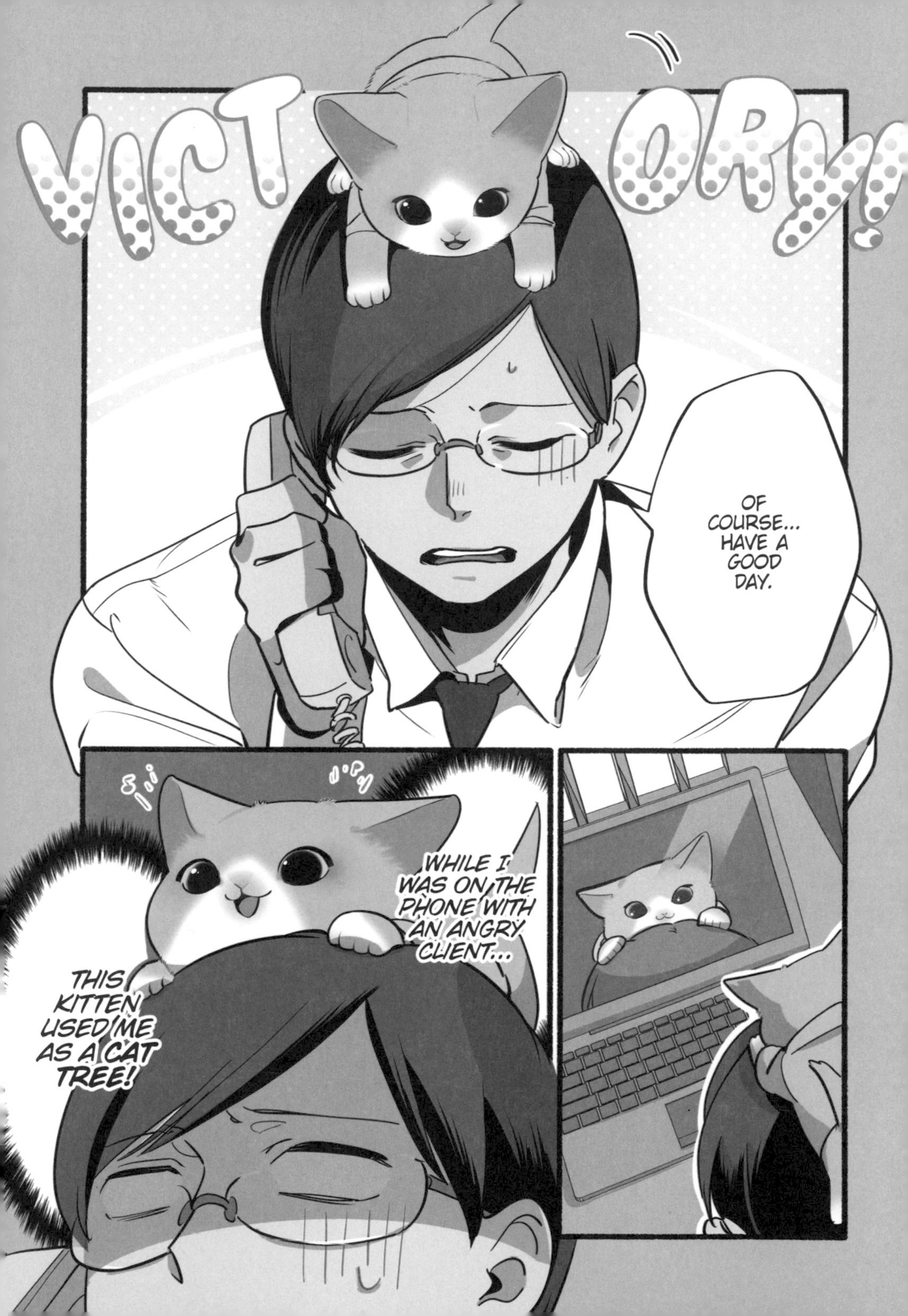
VICTORY!
OF COURSE... HAVE A GOOD DAY.
WHILE I WAS ON THE PHONE WITH AN ANGRY CLIENT...
THIS KITTEN USED ME AS A CAT TREE!

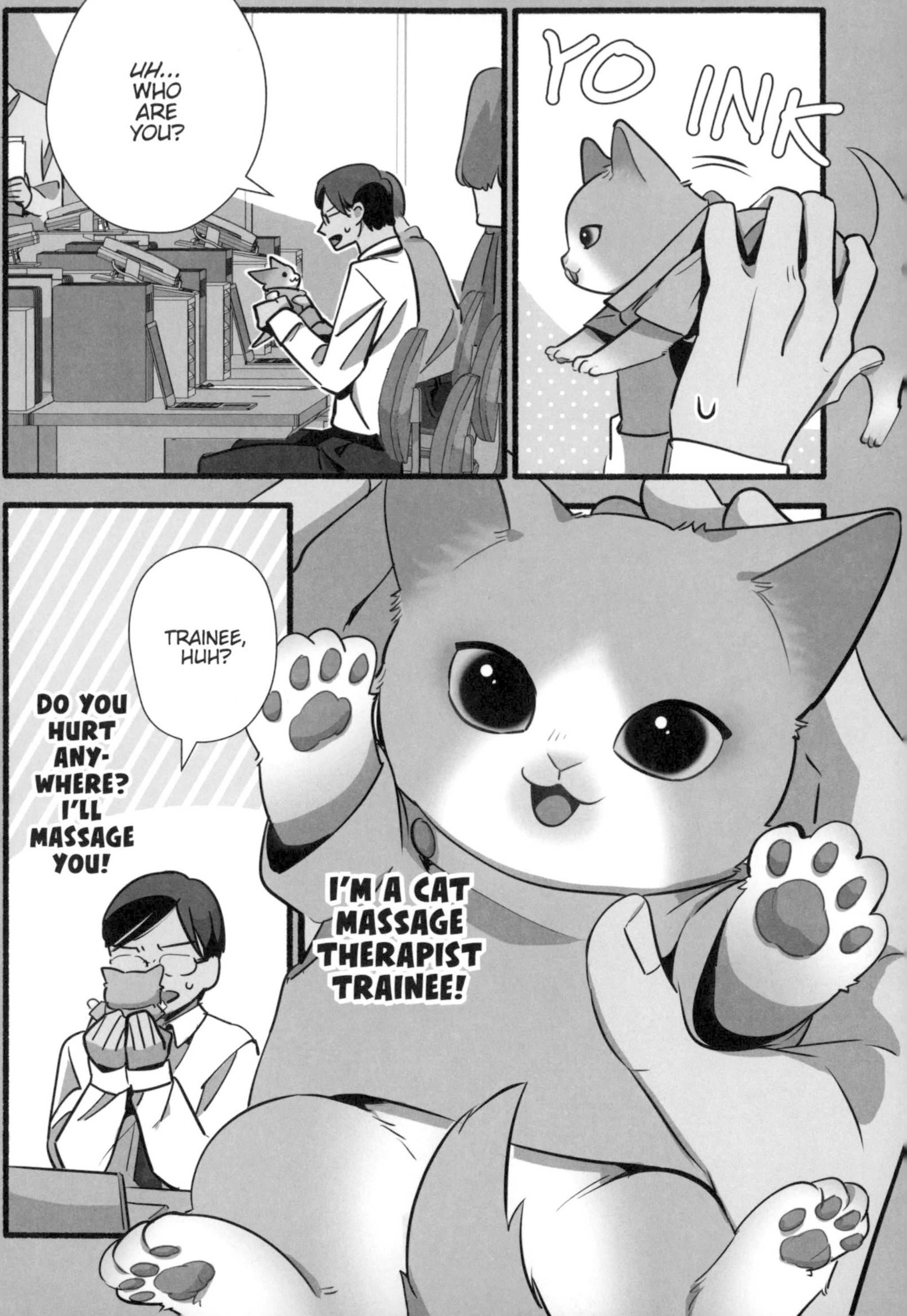
YO INK
UH... WHO ARE YOU?
I'M A CAT MASSAGE THERAPIST TRAINEE!
TRAINEE, HUH?
DO YOU HURT ANY-WHERE? I'LL MASSAGE YOU!

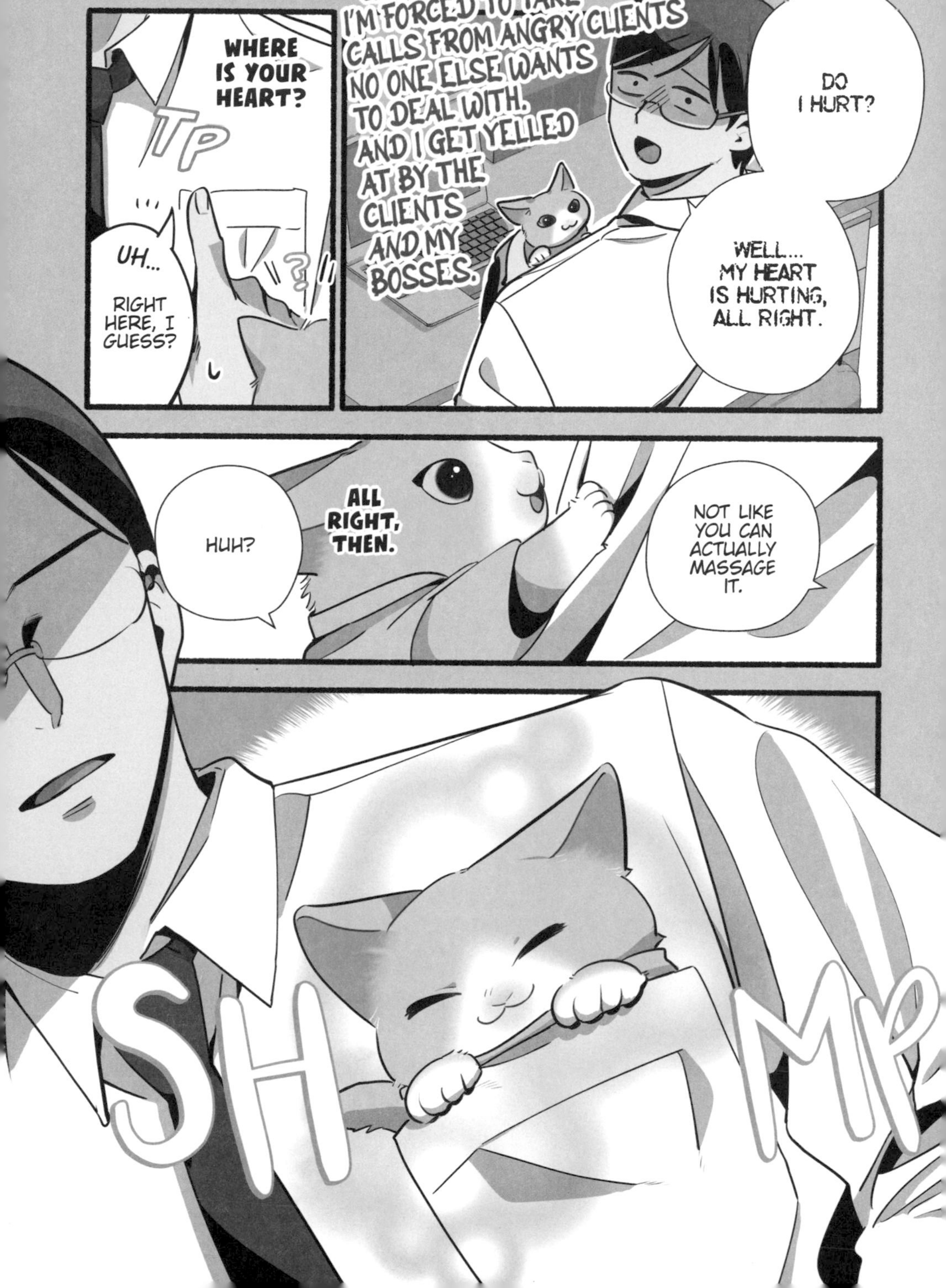
DO I HURT?
WELL... MY HEART IS HURTING, ALL RIGHT.
EVERY DAY, I'M FORCED TO TAKE CALLS FROM ANGRY CLIENTS NO ONE ELSE WANTS TO DEAL WITH. AND I GET YELLED AT BY THE CLIENTS AND MY BOSSES.
WHERE IS YOUR HEART?
TP
UH...
RIGHT HERE, I GUESS?
NOT LIKE YOU CAN ACTUALLY MASSAGE IT.
ALL RIGHT, THEN.
HUH?
SH MP

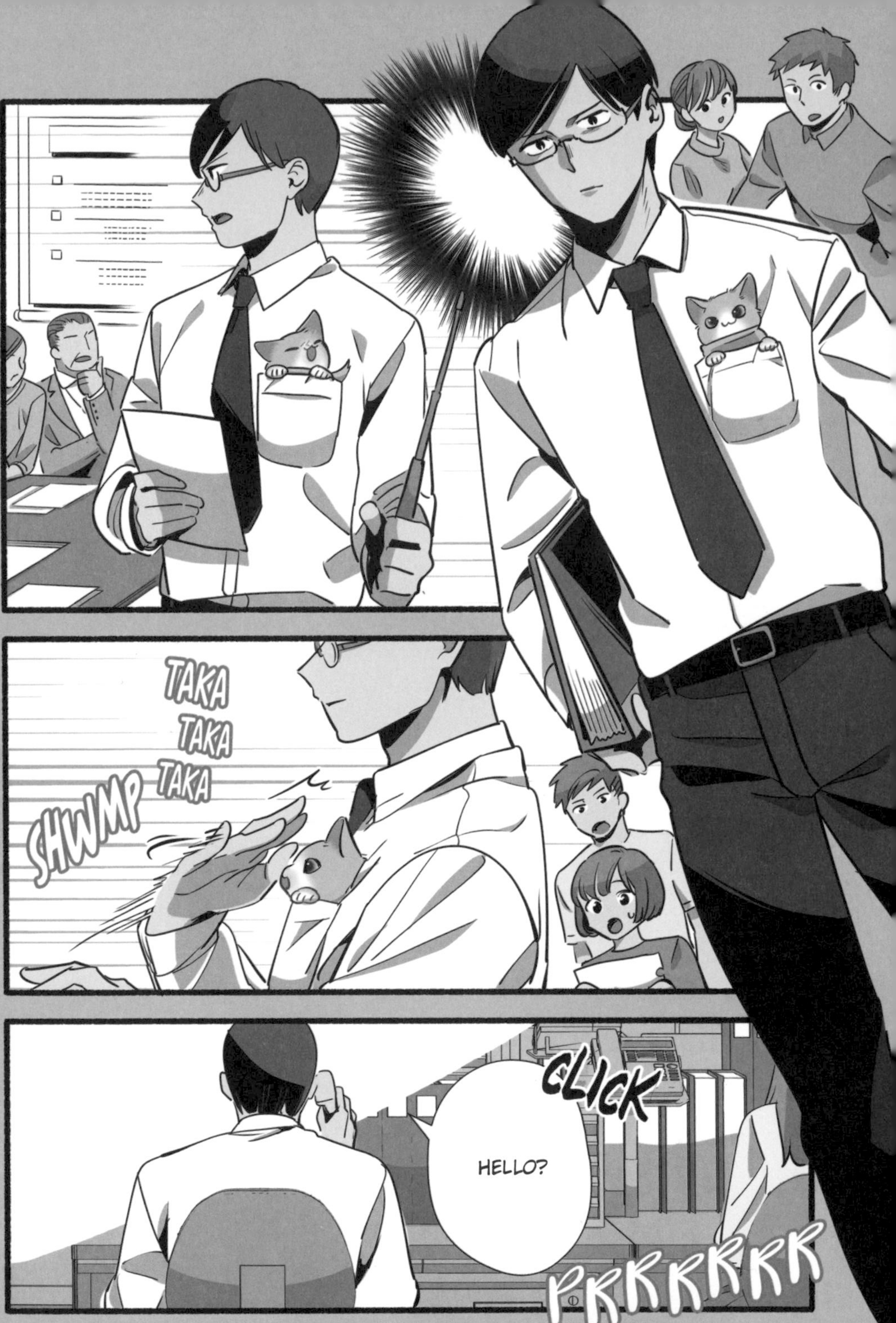
TAKA
TAKA
TAKA
SHWMP
CLICK
HELLO?
PRKRKRKR

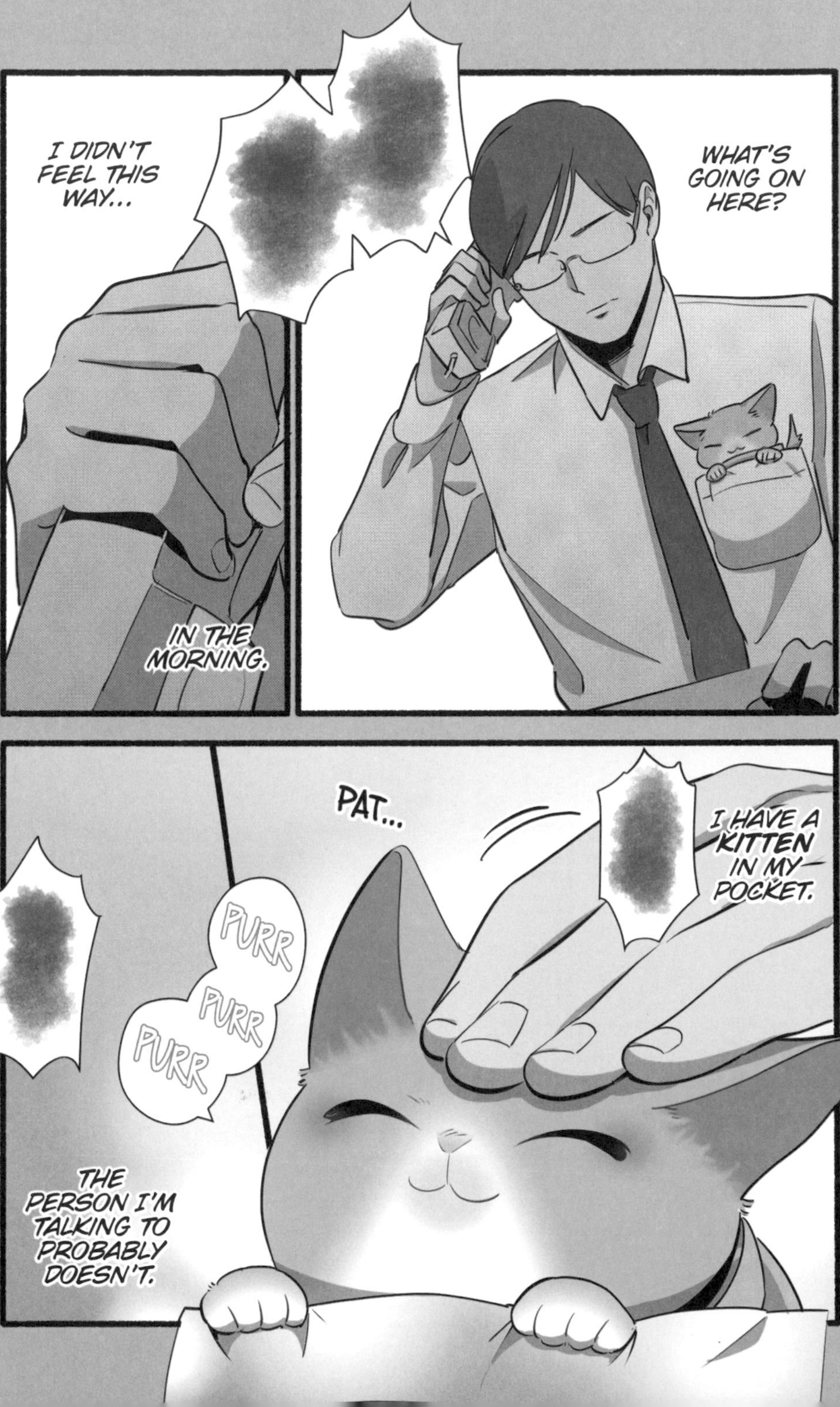
WHAT'S GOING ON HERE?
I DIDN'T FEEL THIS WAY...
IN THE MORNING.
I HAVE A KITTEN IN MY POCKET.
PAT...
PURR
PURR
PURR
THE PERSON I'M TALKING TO PROBABLY DOESN'T.

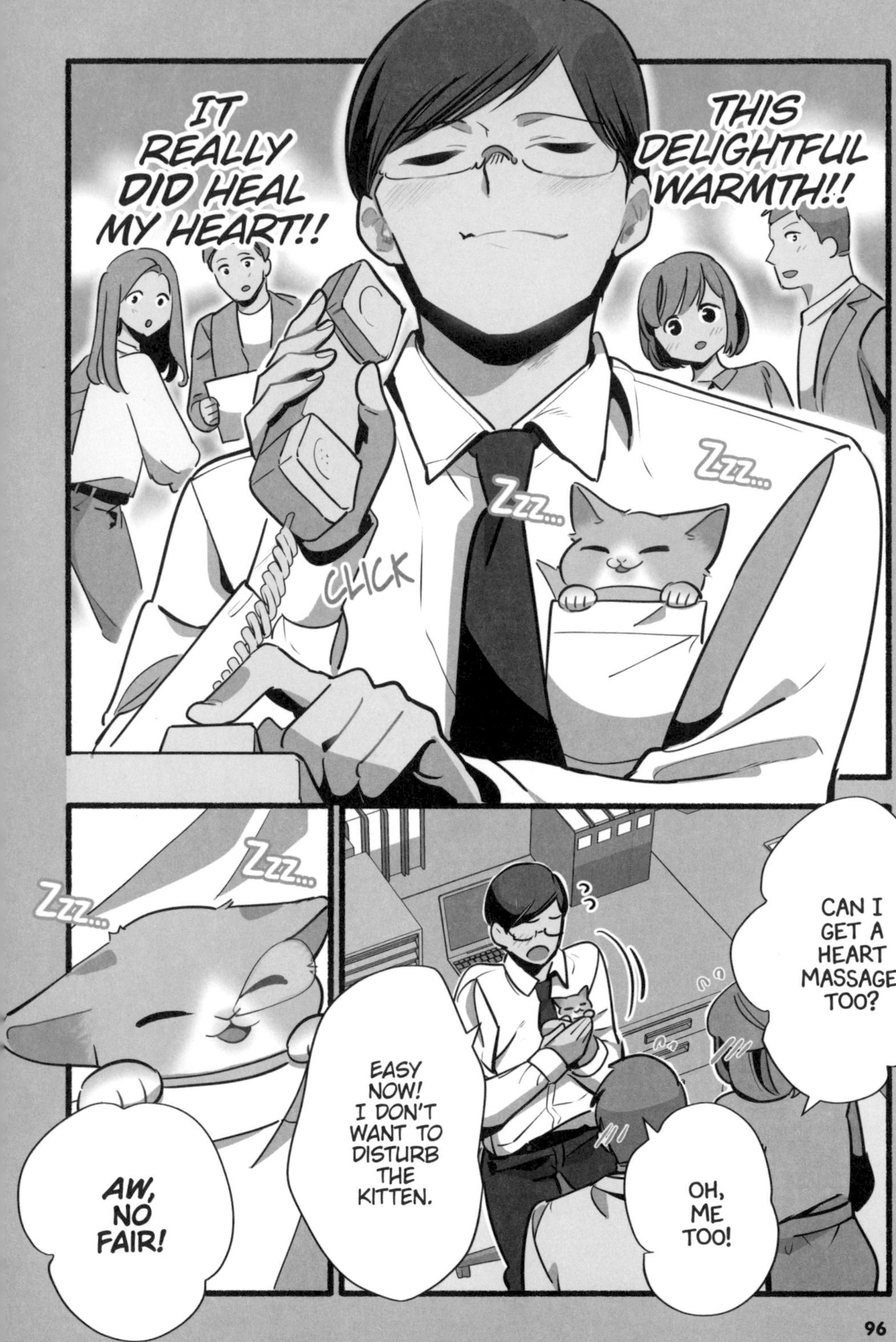
THIS DELIGHTFUL WARMTH!!
IT REALLY DID HEAL MY HEART!!
Zzz...
Zzz...
CLICK
CAN I GET A HEART MASSAGE, TOO?
OH, ME TOO!
EASY NOW! I DON'T WANT TO DISTURB THE KITTEN.
Zzz...
Zzz...
AW, NO FAIR!

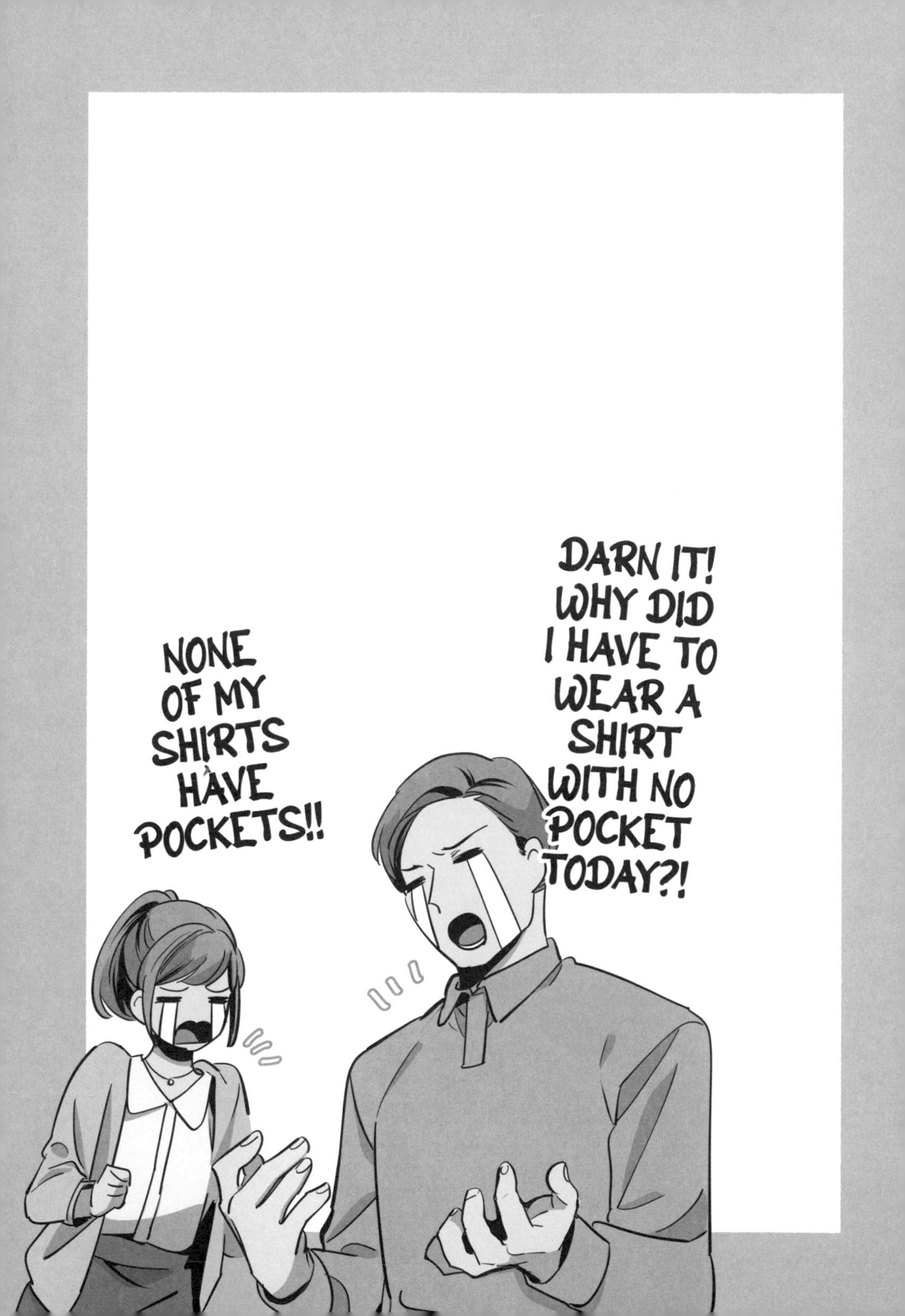
DARN IT! WHY DID I HAVE TO WEAR A SHIRT WITH NO POCKET TODAY?!
NONE OF MY SHIRTS HAVE POCKETS!!

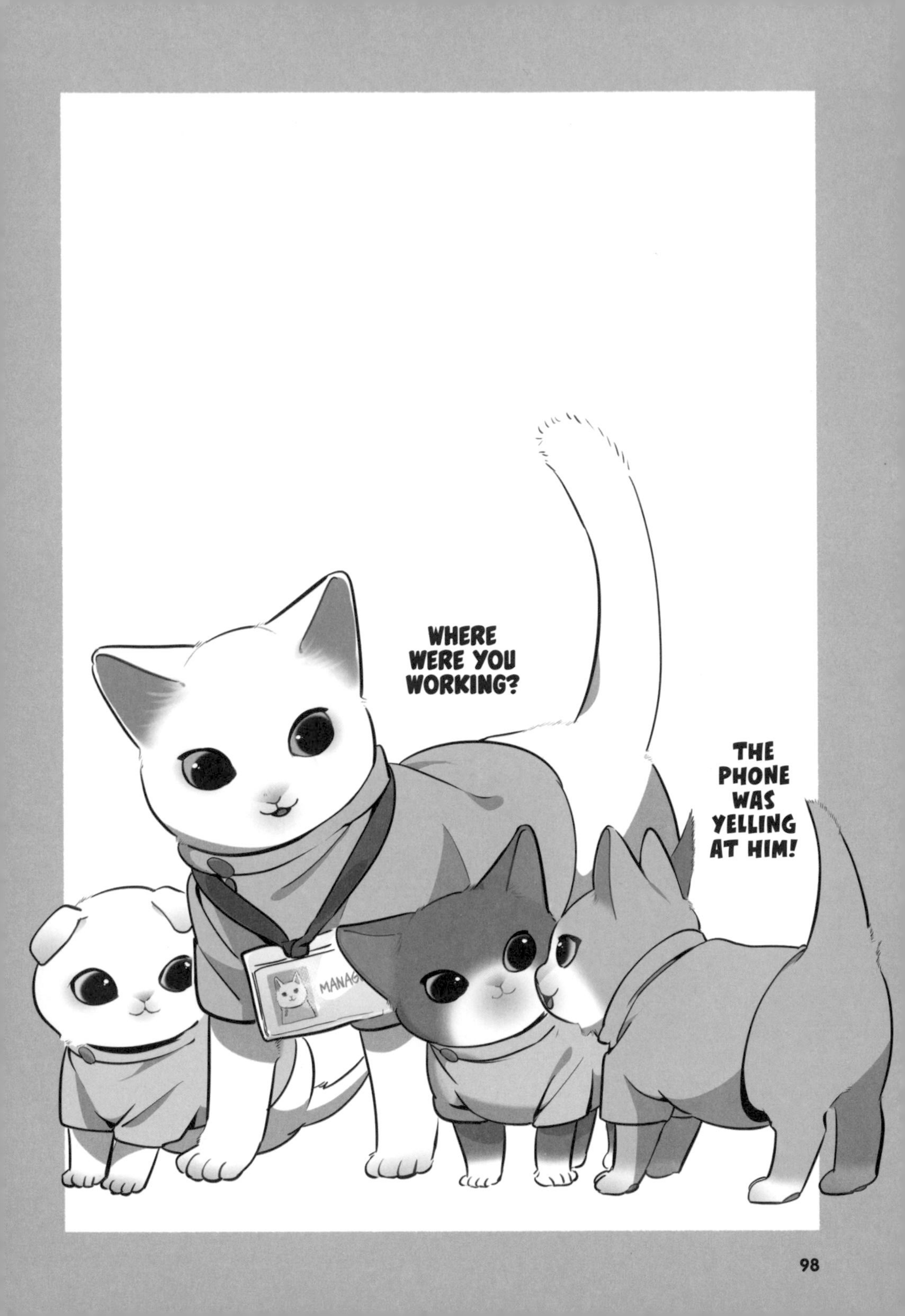
WHERE WERE YOU WORKING?
THE PHONE WAS YELLING AT HIM!

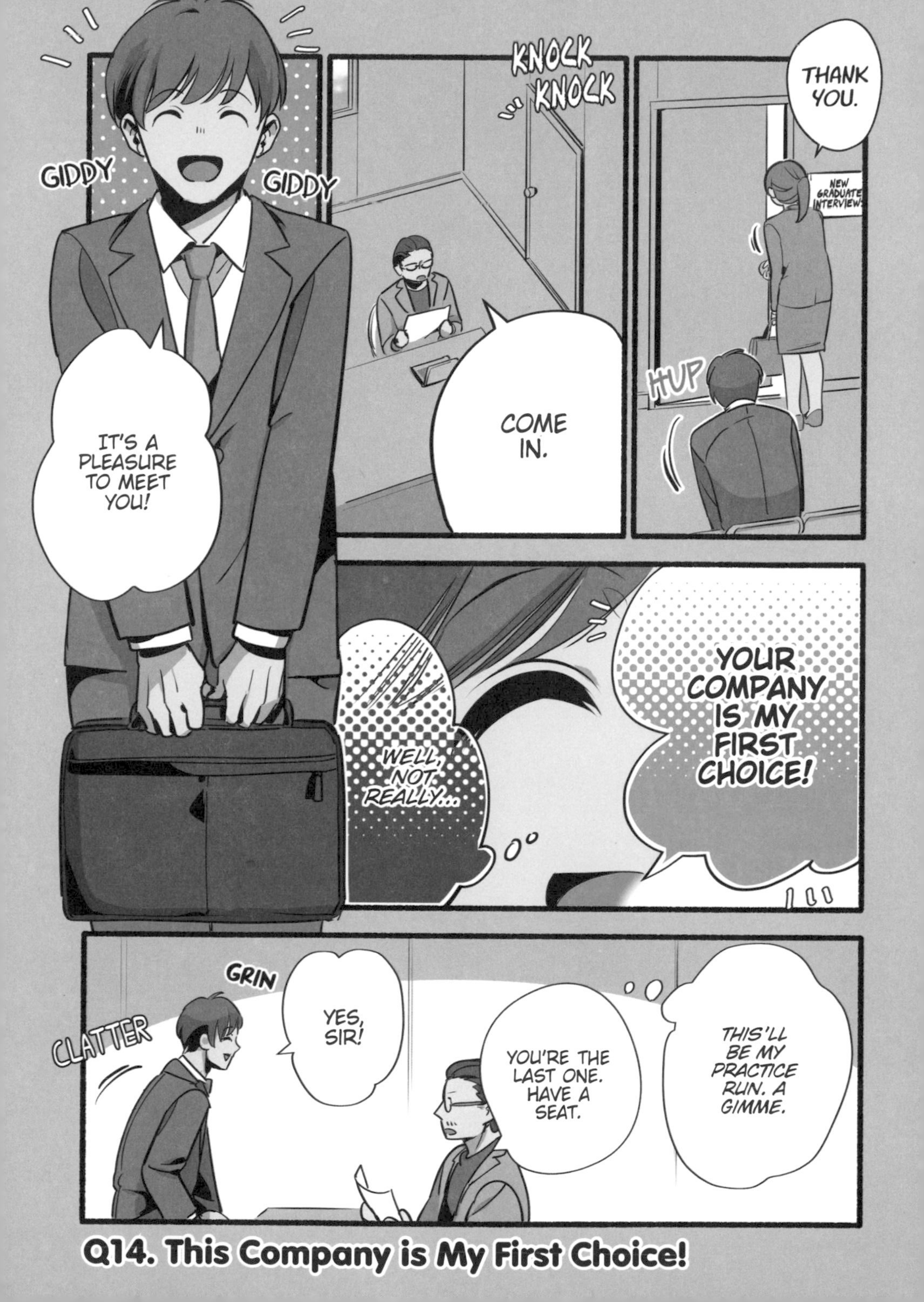
THANK YOU.
NEW GRADUATE INTERVIEWS
HUP
KNOCK KNOCK
COME IN.
YOUR COMPANY IS MY FIRST CHOICE!
WELL, NOT REALLY...
GIDDY
GIDDY
IT'S A PLEASURE TO MEET YOU!
THIS'LL BE MY PRACTICE RUN. A GIMME.
YOU'RE THE LAST ONE. HAVE A SEAT.
YES, SIR!
GRIN
CLATTER

Q14. This Company is My First Choice!

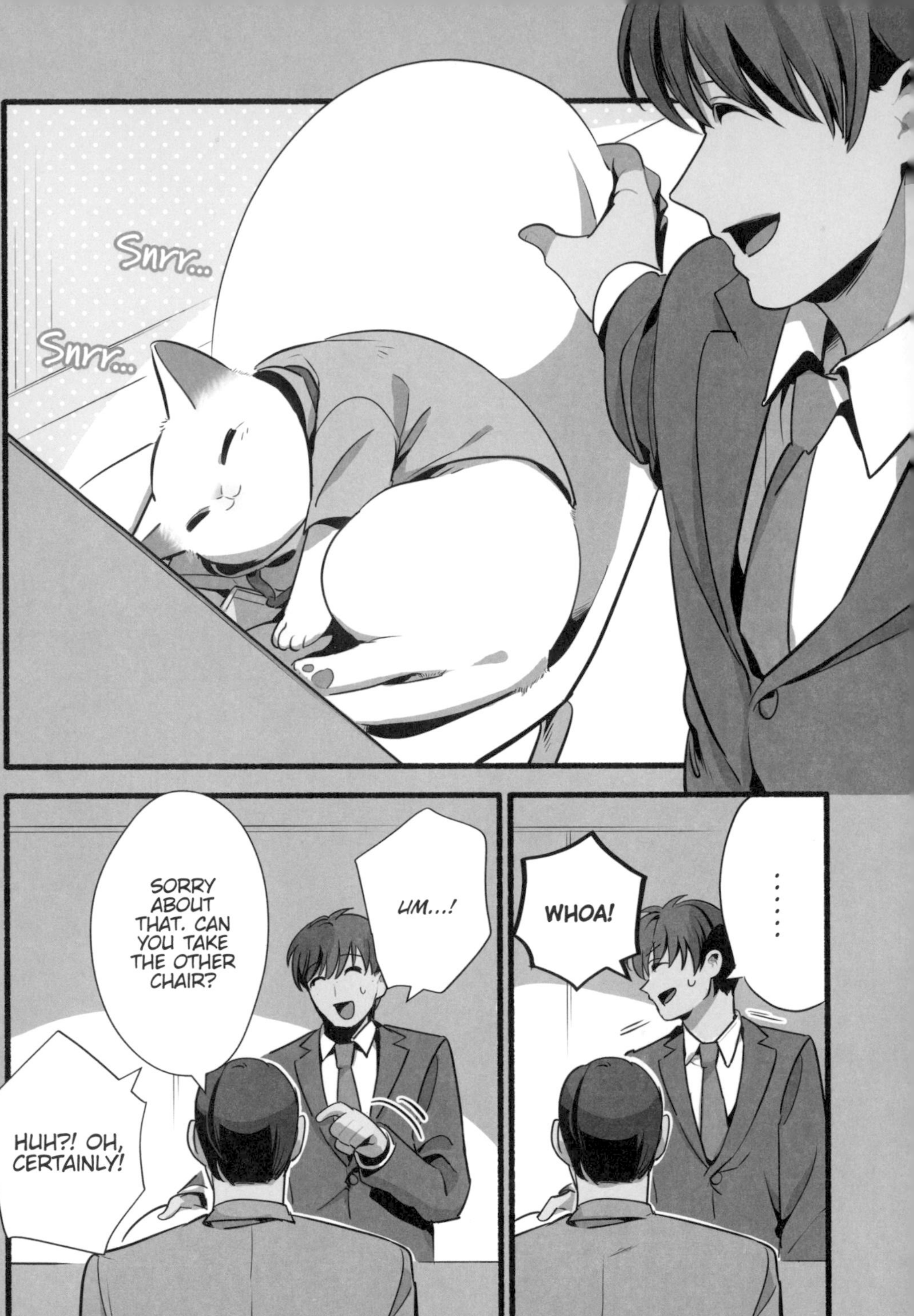
Snrr...
Snrr...
......
WHOA!
UM...!
SORRY ABOUT THAT. CAN YOU TAKE THE OTHER CHAIR?
HUH?! OH, CERTAINLY!

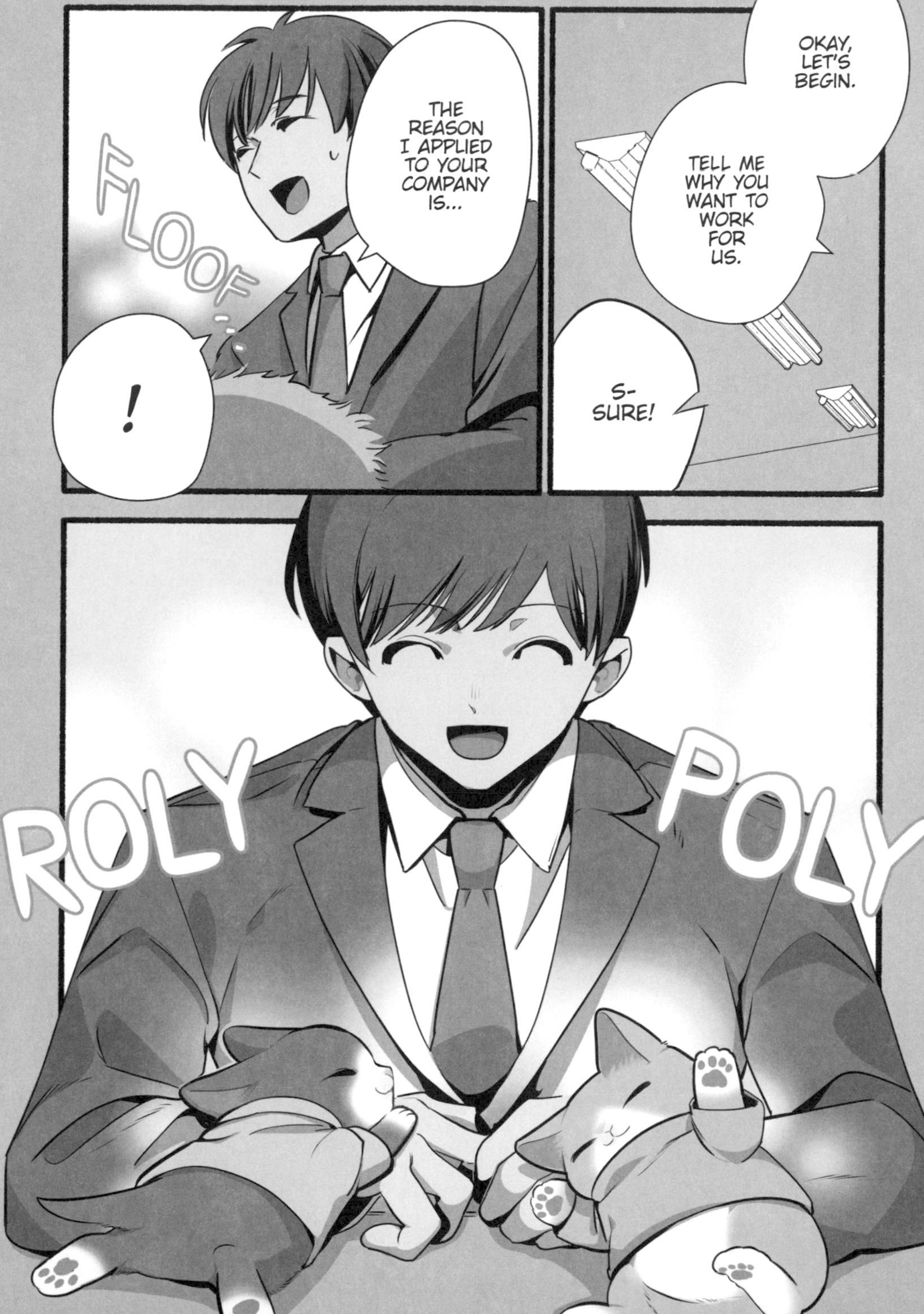
OKAY, LET'S BEGIN.
TELL ME WHY YOU WANT TO WORK FOR US.
S-SURE!
THE REASON I APPLIED TO YOUR COMPANY IS...
FLOOF
!
ROLY POLY

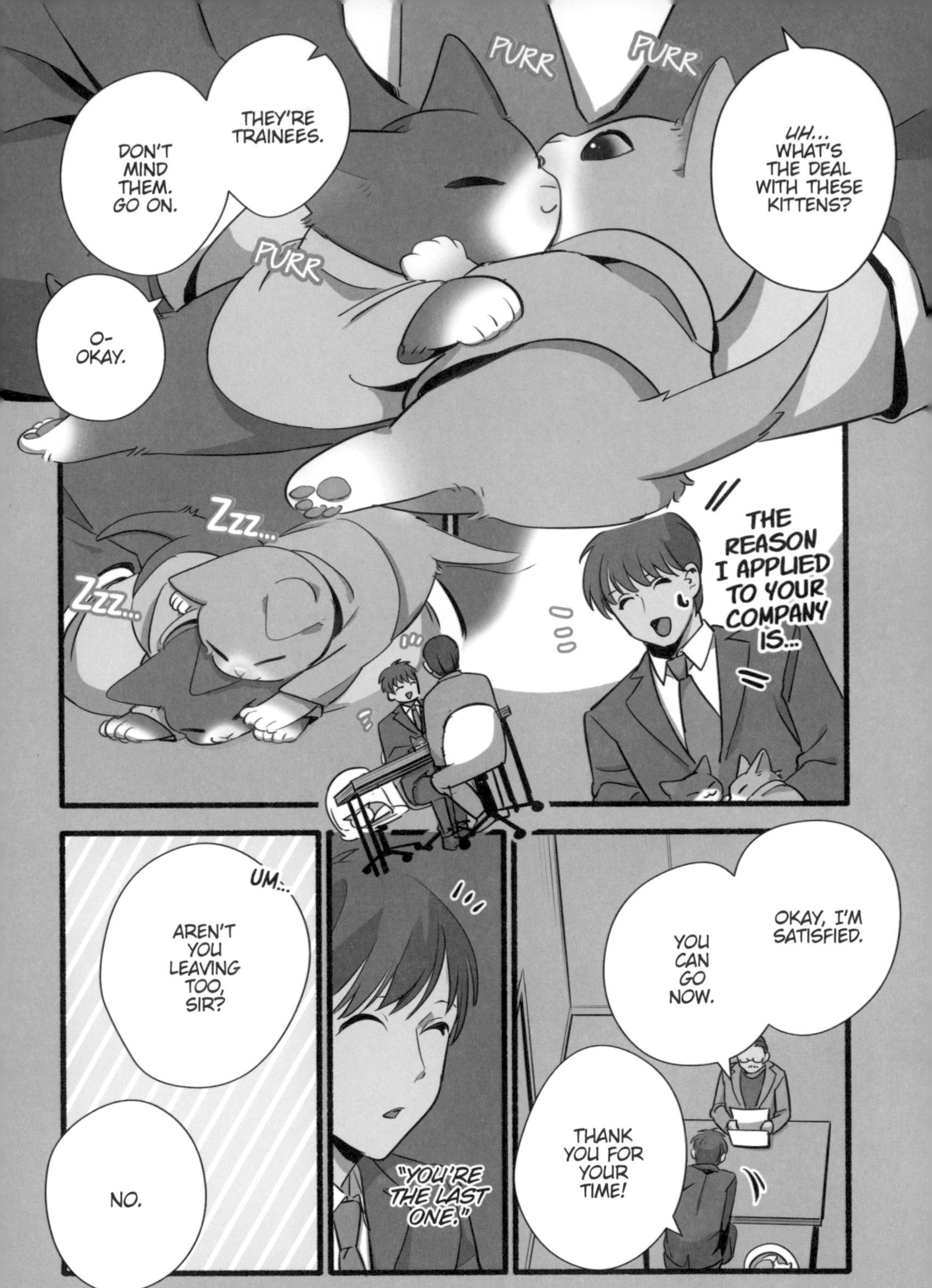
PURR PURR
UH... WHAT'S THE DEAL WITH THESE KITTENS?
THEY'RE TRAINEES.
DON'T MIND THEM. GO ON.
PURR
O- OKAY.
THE REASON I APPLIED TO YOUR COMPANY IS...
Zzz...
Zzz...
OKAY, I'M SATISFIED.
YOU CAN GO NOW.
THANK YOU FOR YOUR TIME!
"YOU'RE THE LAST ONE."
UM...
AREN'T YOU LEAVING TOO, SIR?
NO.

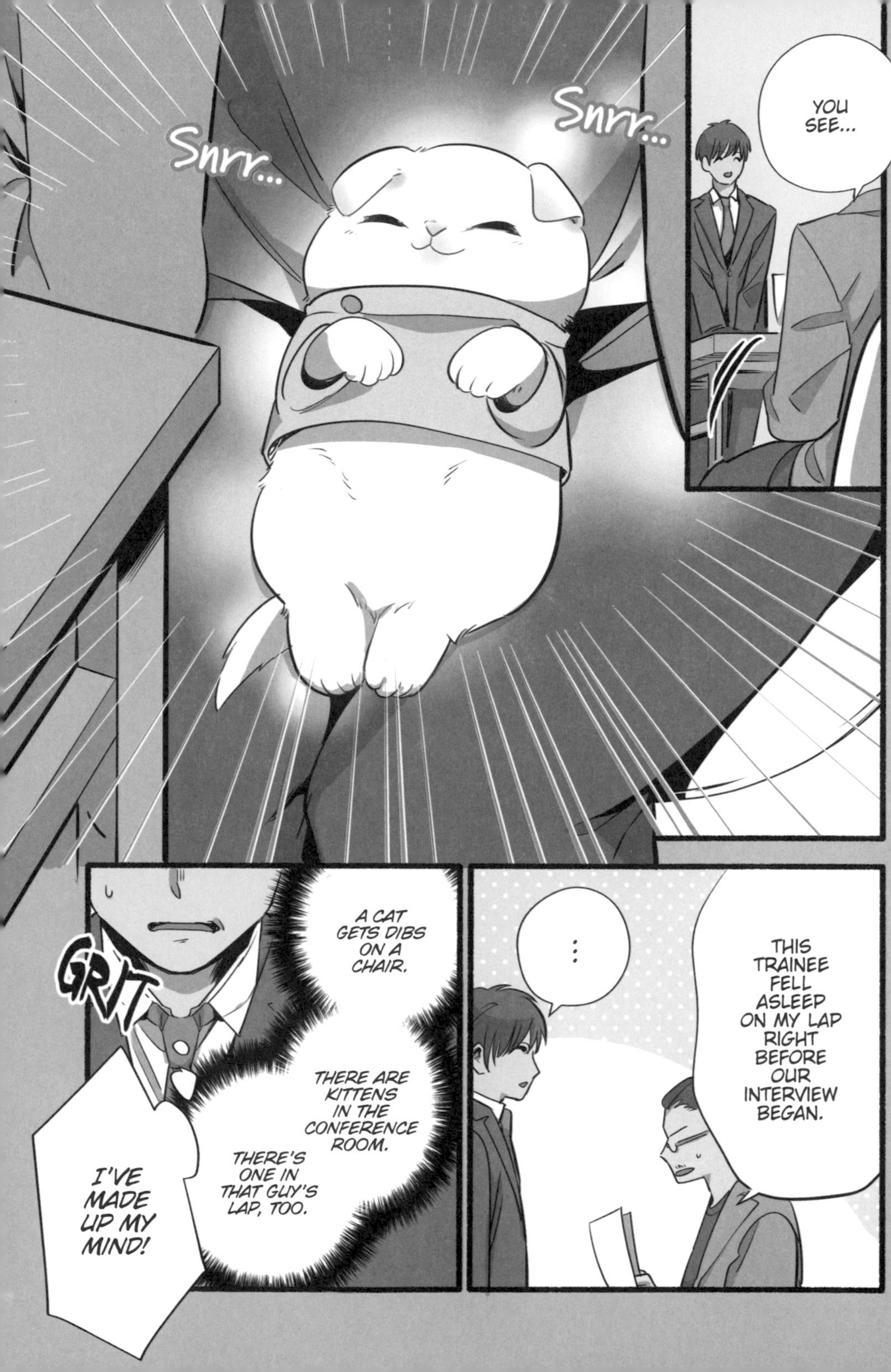
YOU SEE...
Snrr...
Snrr...
THIS TRAINEE FELL ASLEEP ON MY LAP RIGHT BEFORE OUR INTERVIEW BEGAN.
...
A CAT GETS DIBS ON A CHAIR.
THERE ARE KITTENS IN THE CONFERENCE ROOM.
GRIT
THERE'S ONE IN THAT GUY'S LAP, TOO.
I'VE MADE UP MY MIND!

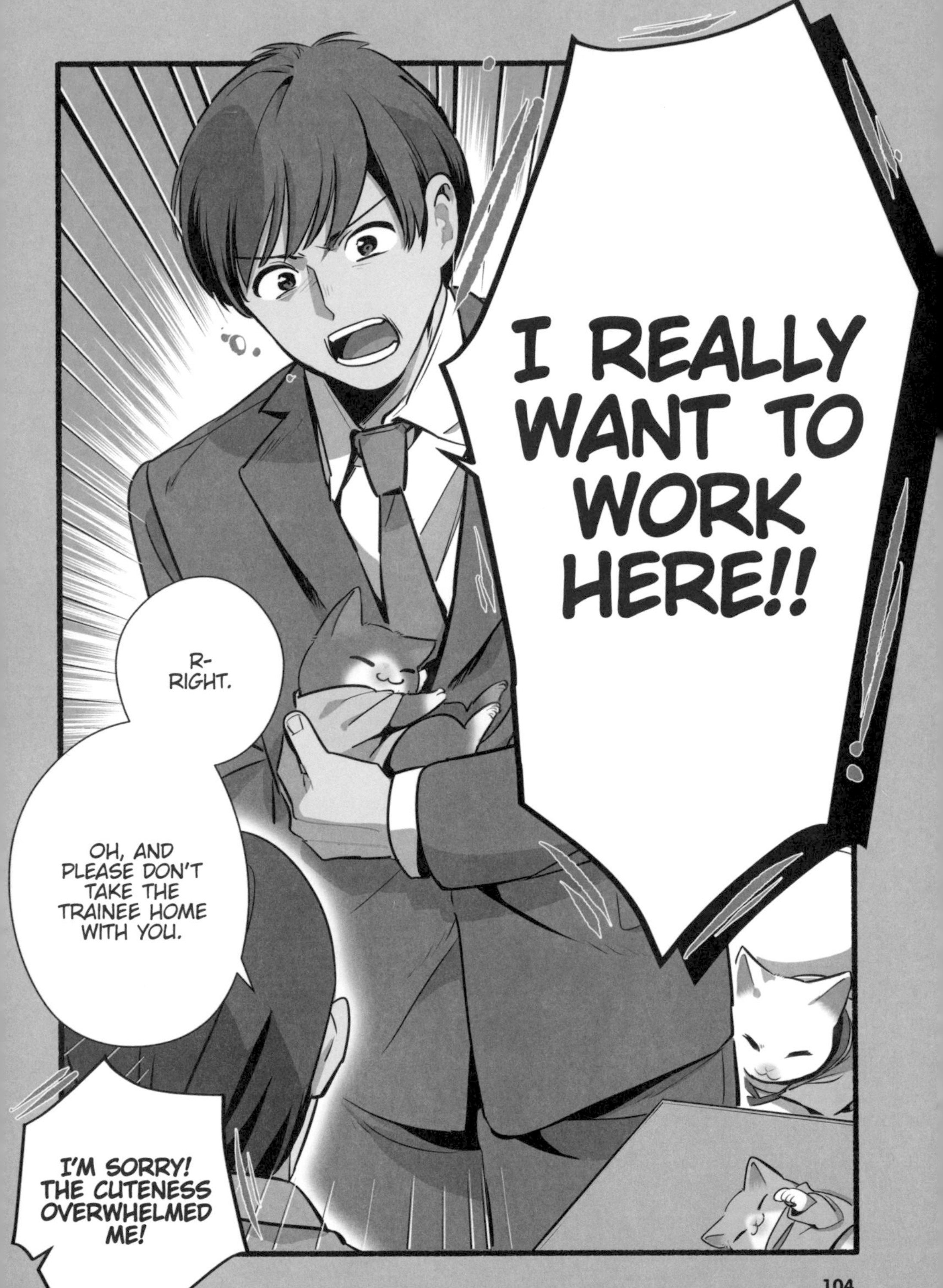
I REALLY WANT TO WORK HERE!!
R- RIGHT.
OH, AND PLEASE DON'T TAKE THE TRAINEE HOME WITH YOU.
I'M SORRY! THE CUTENESS OVERWHELMED ME!

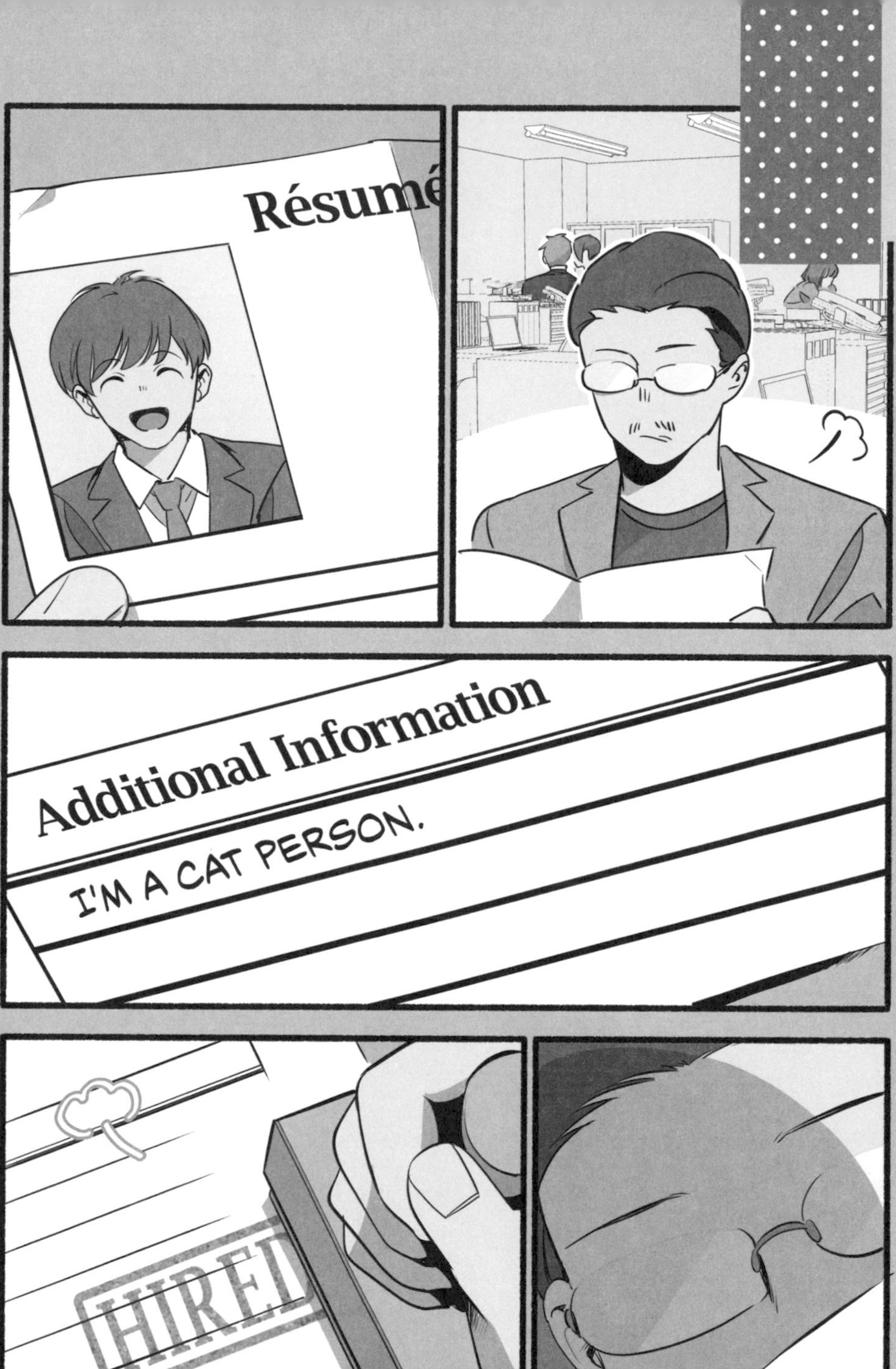
Résumé
Additional Information
I'M A CAT PERSON.
HIRED

Q15. I Look Forward to Your Next Visit

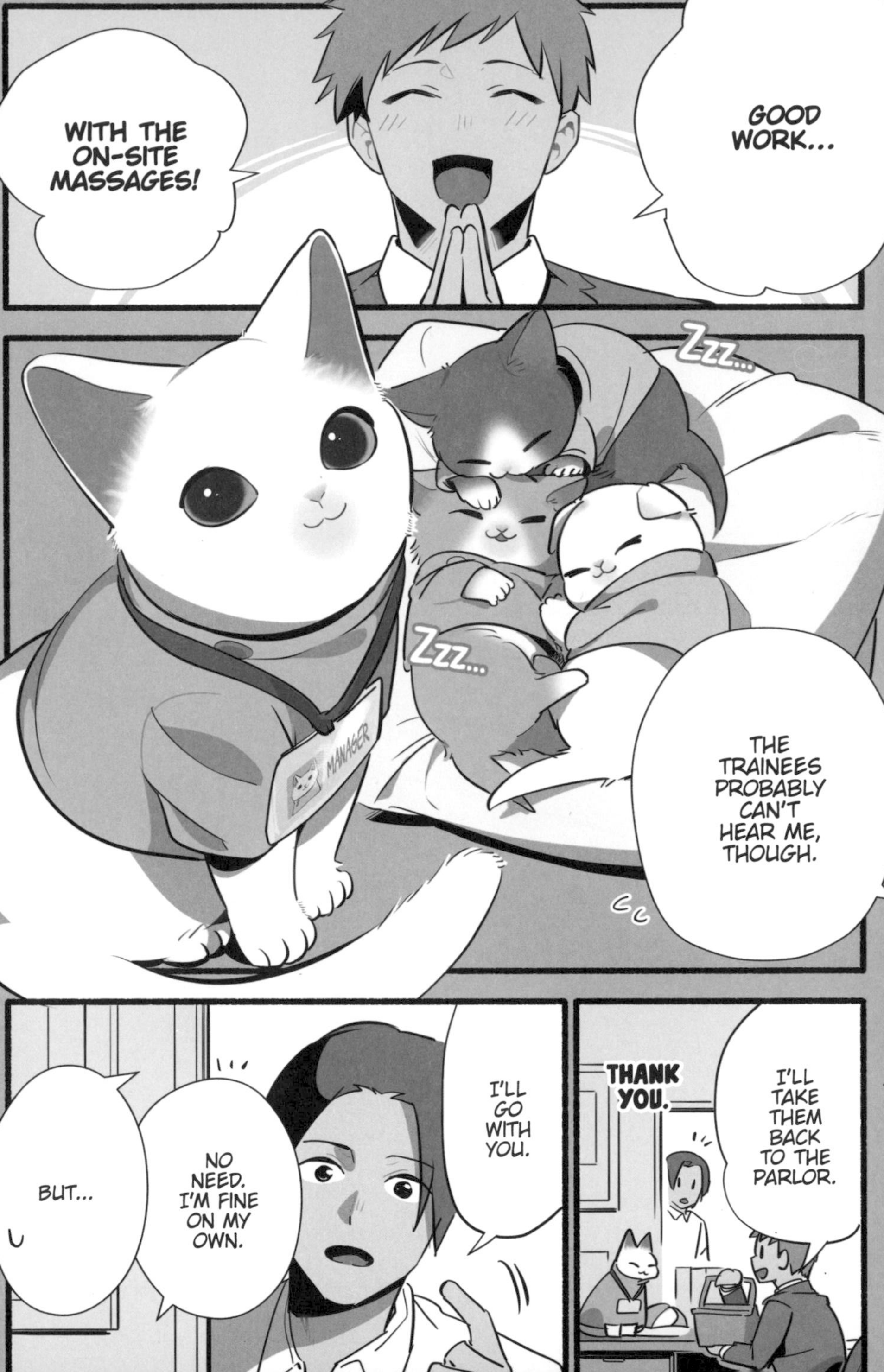

GOOD WORK...
WITH THE ON-SITE MASSAGES!
Zzz...
Zzz...
THE TRAINEES PROBABLY CAN'T HEAR ME, THOUGH.
I'LL TAKE THEM BACK TO THE PARLOR.
THANK YOU.
I'LL GO WITH YOU.
NO NEED. I'M FINE ON MY OWN.
BUT...

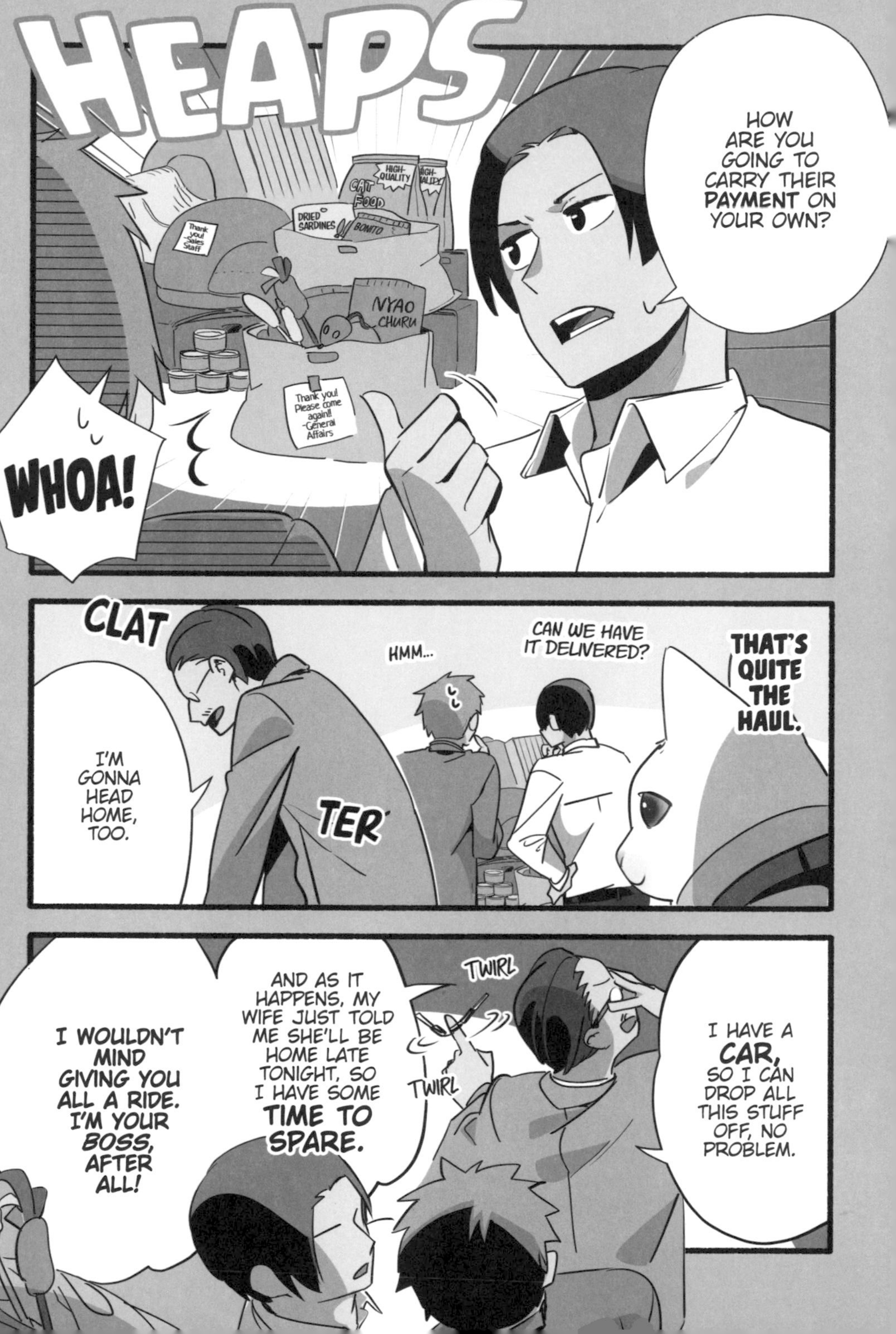
HEAPS
HOW ARE YOU GOING TO CARRY THEIR PAYMENT ON YOUR OWN?
HIGH-QUALITY
HIGH-QUALITY
CAT FOOD
DRIED SARDINES
BONITO
Thank you! -Sales Staff
NYAO CHURU
Thank you! Please come again!! -General Affairs
WHOA!
THAT'S QUITE THE HAUL.
CAN WE HAVE IT DELIVERED?
HMM...
CLAT
TER
I'M GONNA HEAD HOME, TOO.
I HAVE A CAR, SO I CAN DROP ALL THIS STUFF OFF, NO PROBLEM.
TWIRL
TWIRL
AND AS IT HAPPENS, MY WIFE JUST TOLD ME SHE'LL BE HOME LATE TONIGHT, SO I HAVE SOME TIME TO SPARE.
I WOULDN'T MIND GIVING YOU ALL A RIDE. I'M YOUR BOSS, AFTER ALL!

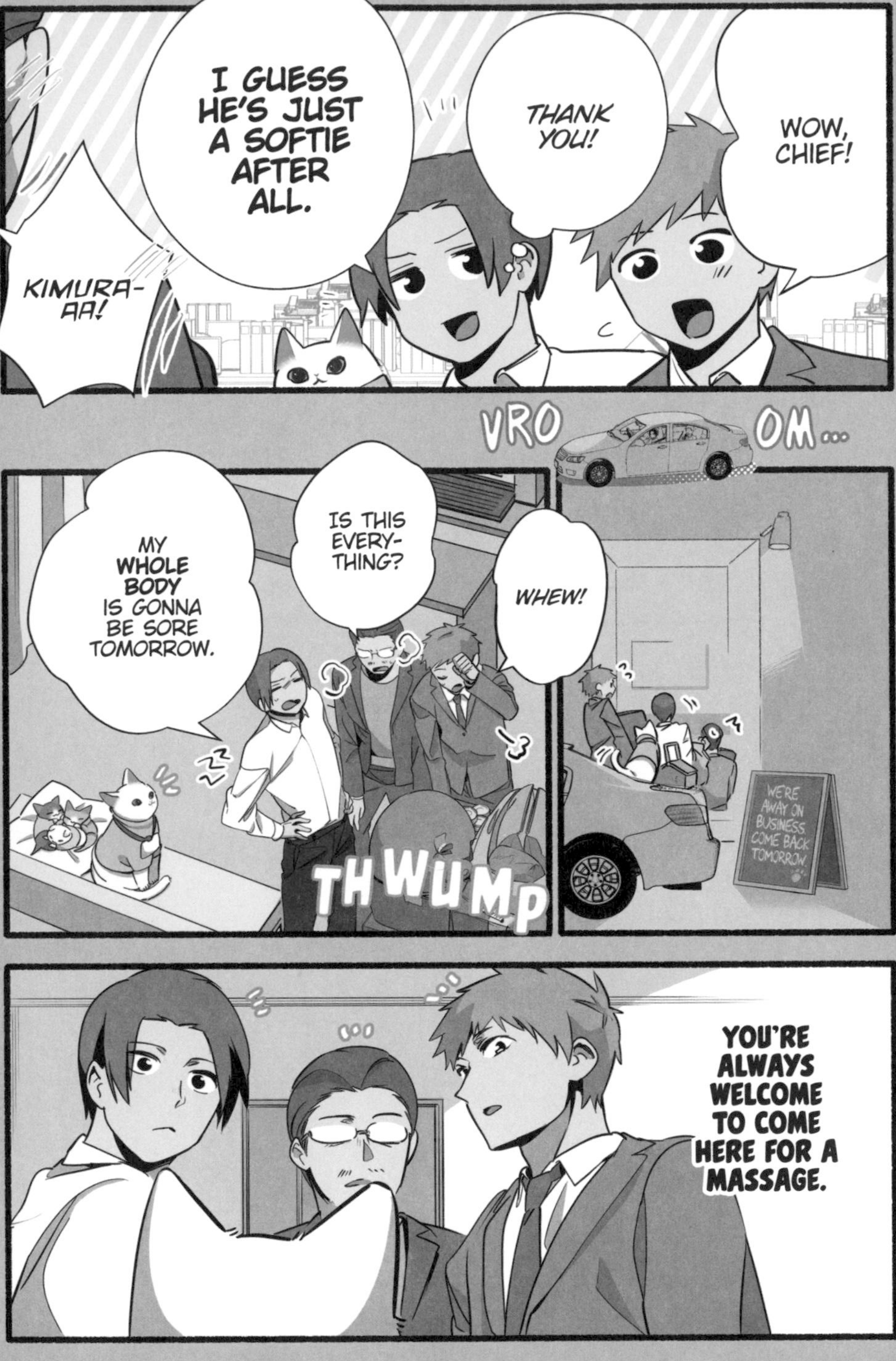
WOW, CHIEF!
THANK YOU!
I GUESS HE'S JUST A SOFTIE AFTER ALL.
KIMURA-AA!
VRO OM...
WE'RE AWAY ON BUSINESS COME BACK TOMORROW
WHEW!
IS THIS EVERYTHING?
MY WHOLE BODY IS GONNA BE SORE TOMORROW.
THWUMP
YOU'RE ALWAYS WELCOME TO COME HERE FOR A MASSAGE.

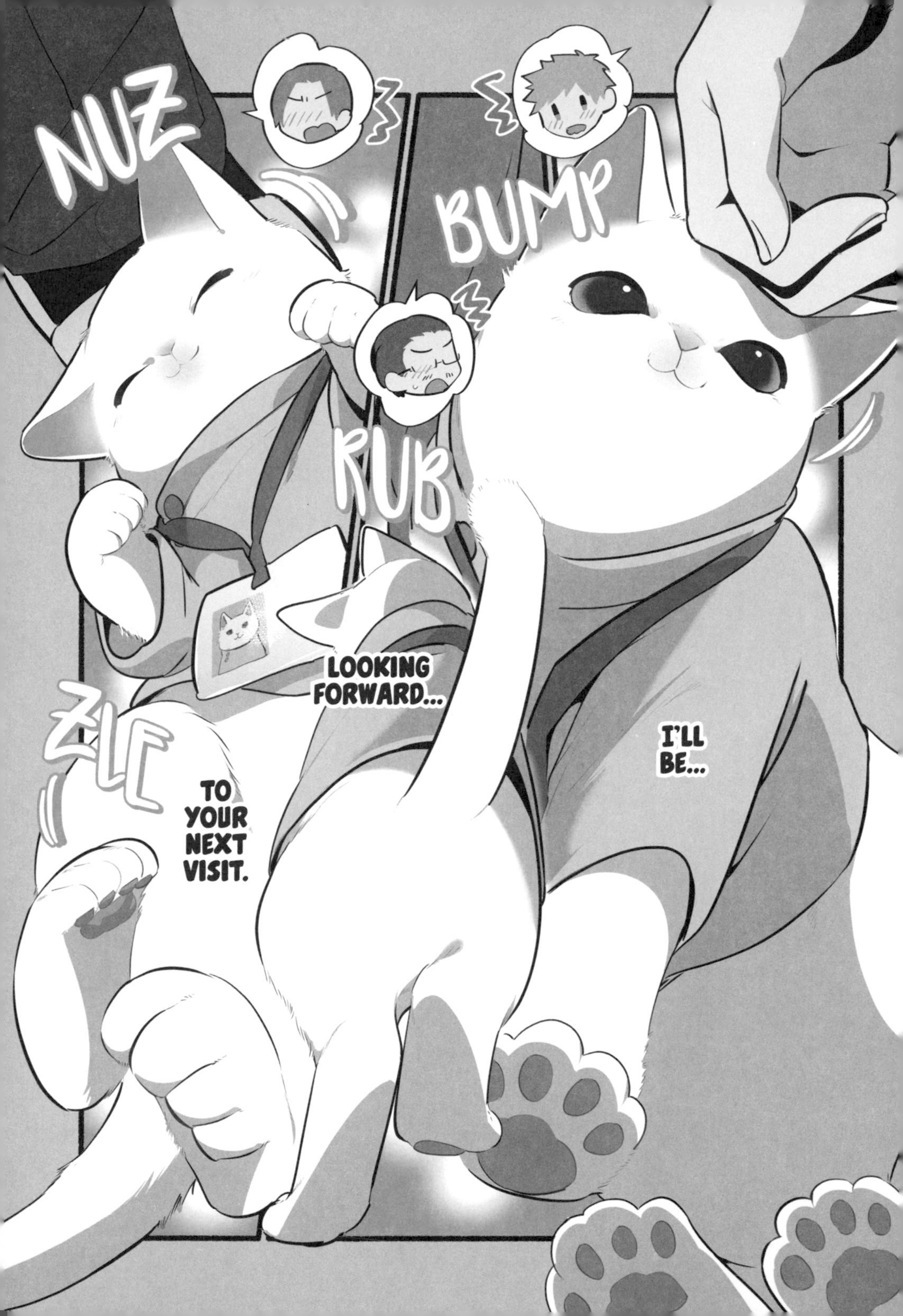
BUMP
NUZ
RUB
I'LL BE...
LOOKING FORWARD...
TO YOUR NEXT VISIT.
ZLE

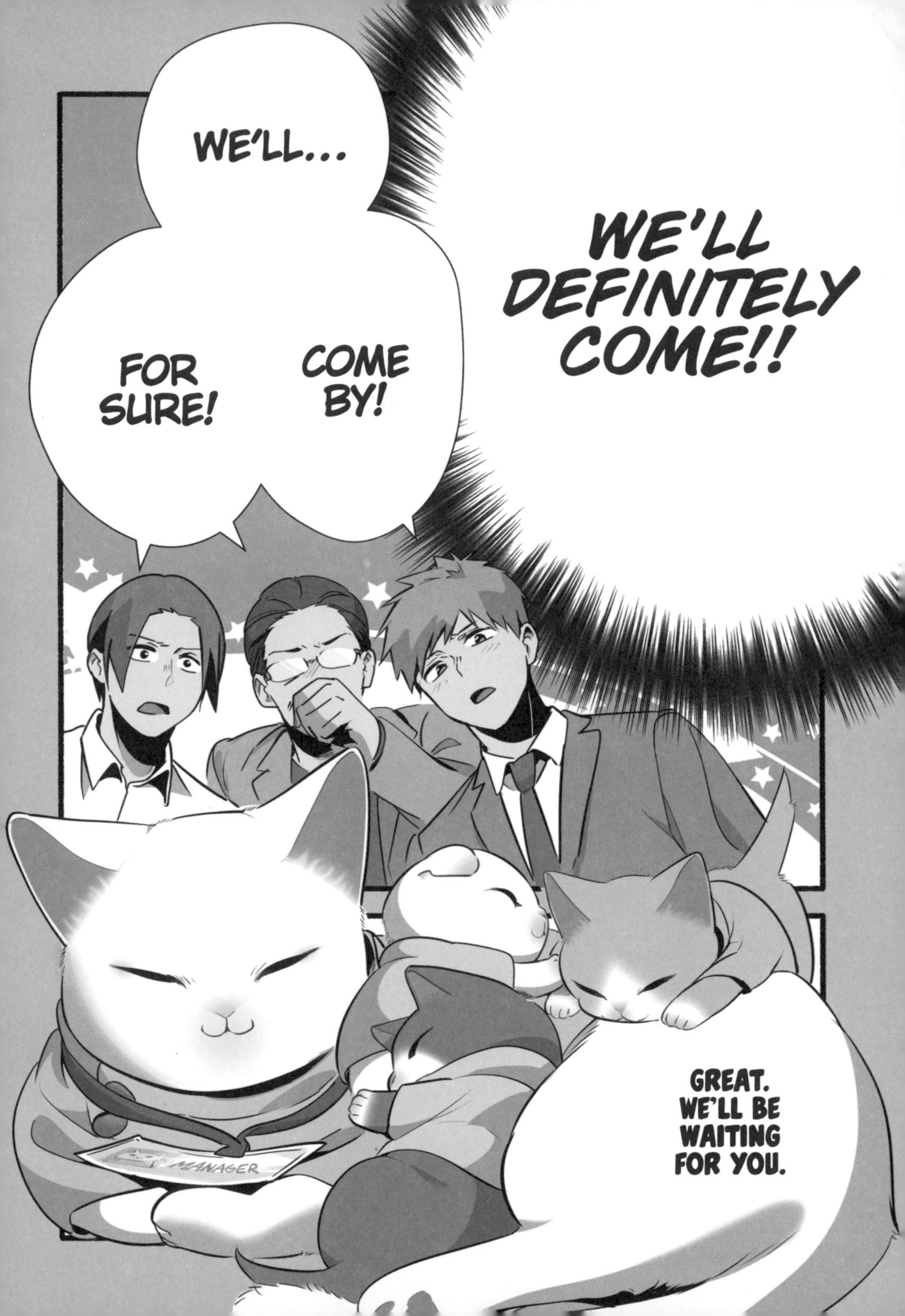
WE'LL...
COME BY!
FOR SURE!
WE'LL DEFINITELY COME!!
GREAT. WE'LL BE WAITING FOR YOU.
MANAGER

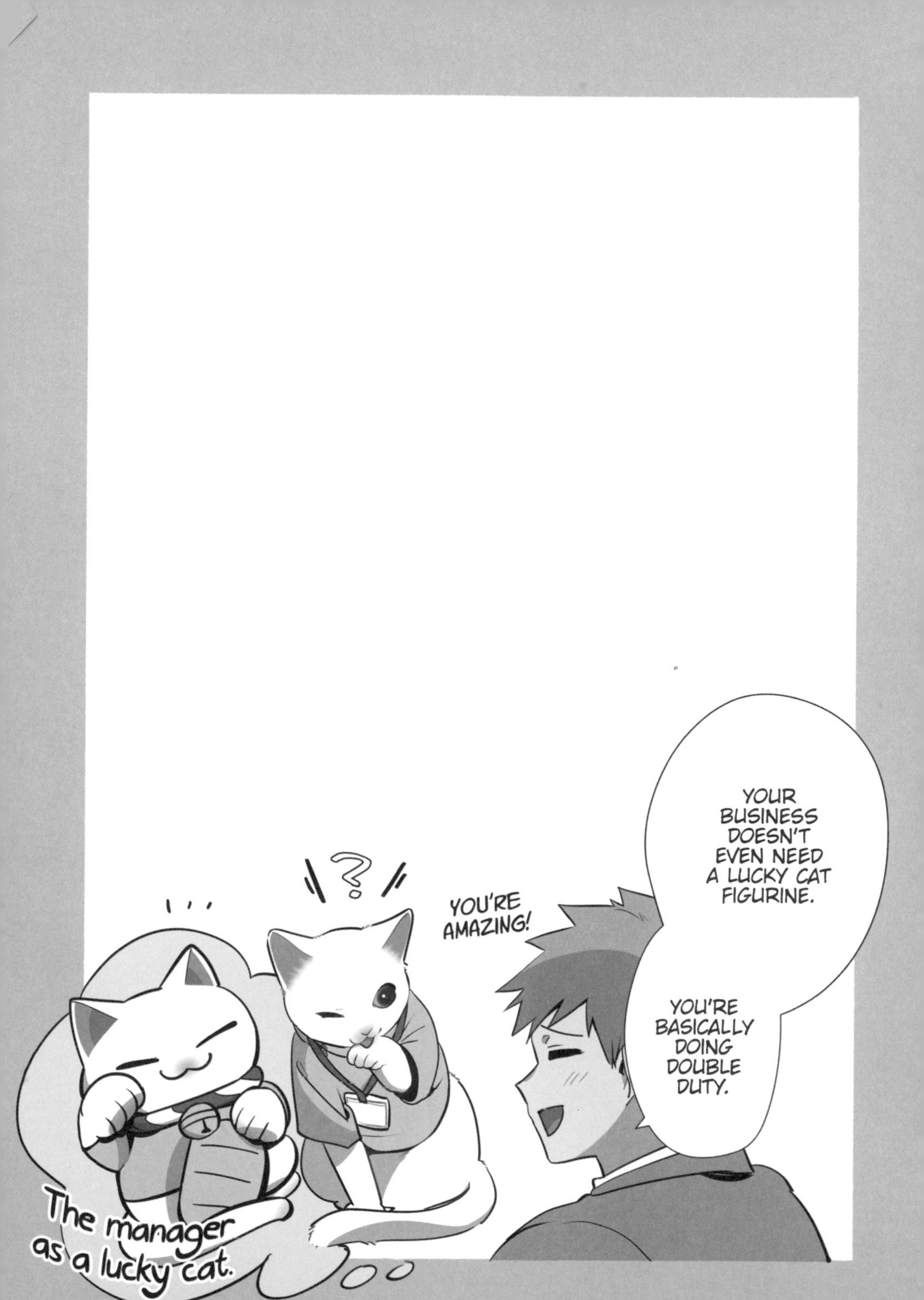
YOUR BUSINESS DOESN'T EVEN NEED A LUCKY CAT FIGURINE.
YOU'RE BASICALLY DOING DOUBLE DUTY.
YOU'RE AMAZING!
The manager as a lucky cat.

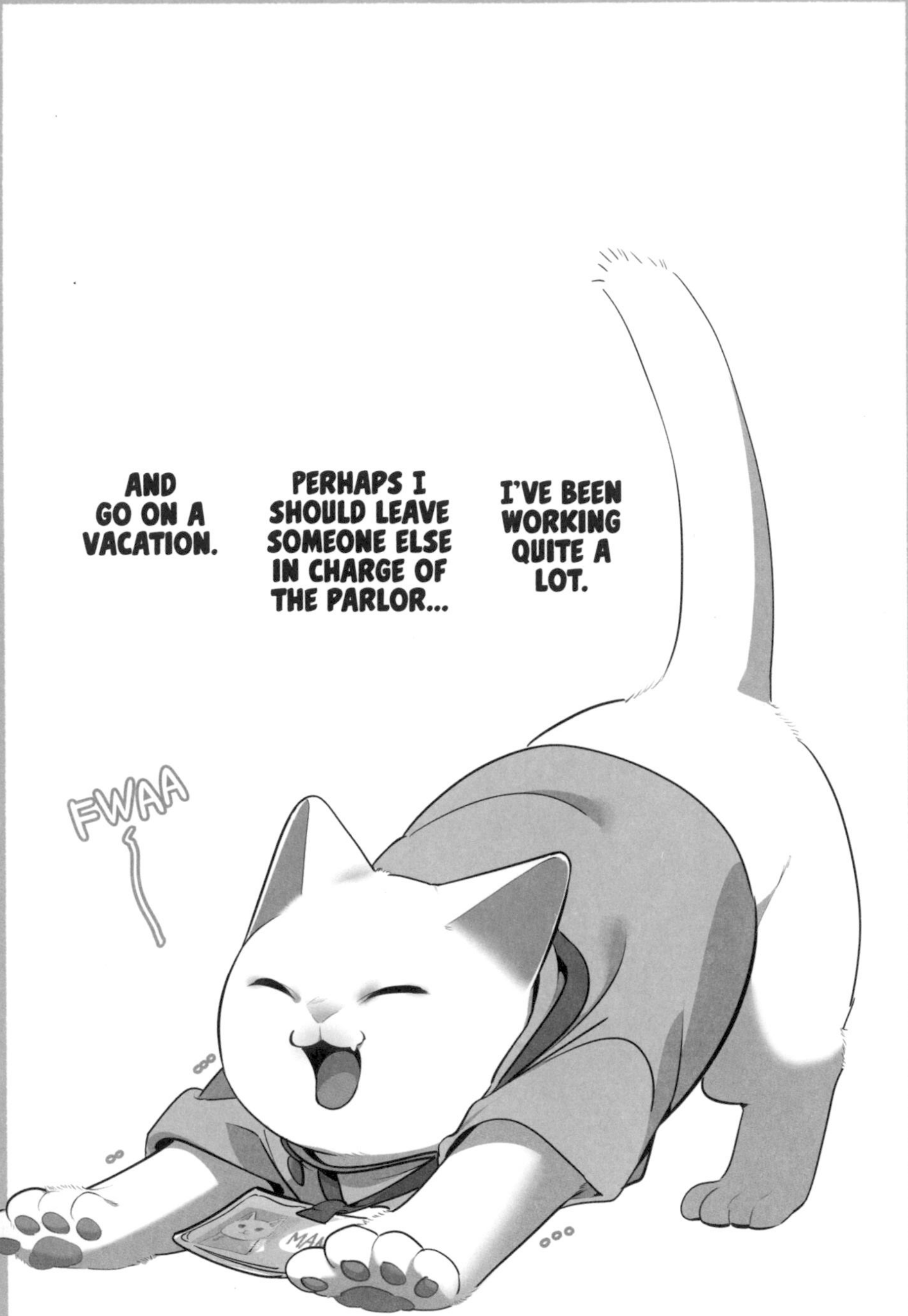
I'VE BEEN WORKING QUITE A LOT.
PERHAPS I SHOULD LEAVE SOMEONE ELSE IN CHARGE OF THE PARLOR...
AND GO ON A VACATION.
FWAA

Q16. A Japanese Bobtail?

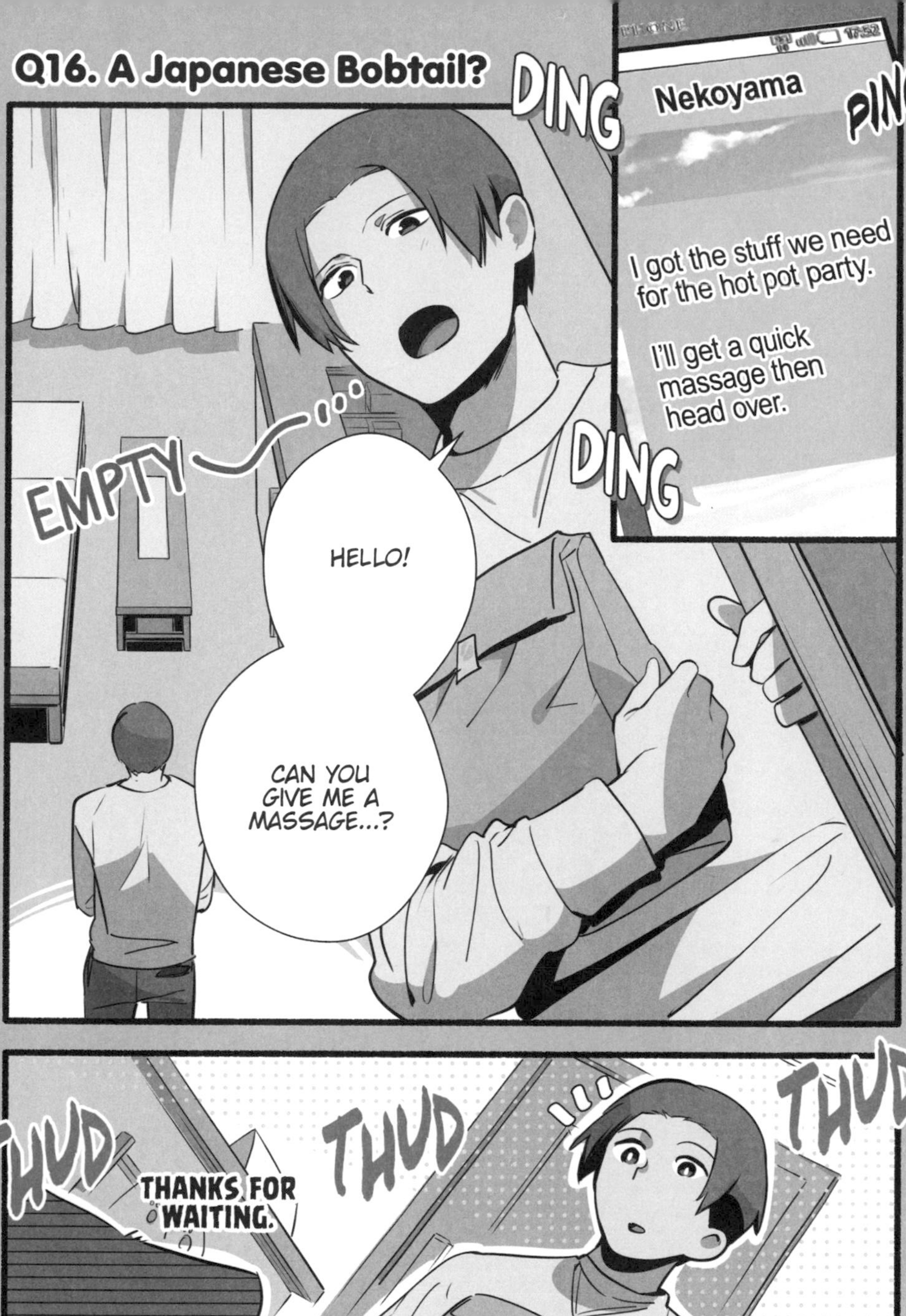
DING
Nekoyama
PING
I got the stuff we need for the hot pot party.
I'll get a quick massage then head over.
DING
HELLO!
CAN YOU GIVE ME A MASSAGE...?
EMPTY
THUD
THUD
THANKS FOR WAITING.
THUD

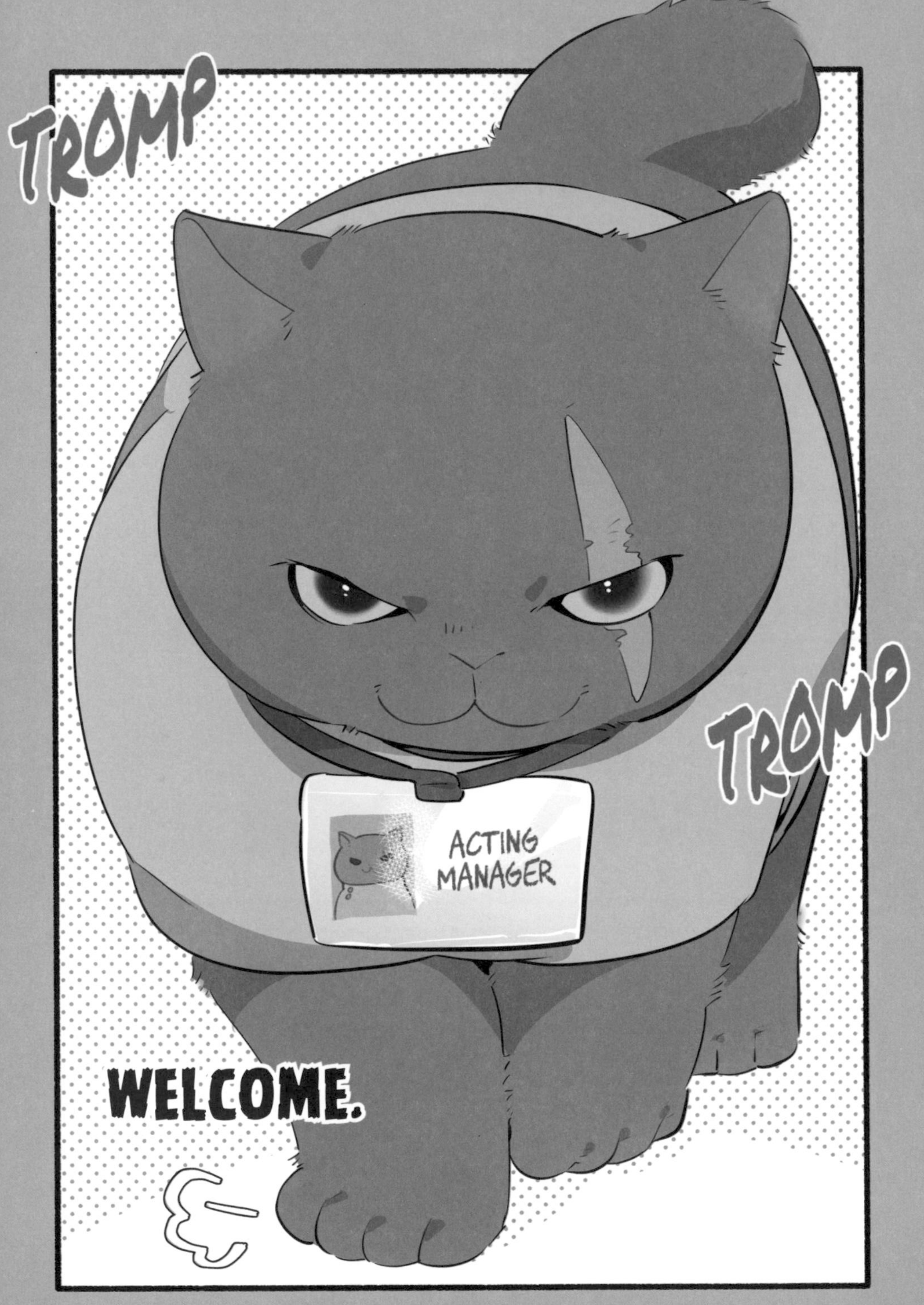
TROMP
TROMP
ACTING MANAGER
WELCOME.

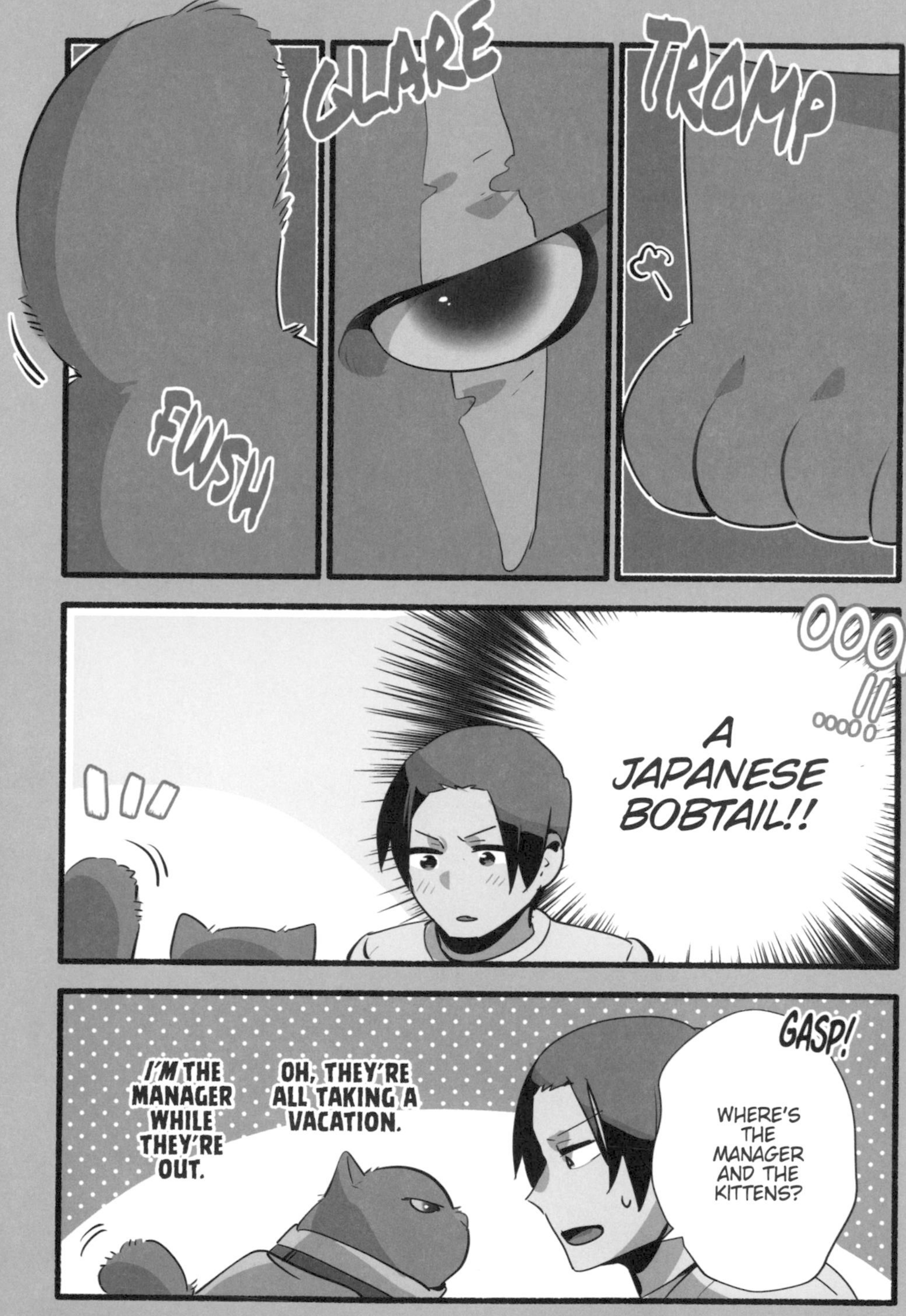
TROMP
GLARE
FWSH
OOOH!!
A JAPANESE BOBTAIL!!
GASP!
WHERE'S THE MANAGER AND THE KITTENS?
OH, THEY'RE ALL TAKING A VACATION.
I'M THE MANAGER WHILE THEY'RE OUT.

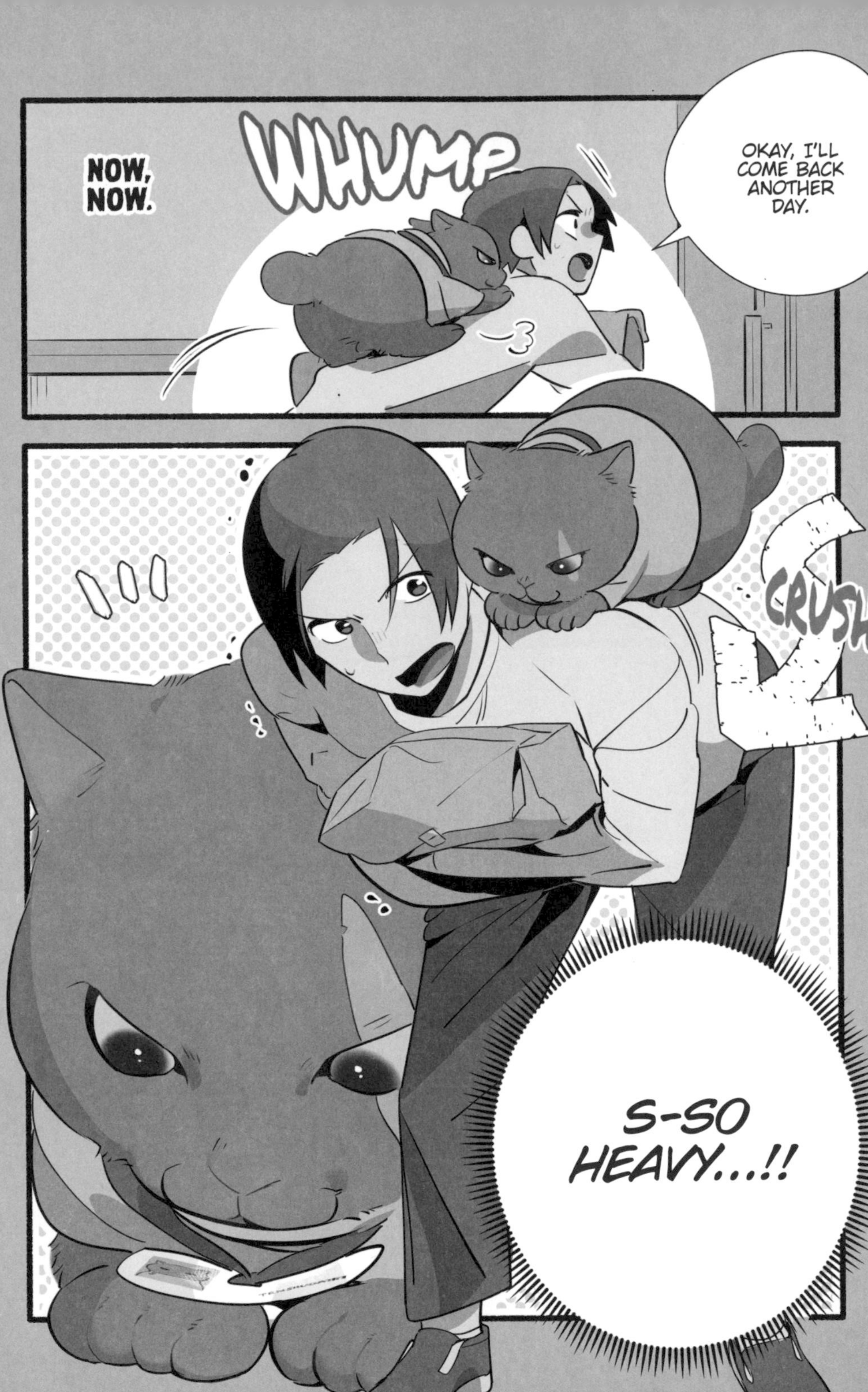
OKAY, I'LL COME BACK ANOTHER DAY.
WHUMP
NOW, NOW.
CRUSH
S-SO HEAVY...!!

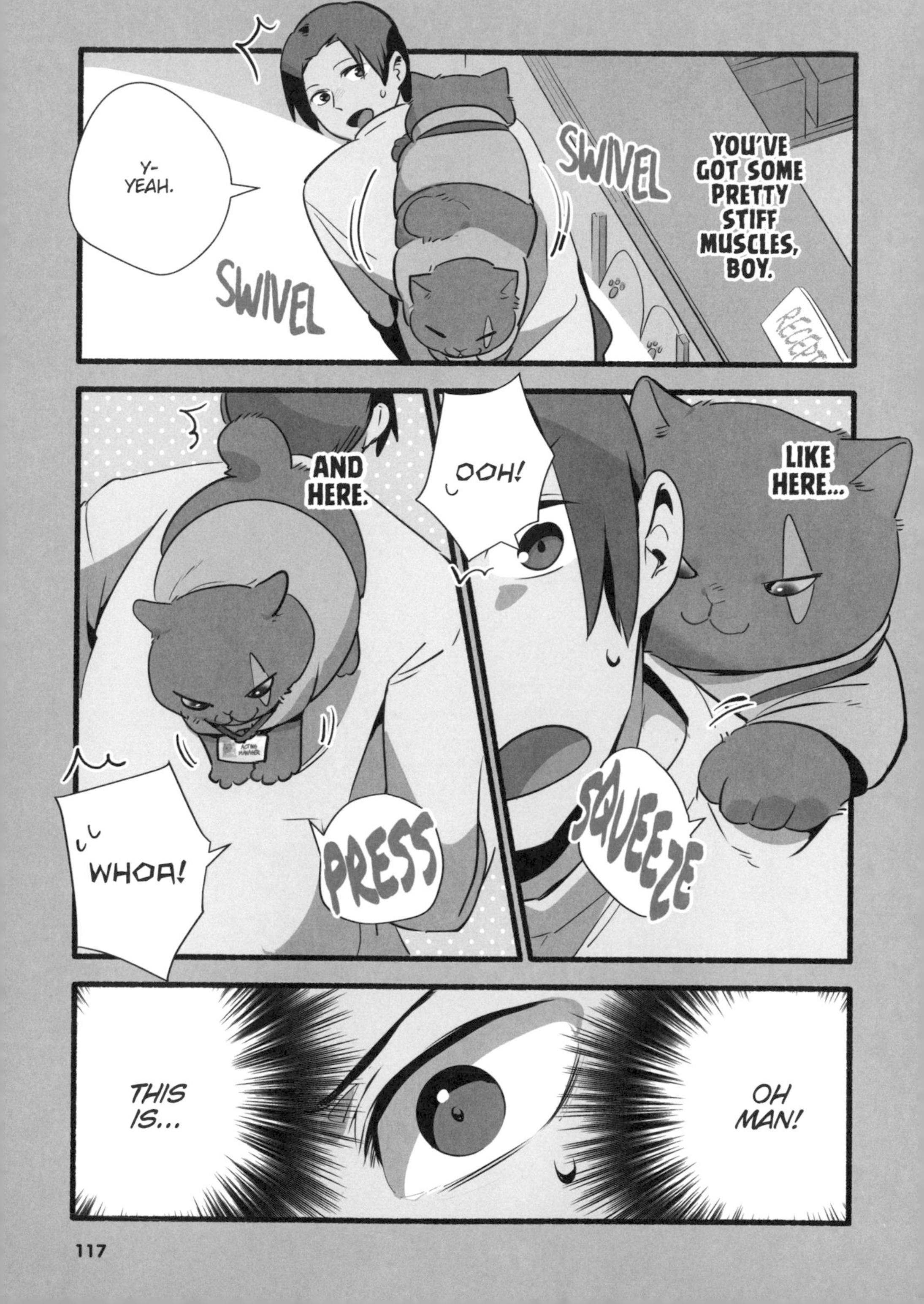
YOU'VE GOT SOME PRETTY STIFF MUSCLES, BOY.
SWIVEL
SWIVEL
Y-YEAH.
LIKE HERE...
OOH!
SQUEEZE
AND HERE.
PRESS
WHOA!
OH MAN!
THIS IS...

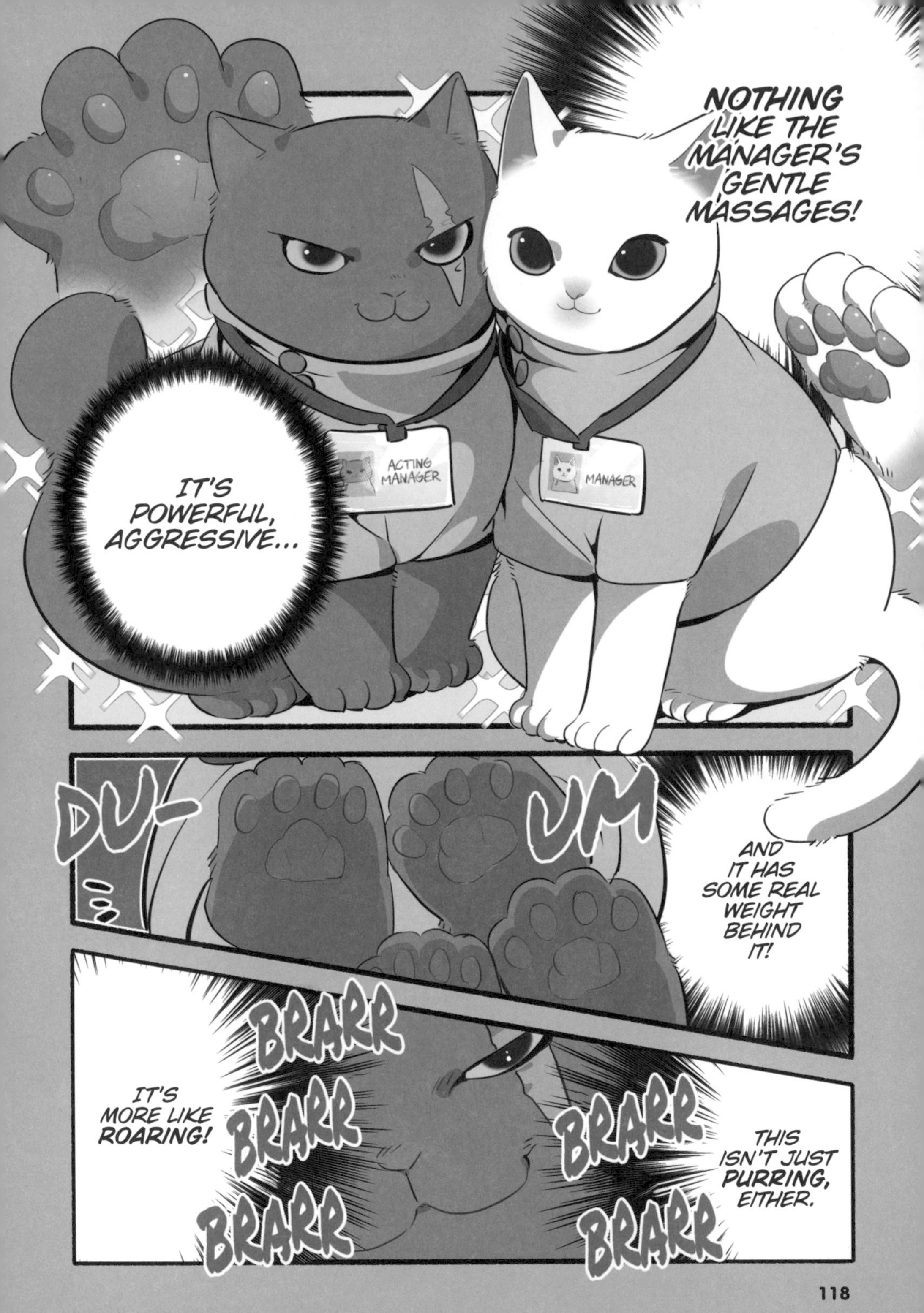
NOTHING LIKE THE MANAGER'S GENTLE MASSAGES!
MANAGER
ACTING MANAGER
IT'S POWERFUL, AGGRESSIVE...
AND IT HAS SOME REAL WEIGHT BEHIND IT!
DU- UM
THIS ISN'T JUST PURRING, EITHER.
BRARR BRARR
BRARR BRARR BRARR
IT'S MORE LIKE ROARING!

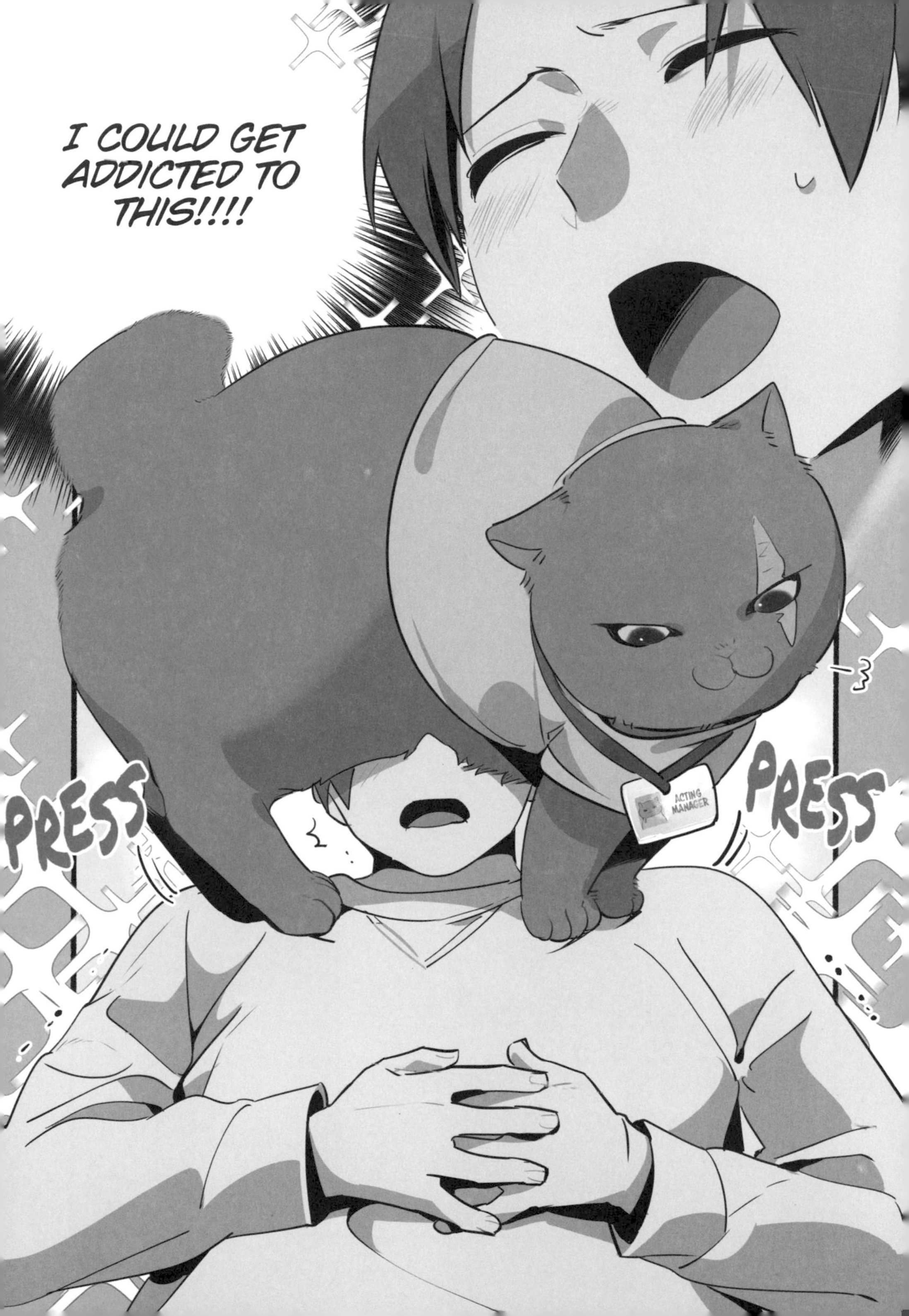
I COULD GET ADDICTED TO THIS!!!!
PRESS
PRESS
ACTING MANAGER

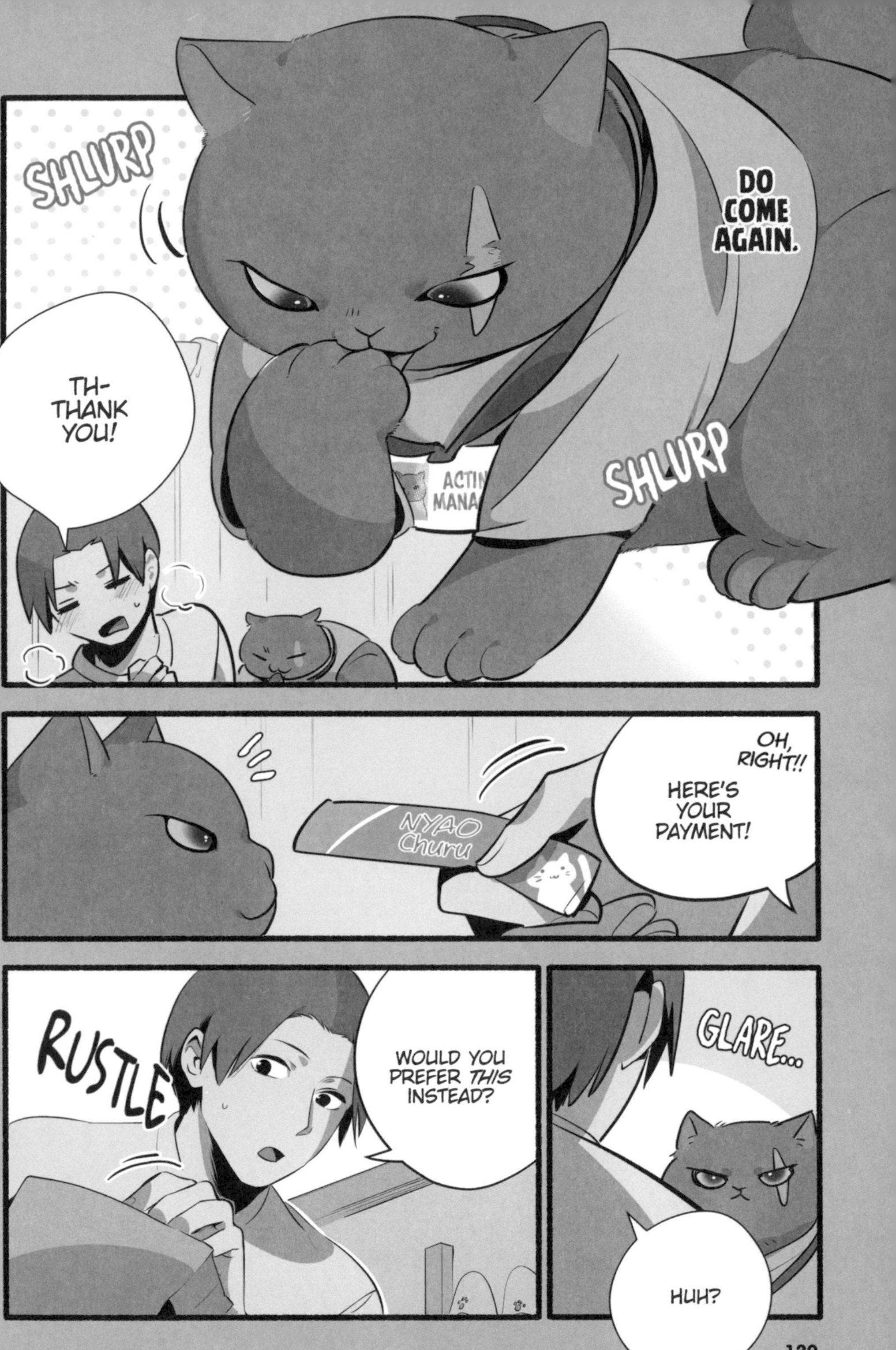
DO COME AGAIN.
SHLURP
SHLURP
TH-THANK YOU!
ACTIN MANA
OH, RIGHT!!
HERE'S YOUR PAYMENT!
NYAO Churu
GLARE...
HUH?
WOULD YOU PREFER *THIS* INSTEAD?
RUSTLE

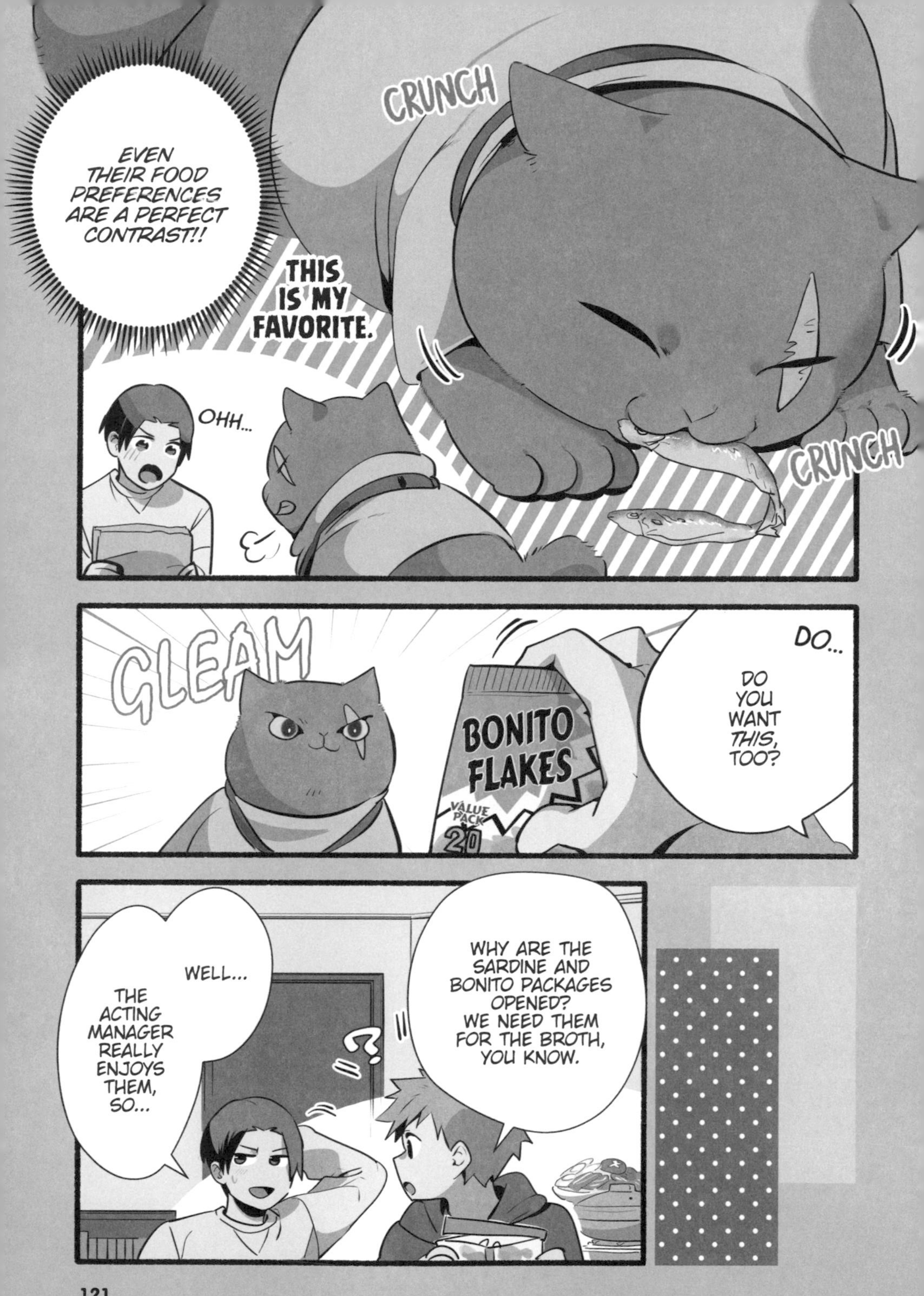
CRUNCH
EVEN THEIR FOOD PREFERENCES ARE A PERFECT CONTRAST!!
THIS IS MY FAVORITE.
CRUNCH
OHH...
DO...
DO YOU WANT *THIS*, TOO?
BONITO FLAKES
VALUE PACK 20
GLEAM
WHY ARE THE SARDINE AND BONITO PACKAGES OPENED? WE NEED THEM FOR THE BROTH, YOU KNOW.
?
WELL...
THE ACTING MANAGER REALLY ENJOYS THEM, SO...

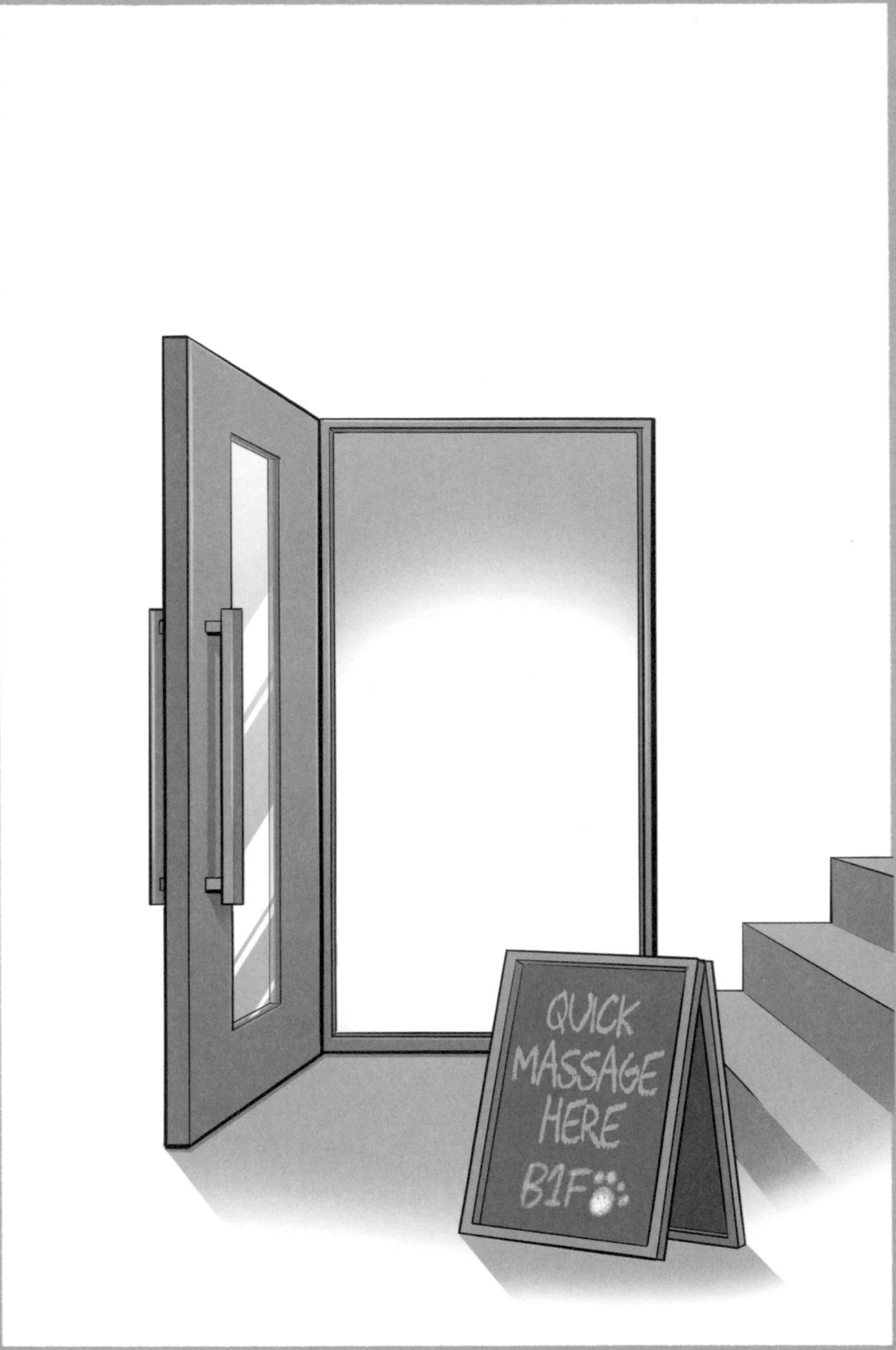
QUICK
MASSAGE
HERE
B1F

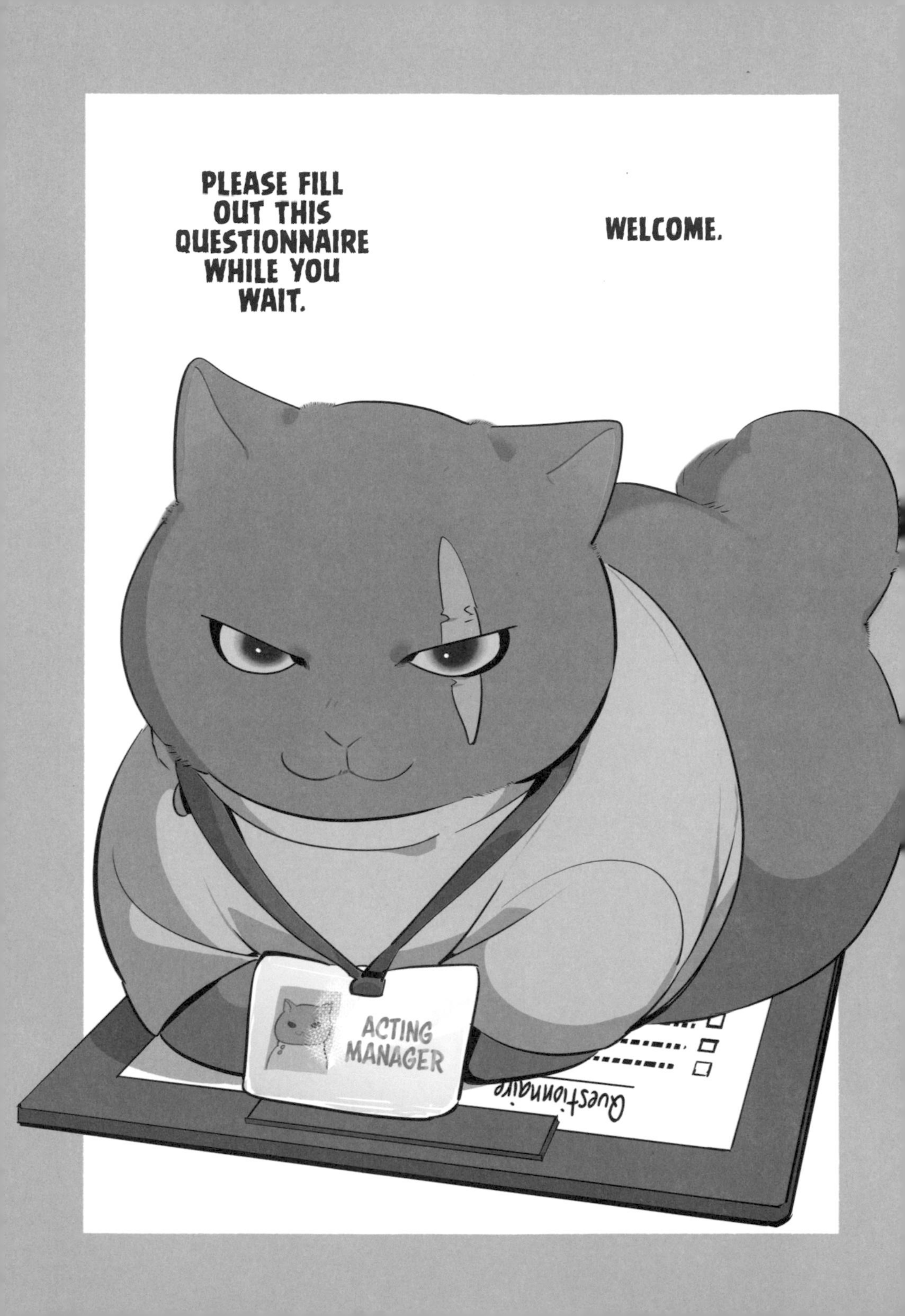
WELCOME.
PLEASE FILL OUT THIS QUESTIONNAIRE WHILE YOU WAIT.
ACTING MANAGER
Questionnaire

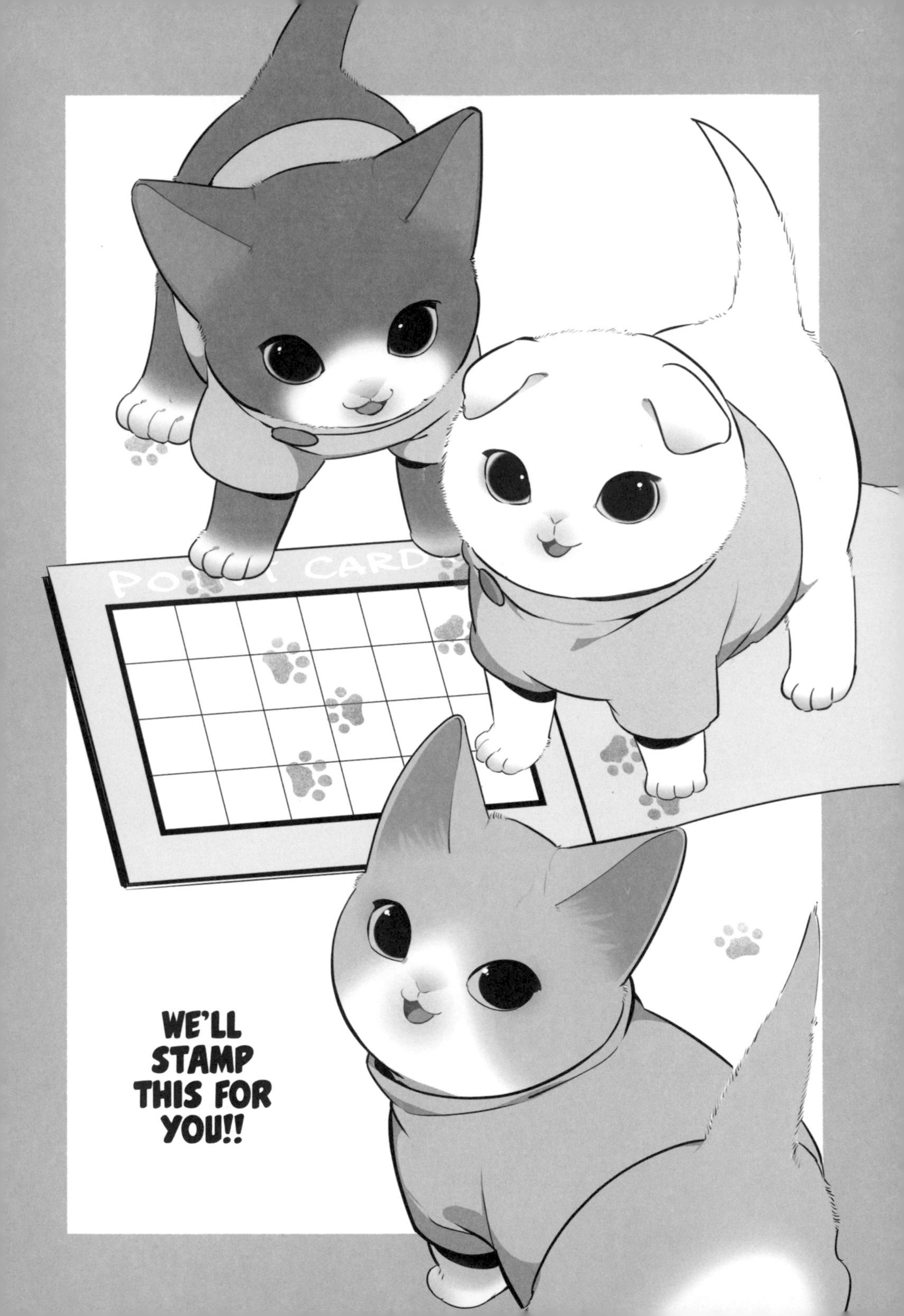
POINT CARD
WE'LL STAMP THIS FOR YOU!!

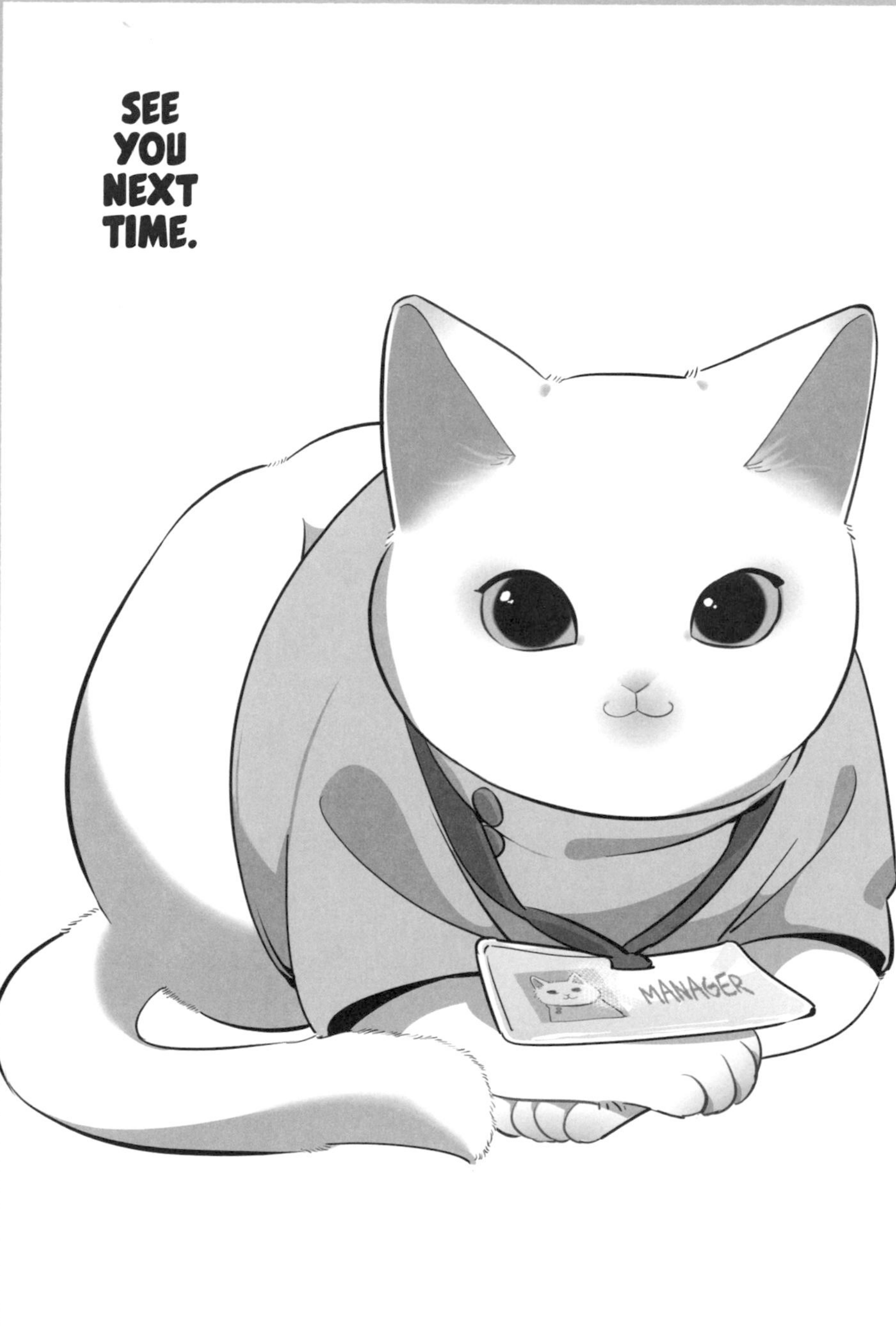
SEE YOU NEXT TIME.
MANAGER

Afterword

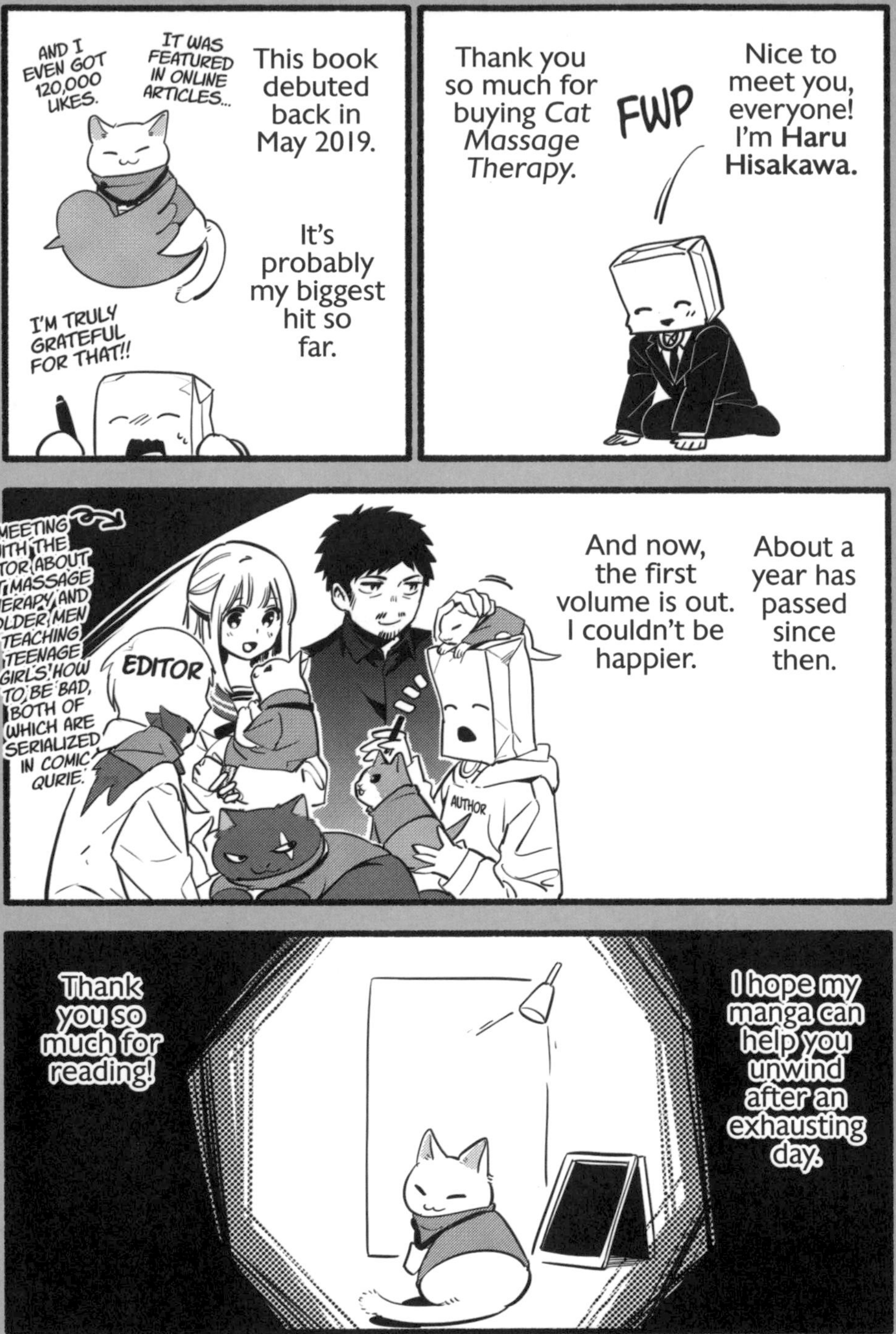
Nice to meet you, everyone! I'm Haru Hisakawa.
FWP
Thank you so much for buying Cat Massage Therapy.
This book debuted back in May 2019.
IT WAS FEATURED IN ONLINE ARTICLES...
AND I EVEN GOT 120,000 LIKES.
It's probably my biggest hit so far.
I'M TRULY GRATEFUL FOR THAT!!
About a year has passed since then.
And now, the first volume is out. I couldn't be happier.
A MEETING WITH THE EDITOR ABOUT CAT MASSAGE THERAPY AND OLDER MEN TEACHING TEENAGE GIRLS HOW TO BE BAD, BOTH OF WHICH ARE SERIALIZED IN COMIC QURIE.
EDITOR
AUTHOR
I hope my manga can help you unwind after an exhausting day.
Thank you so much for reading!

SEVEN SEAS ENTERTAINMENT PRESENTS

CAT MASSAGE THERAPY

story and art by HARU HISAKAWA   VOLUME 1

TRANSLATION
Anh Kiet Ngo

LETTERING
Karis Page

COVER AND LOGO DESIGN
Hanase Qi

PROOFREADER
Danielle King

EDITOR
Shanti Whitesides

PRINT MANAGER
Rhiannon Rasmussen-Silverstein

PRODUCTION ASSOCIATE
Christina McKenzie
Christa Miesner

PRODUCTION MANAGER
Lissa Pattillo

MANAGING EDITOR
Julie Davis

ASSOCIATE PUBLISHER
Adam Arnold

PUBLISHER
Jason DeAngelis

Cat Massage Therapy Vol. 1
© 2020 Haru Hisakawa
First published in Japan in 2020 by OVERLAP Inc., Ltd., Tokyo.
English translation rights arranged with OVERLAP Inc., Ltd., Tokyo.

Seven Seas press and purchase enquiries can be sent to Marketing Manager Lianne Sentar at press@gomanga.com. Information regarding the distribution and purchase of digital editions is available from Digital Manager CK Russell at digital@gomanga.com.

Seven Seas and the Seven Seas logo are trademarks of Seven Seas Entertainment. All rights reserved.

ISBN: 978-1-64827-656-9
Printed in Canada
First Printing: December 2021
10 9 8 7 6 5 4 3 2 1

READING DIRECTIONS

This book reads from *right to left*, Japanese style. If this is your first time reading manga, you start reading from the top right panel on each page and take it from there. If you get lost, just follow the numbered diagram here. It may seem backwards at first, but you'll get the hang of it! Have fun!!

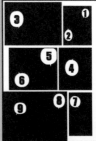

Follow us online: www.SevenSeasEntertainment.com